CW01022585

The Failure of the Free Market and Democracy

And What to Do About It

Daniel Ritter

The Failure of the Free Market and Democracy

And What to Do About It

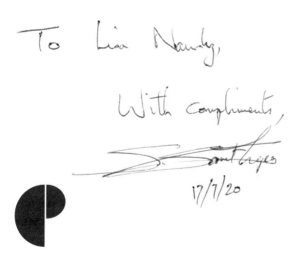

To Lisa Nandy,

With Compliments,

17/7/20

PROFILE
EDITIONS

First published in Great Britain in 2020 by Profile Editions,
an imprint of Profile Books Ltd
29 Cloth Fair
London ECIA 7JQ
www.profileeditions.com

The author and publisher assume no responsibility for the content of websites that are not the publisher's own. While care has been taken to ensure that the web links in the Notes section of this book are accurate at the time of publication, the publisher cannot guarantee that these links remain viable.

10 9 8 7 6 5 4 3 2 1

Printed and bound in Great Britain by Clays Ltd, Elcograf S.p.A

The moral right of the author has been asserted.

A CIP catalogue record for this book is available from
the British Library.

ISBN 978 1 78816 432 0
eISBN 978 1 78283 650 6

Typeset in Garamond

Contents

Introduction

> The ideas of economists and political philosophers, both when they are right and when they are wrong, are more powerful than is commonly understood. Indeed, the world is ruled by little else. Practical men, who believe themselves to be quite exempt from any intellectual influence, are usually the slaves of some defunct economist.
>
> John Maynard Keynes, *General Theory*

Western democracies are under threat economically and politically. Citizens are increasingly disaffected with politicians and institutions that have become dysfunctional and incapable of catering to their basic needs. Real income growth has petered out, public services are stretched, infrastructure is crumbling, well-paying jobs are disappearing. More broadly, the environment is being degraded while inequality is reaching record proportions way beyond most people's sense of justice. Violence is on the rise, in the streets and in political discourse. The social contract between the state and the governed is under threat, as the lopsided and weak recovery since the Great Financial Crisis (GFC) over a decade ago feeds a pervasive sense that something is very amiss. Perhaps most corrosive of all is the realisation that today's young adults stand to be worse off than their parents – unheard of in modern times. There is a gradual loss of optimism for the future. In spite of the marvels of modern technology, the signs are that Western civilisation peaked a generation ago and we are now on an inevitable decline towards its fall.

These are the symptoms of a deep malaise, and piecemeal palliative measures that do not attack the roots of the problem look increasingly like the equivalent of prescribing painkillers for a life-threatening illness. Tinkering with the tax system, hiking the minimum wage or banning plastic bags will not cut it; the forces that are corroding Western society are multiple, interconnected, and have been undermining its foundations for decades. These are the same destructive forces that triggered the GFC of 2008. They are still at work today. We need a root-and-branch diagnosis of how they came about, how they operate and how to stop and reverse them. This book aims to provide that diagnosis and to offer solutions.

Many of my themes are not new. Globalisation, rising inequality, the substitution of machines for human labour, dysfunctional politics and the rise of China have each been written and talked about elsewhere. What has been missing, however, is a coherent explanation of how all these phenomena are interlinked, mutually reinforcing, why they originated together and have led us into crisis.

The challenge to Western society posed by these issues has been aided and abetted by a minor revolution in politics and economics. The post-war consensus on how to run our societies was declared a failure, taken out to the woodshed and shot. In its place, a Darwinian, lightly regulated free-market regime has become the default, the ultimate efficient economic machine and arbiter of social outcomes, banishing politics from its workings. After the inflation of the 1970s, the academic and political pendulum swung firmly against government intervention in the economy and regulation of business practices. In came the era of President Reagan in the US and Margaret Thatcher in the UK, their free-market ideology reinforced and validated by the fall of the Berlin Wall in 1989, the demise of the Soviet Union and the opening up of China to international trade.

The principles of the free market and unfettered international trade were adopted unquestioningly as the optimum way to organise economies. In spite of major changes in society, economic principles set out by Adam Smith and David Ricardo two centuries ago have been used to guide the new dominant political, economic and academic ideology in the West. It is an ideology based on the premise that governments should confine themselves to providing a secure legal framework in which markets can operate seamlessly, and abstain from steering the economy; markets themselves produce the best outcomes in terms of the allocation of resources and the distribution of rewards, and they should be deregulated in order to operate freely.

The deregulation of markets, including that for labour, coincided with the opening-up of a massive supply of cheap labour in countries such as China and those of the former Soviet Union. This has resulted in a visible transfer of income and wealth from most Western workers to the winners in this process: workers in emerging markets and the corporate sector. Globalisation and technological change have boosted the corporations' share of profits in the economy and exacerbated inequalities of income and wealth within countries. Those at the top of the corporate pyramid have reaped the benefits from international trade, the substitution of machines for human labour and lower tax rates, forgetting on the way to compensate those left behind.

This new framework also set in process a powerful debt dynamic. The finance industry was let off the leash as Western households borrowed to increase their living standards in the face of stagnant incomes. This was encouraged by aggressively expansionary banks and ever cheaper credit, courtesy of falling interest rates. Governments and central banks sat watching on the sidelines, unwilling to interfere. Not only was it politically unwise to restrain the rapidly growing mountain of debt, which after all was being created by willing participants in the market, but corporate interests, including the finance industry, began to corrupt the political system in their favour. Campaign finance contributions, lobbying, regulatory capture, or simply the generation of outsize profits that could yield much-needed tax receipts, made governments and political parties reluctant to kill the golden goose. Ironically, economics was re-joined with politics, but through the back door, undermining the very principles and workings of democracy.

According to free-market textbooks, the GFC of 2008 was, by definition, an event that should not have happened. But this was a crisis so deep that the market had to appeal for help to those very institutions that had been so derided as irrelevant: governments and central banks. Without their unprecedented and massive bail-outs of banks and large corporations, the market system would not have been able to right itself and would have collapsed.

In spite of this dramatic refutation of market efficiency and wisdom, free market ideology still limps on today, zombie-like, as the commercial and political elites are reluctant to give it up. It has become so deeply entrenched in our thinking, repeated as a mantra so many times over three decades, that pundits and those in power cannot face up to their mistakes, particularly in the absence of any obviously viable alternative to sell to their disappointed citizens. Worse, the entrenched interests of the winners have made it all but impossible for politicians to steer an independent course. This is especially true in the case of the dominant player in the global economy, the US. From its position of power, America sets the example and the rules of engagement. In an open, globalised world, it is very difficult for other countries to resist and behave differently.

For all the elegance of foundational economic theories, the truth is that politics and economics can never be separated. To attempt to do so is itself a political act and, as we have seen, a path to economic and social disaster. Politics is always about money somewhere along the line, just as economics is always in need of political choices. There is no economic proof of the best decisions for society, not only because economics isn't a hard science like physics, but because there is no proof that one way of slicing the economic pie is superior to another. At best, economists can describe, for example, the trade-off between growth and tax rates or profits and wages, but where to land within these and other trade-offs is inescapably a political decision. In the absence of a world government, there is simply no mechanism for resolving some of these choices when it comes to the allocation of resources for the production of goods and services globally. To simply rely on the market and the goodwill of the winners towards the losers has demonstrably failed.

Put another way, contrary to the orthodoxy of the last few decades, which tried to kick the politics out of economics, we urgently – and *explicitly* – need to re-join the two.

To achieve this, we must recognise how our predicament has been caused by the malign and mutually reinforcing interaction between our political processes and economic and technological developments since the 1980s. Solutions which try to fix individual symptoms in isolation will not work. For example, pumping money into the system to alleviate job redundancies caused by technological change will not work without a wholesale redesign of our attitude to work, taxation, leisure and what are considered socially useful occupations – and the repositioning of international trade on a more level playing field. We can no longer rely on private companies to make decisions about where in the world to produce for short-term gain irrespective of the long-term consequences for all stakeholders.

The solutions proposed in this book follow from this diagnosis. They include measures that can be taken quickly to stop the rot, while others involve a more radical, long-term overhaul of our political institutions.

At one level, we need simply to change incentives and reduce, if not eliminate, conflicts of interest. Governments still have enormous powers to curb corporate greed through taxation and re-regulation. They can raise corporate taxes; disincentivise corporations from transferring production abroad or diverting profits to lower tax jurisdictions; reinvest in society through training, socially useful jobs, public services and legislating for a living wage. Laws can be enacted to reduce conflicts of interest between shareholders and the executive class, including making top compensation packages transparent and legally accountable to shareholders. Banks can be nudged back to being boring financial utilities, safekeeping savings and lending for investment within conservative limits and for small margins.

At the government level, a major upgrade to our antiquated political institutions is now possible and desirable. We can and should cut out conflicts of interest between private capital, elected representatives and citizens. As a first step, all special and private interests should be banned from politics, whether through campaign finance or lobbying. This is not, however, sufficient to guarantee long-term investments in public infrastructure, education and health, the benefits of which will be reaped by future generations. Politicians simply cannot be incentivised that far into the future and are too weak to resist the temptation to bribe the electorate with its own money and short-term policies the bill for which will be presented after they have moved on.

We must also recognise the need to replace our anachronistic institutions with a model of direct democracy that is now technologically possible. Simply put, a well-educated citizenry can vote with their phones or TV remotes. To be successful, this presupposes the education and involvement of citizens in the issues of the day, not to mention a considerable investment in resources devoted to education and training, the key to our future. We need smart citizens to make smart decisions.

Politics on the ground is already chipping away at the political dead wood. Traditional loyalties are disintegrating as conventional parties, prisoners of the current outmoded system, run out of ideas and the ability to deliver. Grass-roots movements attest to the death of tribal politics in which the troops are led by a small group of full-time professional politicians. There seem to be no bounds to how far people will go to break the stale political status quo. This is a first step. No doubt future elections in the US and Europe will debate these issues as the pendulum swings back from the certainties of the last thirty years. We must hope for tangible progress, and that the forces of inertia will not hijack or hold back the yearning for real change. The cost of failure does not bear thinking about.

We need not be resigned to our fate unless we choose to remain timid in our ambition and passive in our response. The time for action is now.

PART ONE

The Twin Challenges of Globalisation and Technology

1

Globalisation and its perversions

Globalisation presumes sustained economic growth. Otherwise, the process loses its economic benefits and political support.

Paul Samuelson

Globalisation is a process of interaction and integration among the people, companies, and governments of different nations, a process driven by international trade and investment and aided by information technology ... Governments also have negotiated dramatic reductions in barriers to commerce and have established international agreements to promote trade in goods, services, and investment. Taking advantage of new opportunities in foreign markets, corporations have built foreign factories and established production and marketing arrangements with foreign partners. A defining feature of globalisation, therefore, is an international industrial and financial business structure.

Levin Institute of International Relations

THE FOUNDATIONS OF ECONOMIC GLOBALISATION

What does globalisation mean in concrete terms? One of its high priests, the International Monetary Fund (IMF), opined in its 2008 *Overview* that people had 'become more globalised', noting,

- The value of trade (goods and services) as a percentage of world GDP increased from 42.1 per cent in 1980 to 62.1 per cent in 2007.
- Foreign direct investment increased from 6.5 per cent of world GDP in 1980 to 31.8 per cent in 2006.
- The stock of international claims (primarily bank loans), as a percentage of world GDP, increased from roughly 10 per cent in 1980 to 48 per cent in 2006.[1]

The central premise of economic globalisation is, according to the IMF, 'that global markets promote efficiency through competition and the division of labour – the specialisation that allows people and economies to focus on what they do best. Trade enhances national competitiveness by driving workers and economies to focus their efforts where they have a competitive advantage.' These theoretical underpinnings of globalisation are not new; as far back as 1817 David Ricardo published his theory of comparative advantage to explain why countries engage in international trade.[2] Notice however that the IMF speaks of *competitive advantage* without specifying whether this advantage is absolute or comparative. But as Ricardo shows, this is a crucial distinction.

Ricardo was trying to improve on his friend Adam Smith's theory of *absolute advantage*,[3] which, in turn, was a better (if imperfect) justification for international trade than mercantilism, the policy of growing an economy through exporting more goods and services than you import. Smith argued that mercantilism could not benefit all countries at the same time because one nation's exports are another nation's imports. Instead, he advocated that countries should specialise according to their absolute advantage, determined by a simple comparison of labour costs. Clearly, though, some nations might have no absolute advantage in anything, meaning that, while some will gain from international trade with absolute advantage, the gains may not be mutually beneficial.

In other words, concentrating production in countries with absolute advantages in everything is really just another form of mercantilism: the higher-cost countries will have to import all they consume, while the low-cost countries, enjoying an absolute advantage, will accumulate reserves – unless their currency rises, in which case their purchasing power will have risen at the expense of the absolutely expensive country that had to import goods and services.

Ricardo's refinement of this argument was to introduce the idea of *comparative advantage*. He argued that, for mutually beneficial international trade, a nation should concentrate resources only on industries where it had a comparative advantage, that is, on those industries in which it had the greatest competitive edge. He even went as far as to suggest that national industries which were, in fact, profitable and internationally competitive should be jettisoned in favour of the *most competitive* industries, the assumption being that subsequent economic growth would more than offset any economic disadvantage from closing these down.

Ricardo attempted to prove his theory that international trade is beneficial by using a simple numerical example relating to the trade between England and Portugal in wine and cloth. In an address to the International Economic Association in 1969, Paul Samuelson famously called the numbers used in this example the 'four magic numbers'.

Comparative difference in cost

A country is said to have a comparative advantage in the production of a good (or service) if its cost of production *relative* to another good is lower than is the case in other countries. This may arise because of natural advantages – for example, Portugal's climate is conducive to the production of wine – or because of long accumulated know-how and technical expertise. A country should be left to specialise in the production of commodities where it has a comparative advantage. For Ricardo, the essence of mutually beneficial international trade is not the absolute difference in production cost between countries, but the comparative difference in costs between two goods in two countries.

Ricardo's theory of comparative advantage

All other things being equal, a country tends to specialise in and export those commodities in the production of which it has maximum comparative cost advantage or minimum comparative disadvantage. Similarly, the country's imports will be of goods having relatively less comparative cost advantage or greater disadvantage.

Ricardo explained his theory with the help of the following (theoretical) assumptions.

1. There are two countries and two commodities.
2. There is *perfect competition* both in commodity and factor (labour) markets.
3. The cost of production is expressed in terms of *labour* – i.e. the value of a commodity is measured in terms of labour hours/days required to produce it. Commodities are also exchanged on the basis of the labour content of each good.
4. Labour is the only *factor of production* other than natural resources.
5. Labour is homogeneous – i.e. identical in efficiency in a particular country.
6. Labour is perfectly mobile within a country but perfectly immobile between countries.

7. There is free trade – i.e. the movement of goods between countries is not hindered by any restrictions.
8. Production is subject to constant returns to scale.
9. There is no technological change.
10. Trade between two countries takes place on barter system.
11. Full employment exists in both countries.
12. There is no transport cost.

Here's how the four magic numbers play out.

The four magic numbers

On the basis of the above assumptions, Ricardo explained his comparative cost difference theory by taking the example of England and Portugal as two countries and wine and cloth as two commodities. The principle of comparative advantage is expressed in labour hours by the following table.

	1 unit of wine	1 unit of cloth
England	120	100
Portugal	80	90

Portugal requires fewer hours of labour for both wine and cloth production. From this it could be argued that there is no need for trade as Portugal produces both commodities at a lower cost. Ricardo, however, tried to prove that Portugal stands to gain by specialising in the commodity, in this case the production of wine, where its comparative advantage is larger. Similarly, England should specialise in the production of cloth, because its comparative disadvantage is lesser than in wine.

Comparative cost benefits both participants

To prove the Ricardian contention that comparative cost-based trade benefits both participants, though one of them has a clear absolute cost advantage in both commodities, we need to work out the domestic exchange ratio.

	Wine	Cloth	Domestic exchange rate		
			W	:	C
England	120	100	1	:	1.20
Portugal	80	90	1	:	0.89

Let us assume these two countries enter into trade at an international exchange rate (terms of trade) of 1:1. At this rate, England specialising in cloth and exporting one unit of cloth gets one unit of wine. At home it would be required to give 1.2 units of cloth for one unit of wine, which is worse. England thus gains 0.2 of cloth, so wine is cheaper from Portugal by 0.2 unit of cloth. Similarly, Portugal gets one unit of cloth from England for its one unit of wine traded as against 0.89 of cloth at home, thus gaining extra cloth of 0.11. Here both England and Portugal gain from the trade, as England gives 0.2 less of cloth to get one unit of wine and Portugal gets 0.11 more of cloth for one unit of wine.

In this example Portugal specialises in wine, where it has a comparative advantage, leaving cloth for production in England in which the latter has a comparative advantage. On this basis, comparative cost theory states that each country should produce and export those goods in which they enjoy most cost advantage and import those goods where they suffer most cost disadvantage.

In reality, however, things didn't work out as Ricardo had predicted. Economist Joan Robinson[4] has pointed out that, following the opening of free trade with England, Portugal endured centuries of economic underdevelopment: 'the imposition of free trade on Portugal killed off a promising textile industry and left her with a slow-growing export market for wine, while for England, exports of cotton cloth led to accumulation, mechanisation and the whole spiralling growth of the Industrial Revolution'.

Robinson also argues that Ricardo's required conditions – such as full employment and a lack of trade deficits and surpluses – were not relevant to the real world. Nor did his theory take into account that some countries may be at different levels of development, raising the prospect of *unequal exchange*, which might hamper a country's development, as in the case of Portugal.

While it is true that specialisation and trade according to relative cost of production can benefit all parties, the conditions under which it actually will, requires preconditions that do not currently exist in the real world. The idea that countries manage who produces what within their borders in coordination with each other is particularly flawed, given that the decision unit in capitalist economies is the company, an institution designed to support its own shareholders rather than coordinate economic policy and planning more widely. Ricardo's theory of comparative advantage implicitly assumes the existence of industry and trade policy at a national level. It does not presume that business decisions are or should be made independently by entrepreneurs on the basis of viability or profit.

RICARDO, COMPETITIVE ADVANTAGE AND TRADE POLICY TODAY

Despite its obvious flaws, Ricardo's model – morphed into the more general concept of *competitive advantage* – has had a significant influence on the laissez-faire international trade policy that has dominated the last fifty years.

World trade increased strongly from 1960 to 2015,[5] as many countries dismantled or reduced their barriers to trade through bilateral agreements and later under the auspices of the World Trade Organization (WTO). Governments were sold on the idea that global trade benefits everyone, and that the obvious benefits to consumers of being able to buy cheaper goods made in low-cost countries would raise standards of living. Rarely was it acknowledged that, in order to consume such cheap imports, consumers also need to be producers who sell enough to pay for their goods.

According to the IMF,

> Global markets also offer greater opportunity for people to tap into more diversified and larger markets around the world. It means that they can have access to more capital, technology, cheaper imports, and larger export markets. But markets do not necessarily ensure that the benefits of increased efficiency are shared by all. Countries must be prepared to embrace the policies needed, and, in the case of the poorest countries, may need the support of the international community as they do so.

In fact, developing countries have done remarkably well from the explosion in international trade, but they were not the ones in need of help. Rather, more traditional economies have often borne the brunt, including the US. Consider, for example, the case of the dramatic decline in decently paid manufacturing jobs there. In a speech in Cleveland, Ohio in 2015, the chair of the US Federal Reserve Board, Janet Yellen, bemoaned the loss of manufacturing jobs: 'Unfortunately, the number of US manufacturing jobs has been generally decreasing since its peak in the late 1970s …This painful trend reflects a number of long-term challenges faced by domestic manufacturers, including the relative costs of labour and investment in producing domestically versus abroad.'[6]

The loss of jobs is an inconvenient truth for the argument that globalisation delivers win-win benefits, with American manufacturing in rude health while its citizens also benefit from cheaper imports. In fact, data published by Susan Houseman and her colleagues in 2011 shows that once you take out computers, the picture is much more complex.[7] The big increases in manufacturing output recorded in the US, even as employment plummeted, were partly due to statisticians adjusting upwards the output for quality improvements such as computing power in the technology sector. If you strip this out, manufacturing output in the US has been stagnant. However, this point has gone largely unnoticed and the assumption remains that the increases reflected healthy productivity growth.

So what happened to all those jobs? Globalists argue that automation has been the root cause, with robot-driven productivity both pushing growth and taking traditional manufacturing jobs. And, according to Houseman et al., automation did happen in manufacturing; we look at its effects in more detail in Chapter 2. However, the extent of its impact, especially in the US, is questionable, as reported by Quartz.com in 2018: 'Consider the shuttering of some 78,000 manufacturing plants between 2000 and 2014, a 22 per cent drop. This is odd given that robots, like humans, have to work somewhere. Then there's the fact that there simply aren't that many robots in US factories, compared with other advanced economies.'[8]

Remarkably, while Germany installed more robots per worker than the US, a study by German academics found that only 274,000 manufacturing jobs were lost in Germany between 1994 and 2014 because of robots, this in a sector that still makes up around a quarter of the economy.[9] Germany lost only 19 per cent of its manufacturing jobs between 1996 and 2012, compared to a third lost by the US. Korea, France and Italy also lost fewer such jobs even though they used more robots per hours worked. Conversely, low-robot-intensive economies such as the UK and Australia saw faster declines in their manufacturing sectors.[10]

When we consider, for example, that the US production of motor vehicles dropped from around 13 million in 1999 to 11 million in 2017, it's difficult to identify a boom in manufacturing output or productivity growth attributable to robots. And if booming robot-led productivity growth wasn't displacing factory workers, then, according to Houseman et al., 'the sweeping scale of job losses in manufacturing necessarily stemmed from something else entirely'. Instead, a good part of the job losses in sectors such as autos is attributable to the rising share of imports.

In other words, contrary to the globalists' thesis, the role of trade in displacing workers is a bigger contributing factor than its defenders are willing to admit.

THE RISE OF CHINA

Of particular importance is China's emergence as a major exporter, which US leaders had encouraged. This has been evidenced in a wealth of research. A study by economists David Autor, David Dorn and Gordon Hanson found that the parts of the US hit hard by Chinese import competition saw manufacturing job loss, falling wages and the shrinking of their workforces.[11] It also found that compensating employment gains in other industries never materialised. The authors drew on detailed studies of the local impact of trade with China to estimate conservatively that at least a quarter of the collapse in manufacturing jobs in the US between 2000 and 2014 was caused by trade with China. These conclusions were mirrored in a second paper, which estimated that competition from Chinese imports cost the US as many as 2.4 million jobs between 1999 and 2011.[12]

The US National Bureau of Economic Research published a report in 2012 on the decline in manufacturing due to the integration of China into the trading system. They summarised their findings as follows:

> According to the Bureau of Labor Statistics, US manufacturing employment fell from 19.6 million in 1979 to 13.7 million in 2007 ... This paper finds a relationship between the sharp decline in US manufacturing employment that occurs after 2001 and US conferral of permanent normal trade relations on China in October 2000. This change in policy is notable for eliminating uncertainty about potential increases in tariffs rather than changing the actual level of tariffs ... these employment declines are associated with relative increases in US imports from China, the number of US firms importing from China, the number of Chinese firms exporting to the United States, and the number of US–China importer-exporter pairs ... Second, we show that elimination of uncertainty is associated with suppressed job creation as well as exaggerated job destruction. The relative importance of the former indicates that analyses of the effect of international trade on domestic employment that focus solely on job destruction may be inadequate ... estimates of employment loss persist even when controlling for industry attributes which might be linked to trends in technical change, particularly industry capital and skill intensity.[13]

In 2017 an Economic Policy Institute report concluded that, since China entered the WTO in 2001, its trade surplus with the US had grown from $83 billion to $367 billion in 2015. That is to say, the US went from rough self-sufficiency up until the 1980s, to outsourcing a lot of its production to low-cost China, at the inevitable cost to American jobs and wages.[14] US manufacturing employment dropped 18 per cent between March 2001 and March 2007.

Figure 1.1: Manufacturing employment, percentage change 1990–2014

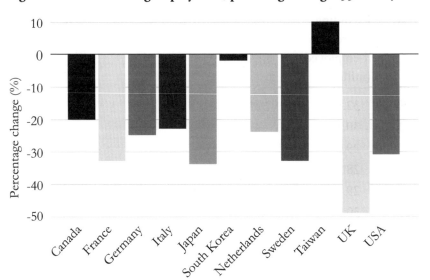

Why did China have such a big impact on US manufacturing employment sparked by granting China Permanent Normal Trade Relations (PNTR) in 2000 and China's accession to the WTO in 2001 – set in motion by Bill Clinton? Because when China joined the WTO, it became a fully protected member of the globalised trading community, reducing the risk that the US might retaliate against the Chinese government's mercantilist currency and protectionist industrial policies by raising tariffs. International companies that set up shop in China therefore enjoyed the benefits of cheap labour, as well as a huge competitive edge from the Chinese government's artificial cheapening of the yuan.

Having peaked around 1977, US manufacturing employment has been steadily retreating for decades, with losses accelerating round about the time of China's accession to the WTO. This is replicated throughout the advanced economies, as shown in Figure 1.1 above.

Table 1.1 Urban manufacturing employment in China, 2000–14

Year	Excluding private and self-employed (millions)	Private and self-employed (millions)	Total (millions)	Share of urban employment (millions)
2000	32.40	n.a.	n.a.	n.a.
2001	30.10	n.a.	n.a.	n.a.
2002	29.07	n.a.	n.a.	n.a.
2003	28.99	10.85	39.84	15
2004	29.60	11.56	41.16	15
2005	30.96	13.30	44.26	16
2006	32.50	15.58	48.08	16
2007	33.58	17.52	51.11	17
2008	33.29	19.01	52.30	16
2009	33.80	19.84	53.65	16
2010	36.37	21.51	57.89	17
2011	40.88	22.91	63.80	18
2012	42.62	23.58	66.20	18
2013	52.58	24.84	77.42	20
2014	52.43	27.17	79.61	20

Coincidentally, in the same period, China has been aggressively taking global market share in manufacturing and, in contrast to the West, manufacturing employment has boomed, even in the face of technology and robots, rising from 32 million in 2000 to 79 million in 2014 for urban workers (see Table 1.1). In addition, rural manufacturing workers increased from 14.5 million to 23.6 million from 2003 to 2014.

Why does China not exhibit the trend of declining manufacturing employment? The key reason is clear: the liberalisation of the economy associated with China's entry into the

WTO led to a huge surge in China's share of global exports and particularly its share of global manufacturing exports, which tripled from 6 per cent in 2000 to 18 per cent in 2012. In contrast, over the same period the US share fell by half, from 18 to 9 per cent.[15]

CHALLENGING GLOBALISATION'S WIN-WIN

The fact is, the globalisation lobby has rarely stated clearly and precisely what they mean by globalisation, nor do advocates differentiate between gains from trade due to absolute cost advantages or from relative or comparative cost advantages. This is because either they do not understand the difference, or if they do, it does not help their case to acknowledge that specialising according to absolute cost means whole nations may lose out. And although comparative advantage is a better justification for trade, as we saw from scrutinising Ricardo's four magic numbers theory, even this does not stand up to scrutiny in the real world.

This does not prevent globalisation's backers from drawing the related false conclusion that putting up barriers to trade is harmful to those that do so. The received wisdom is that restrict-ing international trade – protectionism – will have adverse consequences, for example, raising the prices of imported goods to the detriment of consumers. Broader issues of fairness, or winners and losers, tend not to figure in their arguments. Calculations that the loss of cheap imports might be more than compensated for by the re-establishment of higher-paid jobs in the importing nation go largely unmade.

Nobel laureate Joseph Stiglitz is a prominent critic of globalisation as currently practised. For Stiglitz, globalisation can be either a success or a failure, depending on its management: there is potential for success when it is managed by national governments embracing the characteristics of each individual country; there is a failure when it is managed by international institutions such as the

IMF.[16] He argues that international institutions such as the IMF and WTO are not democratic, do not play the role of a world government and too often favour the interests of big multinational businesses and the financial community.

In the US concerns have also been raised about the North American Free Trade Association (NAFTA), established in 1994 between the US, Canada and Mexico. Writing twenty years later, former US congressman David Bonior claimed that NAFTA had led to 'a fundamental change in the composition of jobs available to the 63 per cent of American workers without a college degree' and a 'ballooning' trade deficit with the other signatories.[17] Manufacturing jobs have either been lost or subject to downward pressure on wages as workers are forced to compete with poorly paid workers elsewhere. Workers made redundant from higher-paid manufacturing jobs have also flooded the market for already lower-paid service jobs, while the threat of further manufacturing shutdowns has effectively closed off wage bargaining, fuelling income inequality. In addition, governments focused solely on improving 'labor-market flexibility' in the name of deregulation have pursued policies that privilege employers' interests over those of workers, by hampering employees' ability to organise.

> The Labor Department's Trade Adjustment Assistance program, which documents this trend, reads like a funeral program for the middle class. More than 845,000 workers have been certified under this one narrow and hard-to-qualify-for program as having lost their jobs because of offshoring of factories to, and growing imports from, Mexico and Canada since NAFTA.
>
> The result is downward pressure on middle-class wages as manufacturing workers are forced to compete with imports made by poorly paid workers abroad. According to the Bureau of Labor Statistics, nearly two out of every three displaced

manufacturing workers who were rehired in 2012 saw wage reductions, most losing more than 20 per cent.

And, for America's remaining manufacturing workers, NAFTA put downward pressure on wages by enabling employers to threaten to move jobs offshore during wage bargaining. A 1997 Cornell University study ordered by the NAFTA Commission for Labor Cooperation found that as many as 62 per cent of union drives faced employer threats to relocate abroad, and the factory shutdown rate following successful union certifications tripled after NAFTA.

This is hardly news; in the early 1990s a spate of studies resulted in an academic consensus that trade flows contributed to between 10 and 40 per cent of inequality increases. Indeed, since NAFTA's implementation, the share of national income collected by the richest 10 per cent has risen by 24 per cent, while the top 1 per cent's share has shot up by 58 per cent.[18]

Some advocates of NAFTA-style pacts acknowledge that they cause the loss of some jobs, but argue that workers win overall by being able to purchase cheaper imported goods. However, when the Center for Economic and Policy Research applied the data to this theory, they found that reductions in consumer prices had not been sufficient to offset losses in wage levels. They found that American workers without college degrees had most likely lost more than 12 per cent of their wages to NAFTA-style trade, even accounting for the benefits of cheaper goods. This means a loss of more than $3,300 per year for a worker earning the median annual wage of $27,500.

The NAFTA data poses a significant challenge for proponents of globalisation. Bonior, himself the House of Representatives Democratic whip during the vote on NAFTA in 1983, is honest enough to recognise that the agreement was not all it was cracked up to be. Not so much because it caused a loss of US jobs, although arguably it did, but because in practice more trade does not always lead to the winners being willing and able to more than compensate the losers. They might if governments of high-cost countries were tough enough to extract good terms from low-cost countries in a fair quid pro quo. But with NAFTA this did not happen. Either Congress and President Clinton simply accepted the prevailing economic orthodoxy of the free traders, even if based on a set of unrealistic assumptions, or they knew that only part of the population would directly benefit but hoped that a trickle-down wealth effect from the main beneficiaries to the rest would eventually compensate for the loss of well-paid manufacturing jobs. Or most disturbingly, they simply carried out the wishes of big business and finance because of the power of the lobbyists and the need to cover election campaign costs.

Another defence of NAFTA and other globalising pacts is that any short-term frictional adjustment costs of unemployment or lower-wage re-employment for workers whose jobs have been outsourced abroad will be offset by the long-term benefits, as the next generation is channelled into the higher-productivity activities that a country specialises in. Unfortunately, the short term is becoming a bit long in the tooth. Stiglitz claimed that 'one of the reasons we [America, but also applicable elsewhere] are in such bad shape is that we have mismanaged globalisation'. Free-trade theory 'only says that the winners could compensate the losers, not that they would. And they haven't – quite the opposite. This is one of the reasons that the real median income of male workers is lower than it was forty years ago.'

In finance, people joke that a long-term investment is often a short-term investment that went wrong. Perhaps the same goes for economic theory.

The fact is, the step-up in the pace of globalisation of the past quarter-century has created winners and losers, and the winners have, by and large, opted to pocket the gains rather than redistribute some of them to compensate the losers. By and large, the winners have been workers in developing countries, and the captains of industry and finance in the developed world whose earning power has been linked to the boost in profitability from outsourcing production and servicing to lower absolute cost countries.

Among other things, this has led to the unprecedented phenomenon that our children's generation looks set to be the first in modern times to end up worse off than its parents', after taking into account higher debt and lower housing affordability. Real median incomes of those aged 15–24 were the same in 2014 as in 1979.[19]

The picture is not much better for the wider working-age population, nor is this confined to America. Even the European model of success, Germany, is subject to the same phenomenon. Real wage growth averaged a paltry 0.43 per cent per annum from 1992 to March 2019, boosted in the early years by German unification,[20] while real GDP per capita rose from $32,337 in 1990 to $46,987 in 2017.[21]

Of course, pay restraint has been a factor driving Germany's competitiveness and export machine. It is the only Western country that has managed to maintain a strong manufacturing base and benefited, as a country, from increased world trade. The question is, as for all Western countries, to whom have those benefits accrued?

While the opening of China to the global production chain has caused a structural decline in Western manufacturing jobs, this does not by itself disprove the benefits of greater international trade. But the evidence of stagnant real wages and the declining share of labour income versus profits in the economic pie, as well as rising income inequality, are hardly consistent with the optimists' belief that new higher-productivity jobs will more than compensate the losers from globalisation. It simply has not happened.

At the same time, the IMF applauds the concomitant explosion in the financial industry:

> The world's financial markets have experienced a dramatic increase in globalisation in recent years. Global capital flows fluctuated between 2 and 6 per cent of world GDP during the period 1980–95, but since then they have risen to 14.8 per cent of GDP, and in 2006 they totalled $7.2 trillion, more than tripling since 1995. The most rapid increase has been experienced by advanced economies, but emerging markets and developing countries have also become more financially integrated. As countries have strengthened their capital markets they have attracted more investment capital, which can enable a broader entrepreneurial class to develop, facilitate a more efficient allocation of capital, encourage international risk sharing, and foster economic growth.[22]

No doubt increased trade necessitates a more extensive global financial infrastructure, including, for example, an increase in banks' capacity to finance trade, corporate restructuring and cross-border reorganisation and takeovers. But we also understand now that international risk sharing also means international contagion and recession when too much risk accumulates in the global financial system. Perhaps one can have too much of a good thing.

There are of course many attractive aspects to a globalised world. It is true that it enables communication across the planet and, combined with the Internet and digital communication, it has democratised access to information. In theory at least it should put more pressure on tyrants and vested interests that benefit from monopolising information. It is also true that it has brought countless people in the developing world out of poverty. Real wages in India and China have risen strongly between 1990 and 2014. The gap is stark between the emerging and developing markets of the G20, where real wages almost tripled between 1999 and 2017, and the developed countries, where real wages rose by only 9 per cent. If we look at individual countries, over the decade 2008–17 real wages have risen 5–9 per cent in Canada, the US and France, but have actually fallen by about 5 per cent in the UK and Italy. Contrast this with China, where real wages almost doubled over the period.[23]

While the number of workers living in extreme poverty in low- and middle-income countries has fallen from 1.3 billion in 1993 to 700 million in 2018, thanks to China's high economic growth,[24] the global middle class has expanded from about 1 billion people in 1985 to 3 billion in 2015. Most of this growth has come from the Asia Pacific region.[25] The developing world's middle class surged by 870 million between 1991 and 2013. These are indeed impressive figures. However, while they suggest that inequality has narrowed *between* countries, it doesn't change the fact that inequality has sky-rocketed *within* countries, as we shall see later.

Globalisation has also had a positive impact on inflation, partly through the availability of cheap manufactured imports from emerging markets and partly the restraining influence on Western wages of workers knowing jobs can be easily moved to cheaper locations. The supply of cheap goods and services has undoubtedly increased the purchasing power and standard of living of Western consumers, *other things being equal.* The problem is, this caveat is spectacularly inappropriate in this context. Globalisation does not just mean cheaper consumer goods. It rearranges all the means of production and their networks, with secondary effects on local producers dependent on the spending power of those engaged in the production of internationally tradable goods and services. This is another example of the multiplier effect – Keynes's insight into the knock-on effects of an initial change in consumption or savings or any other large component of an economy.

The consequences do not stop with the private sector. Changes in aggregate income growth, as well as its composition and distribution, will inevitably affect public finances. Stagnating middle-class incomes in the developed world, coupled with a greater reliance on lower-paid work or government handouts, has also contributed to a structural deterioration in local and national government budgets.

THE WEST IS THE BEST

Promoting globalisation over the last thirty years, however, has been a prime case of pushing against an open door. Rightly or wrongly, the inflationary 1970s led to the rejection of Keynesian economics and governments playing a major role in economies. The collapse of communism in 1989 not only physically liberated people, goods and money to move around the globe, but also constituted the proof, for many, of the supremacy of the Anglo-Saxon free-market model. In a global contest spanning three generations, the West had won by a knockout. The only other option, Keynes's in-between social democratic state interventionism, had been tried and discredited.

In the circumstances the West turned to full-fat free-market capitalism as the only game in town. This promised the most efficient allocation of resources, guided by economist Adam Smith's so-called invisible hand. Smith coined this metaphor to describe how economic agents acting out of self-interest in the market end up promoting the common good, even though that may not have been their intention. The problem is that the conditions Smith described no longer exist. For example, private businesses in sole proprietorships have largely been superseded by limited liability companies, in which ownership is dispersed among shareholders who delegate the running of the businesses to a professional managerial class with its own economic interests.

Similarly, the early version of capitalism described by neoclassical economists consisted overwhelmingly of agriculture and industrial production. The romantic view of the free marketeers has not adapted to the rise of tertiary industries, in particular finance. Unlike primary and secondary industries, finance is fundamentally pro-cyclical and not self-stabilising. It is the cuckoo in the nest. This is because its growth, through the promotion of credit and therefore debt, is inherently destabilising if this takes place at a greater rate than the real growth of the underlying economy.[26] It is also easily prone to speculative excess: higher asset prices perversely attract more demand, fuelled by more credit created on the basis of higher asset prices. This mechanism is not inherently self-correcting as neoclassical economics would wish; quite the contrary.

At some point that is difficult to predict this out-of-control self-reinforcing spiral of debt-fuelled asset or commodity price inflation breaks, threatening a large reversal in prices, causing defaults and threatening debt deflation. This occurs either when the debt load becomes unserviceable, either because of a rise in interest rates or because marginal borrowers do not have the means to service their new debts, interrupting the rise in asset prices required as collateral for the loans, or because growth slows. At this point the whole process goes into reverse and starts to self-destruct as, lacking new buyers, asset prices start to fall, causing more debt to become unserviceable as incomes and confidence fall and asset values fall below the value of some of the loans they support. Defaults rise and debt write-offs lead to forced asset sales and further tumbles in asset values, the tightening of credit conditions and so on in a death spiral that requires the intervention of the state to avert disaster.

Contrary to classical economic theory, falling wages may not restore equilibrium or full employment because a fall in wages will lead to lower prices and profits and, as a result, bankruptcies because of debt. This in turn places further pressure on employment and wages, creating the conditions for a depression. This was also Keynes's central argument for government intervention.

In short, the invisible hand guiding the economy to the most efficient allocation of resources can turn self-destructive. It is arguably the case that all booms and subsequent busts in history not caused by war or disease were caused by the unrestrained excesses of the financial industry – which includes the real estate sector. Nevertheless, it became increasingly obvious during the 1980s that no other system could compete with Western liberal democracy. And what economic system had the winning side employed to win the argument? The capitalist free-market model based on classical economics, including Ricardo's theory of the benefits of greater international trade

But the world confused the collapse of communism with proof of the validity of the unfettered free-market system. It confused the failure of policies in the 1970s that led to inflation with the discrediting of Keynesian economics. And it rehabilitated economic theory born in a world that no longer existed, absolving the authorities of responsibility and the public of the need to make difficult political choices. Everyone, on the left as well as the right, swore allegiance to the market, at least if they were serious about getting elected. Political choices and elections became mild debates on nuances and personalities rather than the big fundamental issues of the past.

Francis Fukuyama captured the zeitgeist in his 1989 essay 'The End of History': 'What we may be witnessing is not just the end of the Cold War, or the passing of a particular period of post-war history, but the end of history as such: that is, the end point of mankind's ideological evolution and the universalisation of Western liberal democracy as the final form of human government.'[27] As if, having solved the riddle of social organisation, there was neither room for further evolution nor for conflict based on ideology: we would all inevitably fall into line and practise the same economic faith.

Fukuyama, however, was smart enough to recognise when things were not quite going according to plan. In 2014, on the twenty-fifth anniversary of the publication of his original essay, he wrote a column in *The Wall Street Journal* to update his hypothesis: while liberal democracy still had no real competition from more authoritarian systems of government 'in the realm of ideas', he was nevertheless less idealistic than he had been 'during the heady days of 1989'.[28]

The biggest problem for democratically elected governments in some countries was not ideological but 'their failure to provide the substance of what people want from government: personal security, shared economic growth and the basic public services ... that are needed to achieve individual opportunity'. Fukuyama also warned of 'political decay', in which corruption and crony capitalism erode liberty and economic opportunity.

In the heat of the late 1980s, it had been easy to confuse democracy with free-market economics; at the time they went hand in hand. In fact, neither requires the other. Russia and China, for example, have grown in leaps and bounds since each adopted some form of market economy without fundamentally changing political systems that remain autocratic. The West recovered from the Great Depression of the 1930s thanks only to massive state intervention. The 'thirty glorious' post-war years saw the creation of welfare states in various forms in the West, with relatively high tax rates and state intervention in economic affairs. This coincided with strong growth, free from the kind of extreme booms and busts we have increasingly witnessed more recently.

WINNERS AND LOSERS: CHINA VERSUS THE WEST

A decade before the fall of the Berlin Wall and the disintegration of the Soviet Union, China, under the leadership of Deng Xiaoping, started to dismantle its state-run communist economic system.

The start of China's emancipation from *economic* communism was the 'open door' policy, begun in 1978. Deng understood that fundamental changes in economic organisation were required if China was to compete with the West. He dismantled collective farms, created free-trade zones and encouraged the foreign investment needed for modernisation. Privately owned businesses sprang up. The policy also permitted Chinese nationals to travel and learn abroad and return to China with newly acquired skills.

As more modern and mechanised farming methods took hold and peasants were incentivised to increase productivity, farming yields went up. Cereal production grew 86 per cent between 1986 and 2005.[29] In turn, this released millions of agricultural workers to seek employment in the growing manufacturing sector. If proof were needed that economic liberalisation worked, China was on its way to double-digit growth rates by the time Deng died in 1997.

Deng's separation of politics from economics was encapsulated in a quote attributed to him: 'It does not matter if a cat is black or white, as long as it catches mice.' Deng possessed the political skill and pragmatism to shepherd his reformist agenda through the Communist Party system. Revolution and the dictatorship of the proletariat now took second place to increasing trade, opening up China's internal market, acquiring technology and management expertise, and, crucially, focusing on export-orientated growth. In 1982 Deng described this process as 'building socialism with Chinese characteristics', arguing that the true socialist revolution could only occur after the bourgeois/industrial phase of economic development, rather than straight from a peasant society.

By liberating the economy from the dead hand of state

ownership and control of prices, the Chinese leadership allowed the economy to breathe, and growth took off. China's accession to the WTO in 2001 cemented its integration within the global economy by providing maximum access to international trade. Even allowing for the size of China's population, and for starting from such a low base, the numbers are staggering. In 1978 GDP per head was $156. From 1980 to 2018, China's average real growth rate was 9.3 per cent,[30] with a high of 15.2 per cent in 1984 and a low of 3.8 per cent in 1990. By 2018, per capita GDP had reached $9,770.[31]

In inflation-adjusted terms, Chinese wages have also grown very strongly, especially since the early 2000s when it joined the WTO. Annual manufacturing wages per head rose from 26,599 yuan in 2009 to 72,088 in 2018. Given that inflation has averaged about 2 per cent per year, this represents stunning growth in real wages, even though China has also massively introduced robots. Clearly, from a national perspective China has been one of the big winners of globalisation.

The story in the West is more complicated. While average pay has gone up over the last twenty years, albeit at a much weaker pace in real terms than for the Chinese, this masks the fact that most of the benefits from trade have accrued to a minority at the top of the income scale. Wages for workers at the lower end of income distribution have either stood still or in real terms gone backwards.

Thomas Piketty argues that we have gone full circle. The top 1 per cent in America collected 25 per cent of income in 1929 at the height of the boom before the bust of the Great Depression, falling to 8.9 per cent in 1976 at the tail end of thirty years of growth, before rising once more to 23.5 per cent at the peak of the last boom before the financial crisis in 2007. In both the 1920s and 2000s there was a sharp increase in the level of debt, which was tolerated because of the belief in the self-correcting nature of markets.[32]

British real wages, while anaemic, did better in the twenty years

Figure 1.2: Median real wage growth, UK and US, 1988–2013

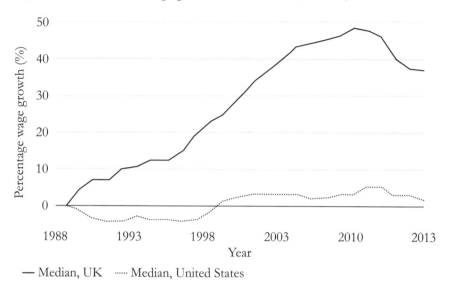

up to the financial crisis but have paid the price since (see Figure 1.2). In countries like Greece and Italy real wages remain stubbornly below pre-crisis levels.

Perhaps most surprisingly, developed economies (like Japan and France) that failed fully to endorse free-market capitalism have shown far better real wage growth than Anglo-Saxon market ideologues predicted.

STRUCTURAL CHANGES IN THE LABOUR MARKET

In the UK unemployment in the decades after the Second World War was low, hovering around 2 per cent from 1950 to 1970 before trending higher. Large-scale structural change came with the disappearance of manufacturing jobs after Margaret Thatcher came to power on an explicitly free-market agenda in 1979: a fall from 7 million jobs producing about 33 per cent of GDP in 1979, to around 3 million producing 13 per cent of GDP in 2008. This was a mirror image of the growth in the finance sector, which doubled to about 7 per cent of GDP from the 1970s to the start of the crisis. Since finance jobs enjoyed much faster wage growth than the rest of the economy, this temporarily dragged up the UK's average wage growth (North Sea oil may have been another contributor), but when the financial crisis burst finance's bubble, the UK's underlying capacity for generating real wage growth was cruelly exposed.

In the Midlands and the north of England growth in government jobs helped to mop up the pool of otherwise unemployed labour, some of which had come from manufacturing. In fact, the UK employment market had a 'good' financial crisis. The unemployment rate never touched double digits and was back down to 5.6 per cent by the fourth quarter of 2014. According to Martin Wolf, a remarkable 73 per cent of the population between the ages of 16 and 65 were in employment, slightly above the pre-crisis peak.[33] However, the bad news is that productivity has stalled. Output per hour worked has flatlined since the crisis, decoupling from the growth of the previous two decades and representing a period of stagnation unprecedented since at least the nineteenth century. At the same time, manufacturing was 4.9 per cent smaller than at the pre-crisis peak, while services were 8.1 per cent bigger.

In the US wages stagnated between 2000 and 2007, but real consumption rose by 20 per cent, financed by debt. And while unemployment oscillated widely between 4 and 10 per cent, and is once again below 4 per cent, this masks the fact that a growing proportion of the population has dropped out of the workforce altogether. Rather than breathing a sigh of relief that America appears to be approaching full employment, we should bemoan the fact that the percentage of the population in work has fallen to around 63 per cent, the lowest level since the 1980s and 2 per cent lower than before the crisis.

It is, of course, difficult to analyse fully the various factors that have contributed to the loss of secure high-paying manufacturing jobs in the West. As we have seen, apologists for globalisation point to technological change as the sole culprit as machines have displaced human labour. Others take a more nuanced approach. What nobody can deny is that the transfer of production to China has resulted in a massive trade imbalance. America's trade deficit in manufactured goods went from virtually nothing in 1990 to several hundred billion dollars just twenty years later. Whereas the US lost about a third of its manufacturing jobs between 2000 and 2009, Germany lost only about 11 per cent. One reason for this is that manufacturing firms in Germany are often privately owned, maybe family businesses, more integrated into their local communities and likely to take a longer-term view of profit generation, so less likely to transfer production overseas.

Research by Harvard Business School's Michael Porter, Jan Rivkind and Rosabeth Moss Kanter shows that the rise of globalisation went hand in hand with a change in how companies organised themselves and rewarded their senior management: 'The basic narrative begins in the late 1970s and the 1980s. Through globalisation, it became possible and attractive for firms to do business in, to, and from far more countries. Changes in corporate governance and compensation caused US managers to adopt an approach to management that focused attention on the stock price and short-term performance.'[34]

In the UK manufacturing jobs shrank from 6.7 million to 2.7 million between 1979 and 2019. Going further back, in 1952 British manufacturing employed 40 per cent of the workforce and represented a third of the economy and a quarter of world manufacturing exports. This has collapsed to 8 per cent of the workforce and 2 per cent of global exports.[35] While this does not amount to proof, it is further strong circumstantial evidence against those who deny globalisation's responsibility for the hollowing-out of good middle-class jobs. This is particularly true in the English-speaking world, which has acted as the cheerleader for the uncontrolled relocation of investment and production to low-cost countries.

Far from being the panacea for all our economic ills, unfettered international trade based on outdated and outmoded neoclassical economic theory has instead sown the seeds of the West's decline. Technological change has undoubtedly played a part in the loss of traditional manufacturing jobs, wage stagnation and an increasing reliance on a less stable services sector. However, on its own it cannot be held responsible for the scale of the decline. Instead, we need to challenge the orthodoxy that globalisation – or at least uncontrolled globalisation – is an inherent and inevitable force for good.

2

What to do with obsolete humans

Other industrial revolutions cost a lot of people their heads, I'm not sure we have the time for the wonderful markets to fix all these problems.

Peter Brabeck[1]

A form of techno-feudalism is unnecessary. Above all, technology itself does not dictate the outcomes. Economic and political institutions do.

Martin Wolf, *Financial Times*[2]

LUDDITES 2.0

Human beings' fear of being replaced by machines is as old as economics itself. Famously, in early-nineteenth-century Britain textile workers known as the Luddites smashed machines in opposition to the introduction of spinning frames and looms, fearing, not without foundation, that mechanisation would leave them without jobs. Their protests did not prevent the Industrial Revolution sparking the greatest jump in production and living standards in human history.

While all agree that short-term unemployment occurs when workers are replaced by machines, the debate on the long-term effects of technological change on labour continues to divide, depending on the health of the jobs market. Optimists argue that, after a while, more jobs are created by new technology through compensation effects than will have been destroyed, although not necessarily for the same people. This process of 'creative destruction' is seen as the only way to move forward. J. B. Say provided the economic rationale for the long-term optimists. His central idea is that, as technology increases efficiency and productivity and so the economy's output, the implied rise in real incomes fuels the means to buy the increased production. Keynes turned this into a catchy sound bite: 'supply creates its own demand'. Eventually, advances in technology allegedly raise the wages of most, if not all, workers. The evidence for this includes the increased demand for labour during the Industrial Revolution and dramatic increase in living standards in the West over the last century and a half.

More recently, the optimistic consensus has been challenged by weak labour markets and stagnant wages in many countries. This has led to an argument between those who lay the blame for this economic malaise at the door of globalisation and international competition and those who focus on labour substitution by increasingly smart machines. The reality is that it is difficult to disentangle the effects of exporting jobs to low-cost countries from that of automation; in fact, they go hand in hand.

Erik Brynjolfsson and Andrew McAfee, in their book *Race Against the Machine*, cite Michael Spence, who makes the link between globalisation and technology. Technology has all but eliminated geographic barriers, gradually equalising factor prices and forcing American labour to compete with developing nations. Brynjolfsson cites the following dispassionate assessment by NASA of the advantages at the time (1965) of manned space flights: 'Man is the lowest cost, 150-pound, nonlinear, all-purpose computer system which can be mass-produced by unskilled labour.' The key question is how we respond to these two seemingly unstoppable forces that challenge fundamentally the way we work and are remunerated.

Technology pessimists have been gaining ground in the last few years. A Pew Research survey of technology experts revealed a split on the adverse long-term effects of technology on employment with 52 per cent thinking that technology will not displace more jobs than it creates by 2025, while 48 per cent thought it would.[3] Former US treasury secretary and Harvard professor Lawrence Summers has stated that he no longer believes automation will create new jobs. And although recent research covering seventeen industrialised countries from 1993 to 2007 by Georg Graetz and Guy Michaels concludes that technology has not led to a fall in aggregate wages or employment, they agree that it has affected the *distribution* of employment: 'While we find no significant effect of industrial robots on overall employment, there is some evidence that they crowd out employment of low-skilled and, to a lesser extent, middle-skilled workers.'[4]

Even if aggregate wages have risen, the trickle-down effect certainly seems to have dried up. The distribution of gains from technological change has become more skewed to those with higher skills and incomes, to the extent that large swathes of the population are unemployable except in low-skill low-pay jobs, and have ceased to progress in real inflation-adjusted terms for many years.

THIS TIME IS DIFFERENT
While anxiety over the effects of technology coincided in the past with weak labour markets and subsequently proved unjustified, it may well be that, like the many false alarms raised by the boy who cried wolf, this time is actually different.

In the late nineteenth and twentieth centuries new machines needed armies of people to use and maintain them, the automobile industry being a prime example, absorbing millions of people who migrated from the countryside in the 1950s and 60s to work in giant mechanised factories that vastly increased productivity.

During this age of mechanisation machines were replacing physical muscle power and therefore complemented labour, making it more efficient and increasing its productivity. In the US nominal GDP per head increased steadily between 1960 and 1980, initially in lockstep with median income per head. Most of that productivity growth accrued to workers as higher wages. According to Martin Ford, real household median incomes in the US tracked per capita GDP and doubled from $25,000 to $50,000 between 1948 to 1973.[5] This was indeed a golden era of technological change working *with* the labour force.

But from around 1980 productivity began to far outstrip growth in median income per head and real median household income. Median income is a less misleading measure of those in the middle, representing the individual halfway up the income distribution scale, since, unlike mean or average income, it is not distorted upwards by the super earners right at the very top.

This period is significant since it coincided with a three-decade fall in the cost of capital in the form of declining interest rates, as well as the entry of China into the global supply of labour. This in turn facilitated the steady leveraging up of most developed economies to an unprecedented level. Growing debt enabled a continuation of rising consumption and living standards among many poorer households, and masked the slowing momentum of rising real wages. At the top end of income distribution, borrowing was used to increase wealth through the acquisition of assets rising in value faster than nominal GDP, turbocharged by cheap money.

Studies carried out in the US show that in the thirty years after 1973 real median household income increased, due mainly to the increase in female participation in the labour force, but only by about 22 per cent compared to GDP growth of 50 per cent. The fruits of increased technological change began to accrue less and less to those in the bottom half of the distribution scale. In fact, in real terms, which is what matters, the top half all but ceased to share out any of the benefits of growth with those beneath them, an issue we'll explore in more detail in Chapter 4. Today, the cost of machines has come down enough, and their sophistication has improved so much, that the symbiotic relationship to labour is completely breaking down.

Writing in Germany's *Süddeutsche Zeitung* in 2014, Horst Neumann, Volkswagen board member for human resources, said robots would fill some of the retiring baby boomers' jobs, not people. He added that robots that carry out routine tasks cost the company five euros an hour over their lifetimes including maintenance and energy costs while Chinese workers cost ten and Germans (including wages, pensions and healthcare) about forty euros an hour.[6] Foxconn, a Chinese contract manufacturer for brand names such as Apple, has embarked on a process of replacing part of its workforce with robots. By 2017, China had become the world's largest market for industrial robots, representing 58 per cent of the world's sales, compared to 6 per cent in the US and 8 per cent in Germany.

Part of the recent 'onshoring' trend of returning production to the US is due to the fact that machines are now competitive with what was cheap foreign labour. That does not, of course, mean that ex-manufacturing workers are getting their old jobs back. This begs the question of where this trend will take us economically and socially. Not only are machines displacing labour in manual and repetitive tasks, but their inexorable advance even threatens jobs that require intelligence or higher education.

MOORE'S LAW

Gordon Moore, the co-founder of Intel, postulated that the number of transistors you could fit on a semiconductor chip would double roughly every eighteen months. The exponential rise in computer power following Moore's law has qualitatively changed the relationship between man and machine for three reasons. First, the cost of producing machines is falling, thereby making more tasks open to the substitution of robots. Second, the progress of technology in production is faster than the speed at which displaced humans are being retrained into jobs that are not yet economically mechanised. Lastly, it is doubtful that workers displaced by machines can migrate into higher-skilled jobs that are not amenable to technological substitution.

The writing has been on the wall for some time now.

Way back in the 1980s, Nobel prize-winning economist Wassily Leontief foresaw that humans' role in production would diminish, just like the horse in agriculture. While machines would replace muscle, humans could still find productive jobs using their brain power, although this was also now under threat.[7] Indeed, the rise of ever smarter computers is eating away at the need for human brain power. As well as factory work, many white-collar jobs, the domain of the middle classes, are at risk. And if that is the case, so are the middle-class incomes that have been the engine for economic growth in the past. The remedies he proposed included sharing work time and subsidising employment through social security.

A study in the UK by the Chartered Institute of Personnel and Development claimed that the increase in the number of university graduates has outstripped the growth in higher-skill jobs, resulting in many graduates' aspirations to embark on a secure middle-class career being dashed, and many ending up working in low-skilled jobs where their degree in not required.[8] In 2014 Google's co-founder Larry Page went as far as to suggest a four-day working week, so that as technology continues to displace jobs, more people can find employment.[9] Google chairman Eric Schmidt is on record as saying, 'The race is between computers and people, and people need to win … it is very important that we find the things that humans are really good at.'[10] That did not prevent Google from purchasing UK AI company Deep Mind, and US robot maker Boston Dynamics.

In 2009 Martin Ford suggested that machines will do the work of many people who will not be able to find alternative employment.[11] Already, many industries such as retailing are being transformed by online shopping and delivery. Large automated warehouses greatly reduce the need for human intervention, although some employment is created for truck drivers – for now. Intelligent vending machines and checkout counters also reduce the need for staff, as do automated passport controls and departure gates at airports. Successful new industries will make use of advanced information technology and are unlikely to be very labour intensive.

However, according to Ford, by the early 2020s the size of individual elements on computer chips will be reduced to about five nanometres (billionths of a metre) 'and that is close to the fundamental limit beyond which no further miniaturisation is possible'. In other words, we are fast approaching the end of the advance of computer hardware using current technology. However, that does not take into account potential breakthroughs in new technologies such as quantum computing.

Furthermore, that is not the end of the story, since there is still room for more efficient software. According to Charles Simonyi, the man behind the development of Microsoft Word and Excel, this will enable us to eliminate the need for humans to do repetitive tasks that account for a lot of work. Indeed, Ford argues that knowledge-based jobs are more susceptible to replacement by improved software using algorithms than jobs requiring physical manipulation and fine motor skills (try building a robotic tennis champion). You can imagine a computer whose memory includes all past legal case histories that it can scan in order to select those that are useable to make a case based on precedent, for example; hence Marc Andreessen's slogan, 'Software is eating the world.'[12]

There is nothing to stop computers using algorithms from uncovering significant statistical relationships and employing those to improve themselves and what they can do. One of the principles of big data analysis is that the sheer power to crunch vast amounts of data can replace human (fallible) judgment and experience.

Ford also gives the example of a composition played by the London Symphony Orchestra in 2012, called *Transits – Into an Abyss*, which a reviewer praised as 'artistic and delightful'.[13] It was composed by a computer. So much for humans maintaining their monopoly on creativity.

PERMANENT UNEMPLOYMENT

What happens when computing power replaces professions employing human intelligence, especially in an age of globalisation? Keynes foresaw the possibility of long-term technological unemployment in the 1930s but considered this to be a good thing as it would liberate many from dreary and unpleasant jobs. Human beings would be able to spend more time on leisure and the arts and lead more enjoyable and fulfilling lives.

While this sounds attractive, society would need to overcome two problems. First, the political system would need to accept and put in place a permanent and sufficient income for doing nothing or very little – those no longer needed in the productive process. As Ford correctly points out, 'we run the risk that a large and growing fraction of our population will no longer have sufficient discretionary income to continue propelling vibrant demand for the products and services that the economy produces'.

At the very birth of the manufacturing golden age Henry Ford famously increased his workers' wages so that they were able to buy the goods they were making. Perhaps unusual among industrialists, he understood that workers were also consumers. While it may appear rational for one company to maximise profits by minimising labour costs without fear of the consequences, this logic breaks down if generalised across the economy, since my costs are your revenue. Keynes saw that Smith's invisible hand did not always produce socially or economically optimal outcomes by each economic unit rationally pursuing its own self-interest. The machine carries the seeds of its own instability and breaks down, as economist Hyman Minsky has argued, because each economic agent does not take into account the consequences of the replication of its behaviour by its peers.[14] Laying off workers may work for one company, but it also carries with it the danger of negatively affecting companies whose goods those workers can no longer afford to buy.

Second, and perhaps more challenging, individuals' identity and sense of self-worth is often tied to their role within the economy. The involuntary unemployed suffer from loss of self-esteem, sometimes associated with worsening health. It is difficult to overcome the feeling that you are no longer needed by society, living a life that is useless economically and dependent on permanent handouts. This is hardly a recipe for healthy individuals and social cohesion.

A whole new culture, very removed from our current competitive, individualistic, materialistic and consumerist mindset would have to take over. But if, as many have observed, those with power and wealth shape our values and have a vested interest in pumping up a system that has served them so well, it is difficult to imagine such a transition being promoted by those at the top who have the most to lose, and occurring peacefully.

In the US the information technology age has arrived at a time when productivity growth and job creation are already slowing. Robert Gordon documents how productivity growth actually started slowing in the 1970s. The digital-tech revolution has not been all that it has been cracked up to be, showing nothing like the positive, generation-changing effects of electricity or the internal combustion engine. Its most positive effect in the developed world – the widespread use of the PC – was done by 1994.[15] What is undeniable is that since 2008 average annual growth of GDP per hour worked in the US has retreated from about 2.5 per cent to a little over 1 per cent,[16] while real median incomes in the US hardly rose from $29,998 in 2000 to $31,099 in 2016.[17]

Sluggish productivity growth is not only a problem in the USA. As we saw in Chapter 1, the UK's productivity has recently plunged, a pattern replicated elsewhere. This is not good news for the 'more tech is best' brigade, and it's fair to say that there is a considerable degree of confusion on the subject. The *Financial Times*, one of a few truly global daily newspapers, trotted out the pro-tech view in a 2015 leader article: 'The advance of the internet and mobile technology … has generated new services and raised productivity,' while also acknowledging, 'The rapid advance of automation and artificial intelligence poses real challenges to how advanced industrial societies are organised.'[18] Earlier that same year, Brian Groom claimed, 'Weak productivity has been the main factor behind a decade of falling real wages in the UK since the [financial] crisis, the longest sustained drop for at least 50 years … Employers have expanded output by hiring extra workers, rather than investing in labour-saving technology or squeezing more efficiency out of their existing staff.'[19]

Hiring humans rather than machines, how retro! It seems we have suffered from too little labour-saving or efficiency-squeezing investment in the current decade, but this does not explain earlier diminishing productivity growth when Moore's law was powering the exponential advance in information technology. Yet back in 2014 another *FT* leader described how manual and clerical workers in wealthier nations have struggled as a result of growth in trade and technology over the past three decades. Entrepreneurs and the

'1 per cent' have gained most, but 'now the chill wind of automation may blow on the peaks'.[20]

So, you're damned if you do and damned if you don't. Not enough investment, and productivity and growth in living standards stall, but too much labour-saving investment, and (real) wage growth stalls. This sounds like a lose-lose situation.

In 2013 Carl Frey and Michael Osborne predicted that up to 47 per cent of US jobs were at risk from automation, with workers in transport and logistics, office and administrative support most at risk.[21] This will increase inequality as income is transferred to the owners of robots. Meanwhile those clinging to the hope that improving education to shoe-horn workers into higher-skill occupations simplistically assume that we can predict what kind of skills will be needed several decades down the road. However, cold realism argues for many more living a life of leisure, which probably requires some redistribution of income and wealth from the few who reap the rewards from new technology.

Perhaps, as Ford and others argue, we have simply been experiencing the wrong kind of technological change. Information technology and computers don't fundamentally change our lifestyles and quality of life the way electricity, the motor car and jet planes did. Perhaps the pace of truly transforming innovation has slowed since the first half of the twentieth century, when its fruits were more widely distributed.

WINNER TAKES ALL

Pessimists believe that information technology enables a small minority to prosper. Instead of a free market where the constant pressure of competition prevents firms and individuals from earning and maintaining excessive profits, technology seems to create a small number of players who wipe out or buy out their competitors. You only have to consider the dominant technology brands –

Microsoft, Apple, Google, Amazon, Facebook, Netflix – to see that once established, these businesses have the means to extend their competitive advantage and crowd out competitors.

This is hardly the land of competition anticipated by Adam Smith's invisible hand and totally inconsistent with economic theories which assume that abnormal profits will be arbitraged away by new entrants into the market. But if we are not in a world of perfect competition, what guarantee is there that the invisible hand of the market will guide us to optimal and efficient outcomes? None. Instead, is it not more likely that entrenched and dominant firms will be shielded from the pressure to improve, earning rent from their dominant position and relieved from the pressure to compete to provide the best-quality products? Some might view Microsoft's dominance of the computer operating system market as a case in point.

At the individual level, in a winner-takes-all system aided and abetted by global communications, top sports, entertainment personalities, financiers and CEOs can leverage their earning power to unprecedented global levels.

Brynjolfsson and McAfee argue that it is wrong to lay the blame for the loss of earning power of much of the working population entirely on the effects of globalisation. The fact is, the degree of interconnectedness needed for globalised production and distribution would not be possible without modern technology for transport and communications. Technology has been the hand-maiden of globalisation.

Ford lays the blame for the loss of manufacturing jobs in the US squarely on technology rather than globalisation, since the downward trend in manufacturing employment started decades before China joined the global marketplace. He argues that the US actually produces more now, but with fewer workers, even if the rate of productivity growth has slowed.[22] General Motors, the erstwhile car manufacturing giant, employed around 618,000 workers in the US at its peak in 1979, out of a total global workforce of around 850,000. Today, a little over 55,000 jobs have survived at its US plants. US Steel jobs peaked at 340,000 in 1943 and have shrunk to around 29,000 in 2018. But this analysis does not take into account the obvious point that both of these companies have lost market share, as their industries have been invaded by imports and foreign-owned plants; Toyota alone now operates around a dozen factories in the US.

The leading technology companies of today also employ fewer people than the old industrial companies. Microsoft employed around 80,000 workers in the US in 2018, compared to Facebook's 35,000 and Netflix's 7,000. Apple employed 84,000 US workers in 2018 and Google around 90,000. This represents a huge jump in productivity compared to the old manufacturing industries, but the flip side of the coin is that it no longer requires many people to produce a given unit of *measured* economic output – sidestepping the technicalities of how to measure the economic output of a Google or Facebook.

There is no way the numbers of old-economy workers that are now superfluous to requirements can be employed in the new knowledge industries. Even Amazon, the number-one online retailer, which has added workers over the last five years and in 2019 employed around 647,000 worldwide (including part-time and low-paid order fulfilment workers in its warehouses), is still dwarfed by the largest bricks-and-mortar retail chain Walmart, which boasts 1.5 million employees in the US alone.

If technology is one of the culprits for the loss of employment, particularly in manufacturing, it is difficult to point to the commensurate creation of secure high-paying, high-value jobs elsewhere to compensate for these losses. Even where other jobs have taken up the slack, in many cases the replacement jobs have not commanded decent wage levels; they're effectively downgrades.

Optimists, on the other hand, continue to believe the opposite. Since unprecedented growth has occurred thanks to the advent of machines over the last 150 years, if structural growth and real income growth have slowed in the last ten years, it is because our rate of technological innovation has slowed down. There has been no new 'big thing' since the high-speed Internet and mobile phones. What we need is *more* technological change, not less.

This seems counter-intuitive given the continued growth in computing power and its application to more and more tasks. Examples abound: automated transport systems, driverless cars and drone deliveries are just the tip of the iceberg. Even the traditional bobby on the beat has been superseded by CCTV and controllers in front of their monitors directing a few rapid-response units. The effects of today's technology are present everywhere, so that fewer and fewer jobs seem immune to substitution by machines.

There has been very little discussion by the authorities of the possibility that the relationship between technological innovation and employment and wage growth may have been turned upside down by computing power. Is it because they are in denial? Or perhaps they don't know which way to turn so it is better to keep silent and await developments. Economist Jeffrey Sachs, in a 2018 interview, warned that a 'tech tax' is necessary if the world is to avoid a dystopian future in which AI leads to the concentration of wealth in the hands of a few thousand people. He argues that new technologies are dramatically shifting income distribution worldwide 'from labour to intellectual property (IP) and other capital income'.

END GAME
Suppose for a moment that Moore's law comes to an end and the rate of advance of computing power slows or even grinds to a halt,

constrained by the sheer physical limits of making the building blocks of computers' brains smaller and smaller. Should we welcome this because it will give humans a breathing space to up their skills and work with machines in large numbers once more? Or should we fear the approaching end of the digital revolution? Could it be that the huge gains in productivity and living standards of the last 150 years are coming to an end so that from now on the cake will no longer grow, especially if population growth is constrained by environmental pressures? If that happens, what happens to the free-market economists' trickle-down effect, which was supposed to support the social contract? If the masses can't benefit from at least some of the growth as the pie expands even if their share shrinks, won't social peace break down as it becomes a question of how the rewards are shared out? Are we already in the foothills of this phenomenon?

Conventional economists and politicians ridicule such notions as unfounded and alarmist. But they are no less well founded than the mass of dumbed-down free-market beliefs that have been accepted as valid these last thirty-five years. And we have just witnessed the lack of imagination and prescience exhibited by these same conventional thinkers ahead of the greatest financial and economic crisis since the 1930s. As conventional living standards level off, it is at best complacent to do nothing and not rethink our framework for understanding how the economy works.

One conclusion is that we must come round to the notion of a guaranteed living wage for part of the population. As far back as the 1960s, a group of distinguished academics and journalists, including Friedrich Hayek, proposed this in order to neutralise the effects of rising unemployment and inequality. More recently, thinkers ranging from Martin Ford[23] and Erik Brynjolfsson[24] to Robert Reich[25] and Guy Standing in the UK[26] have also started to advocate some form of basic income as a solution to technological unemployment. Given the vast output of machines, it would be possible to put this in place at little real cost. We will return to this theme in the concluding chapter.

PART TWO

Dysfunctional Economics and the Decline of the West

3

The falling share of labour in the economy

If corporate investors, in aggregate, are going to eat an ever-growing portion of the American economic pie, some other group will have to settle for a smaller portion. That would justifiably raise political problems.

Marc Faber

The data is unequivocal. The income share of the national economic pie going to labour has been shrinking for around three decades (see Figure 3.1 overleaf).

This phenomenon should not be confused with rising inequality in the distribution of that income among working people. Neither does one imply the other. You could have a more equal distribution of income from wages (from CEOs down to the lowest employee) even if the total take from wages fell as a percentage of national income. However, they are linked historically and the effects of each on consumption and growth is similar. Other things being equal, each has a depressing effect on the incomes – and so purchasing power – of the less well-off, whose propensity to consume out of income is greater.

Clearly, a decline in labour's share of national income means that, even in a growing economy, growth in consumption will be

Figure 3.1: Changes in labour share in G20 countries plus Spain 1970–2014

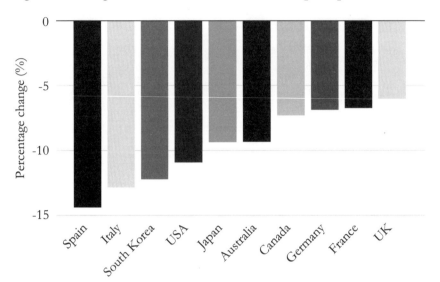

weaker, unless households spend more as a proportion of income. In other words, in order to keep up, households will need to either save less or borrow more. Similarly, an increasingly unequal distribution of income within the labour market has well-known depressing consequences for consumption. We will look at the latter in more detail in Chapter 4.

How and why has this retreat by labour taken place and what does it mean for the developed economies and investments in the future? And crucially, how does it link to globalisation, technological change, rising inequality and the erosion of trust in mainstream politicians and the democratic process?

WAGES AND THE EQUITY MARKET
Looking at the relationship between labour and capital another way, in the 1960s it took American workers about 30 hours of work to buy the value of the S&P 500 stock market index.

Figure 3.2. Hours of work to buy the S&P 500

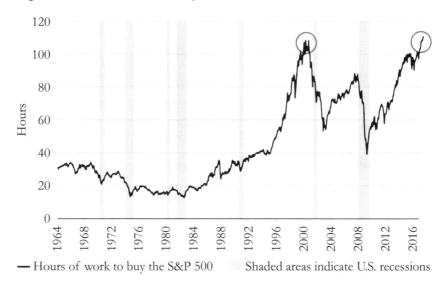

— Hours of work to buy the S&P 500   Shaded areas indicate U.S. recessions

This ratio fell to about half that during the 1970s, when the market fell and workers had the upper hand in wage bargaining, before rising to around 74 at the market peak in 2007 (S&P 500 at 1,565/$21.05 average private-sector hourly wage). The GFC brought the ratio back down to about 30 in March 2009. Fast-forward to end of July 2019, and it has soared to 106, underscoring how well capital has done relative to labour in the aftermath of the crisis.[1] A related factor is that company earnings have been so strong partly because wage growth has been so weak. The bulk of growth is being captured by corporate earnings and shareholders.

PROFITS AND GDP

According to a McKinsey Global Institute report, global corporate net income rose fivefold between 1980 and 2013, compared to world GDP growth of a mere 70 per cent.[2] Profits as a share of GDP rose to 11.6 per cent in the US, which is the highest level since 1929 and double the rate of the more egalitarian 1990s. In the UK a similar trend is clearly visible.[3]

The McKinsey Institute is not alarmed because it believes that the share of corporate profits *globally* will revert towards the mean as growth becomes concentrated in emerging markets. Because of the preponderance of family-owned or controlling-shareholder companies in these markets, companies are less driven to pursue short-term profits or squeeze their employees, and are more inclined to take a long-term view and reinvest profits to build position in the market and pursue growth. According to the institute, emerging-market companies only returned 39 per cent of earnings to shareholders between 1999 and 2008 compared to 80 per cent for developed-market companies. Even if developed-market companies eventually lose the long-distance race, they have certainly made out like bandits over the last thirty years, scant consolation for their workers.

If sales and revenues don't grow much, the only way to grow corporate earnings more impressively is to expand margins by cutting costs. This drives up share prices, which benefits owners and managers of capital. Since labour often represents a major part of costs, company managements have been busy 'improving efficiency' by shedding expensive labour in the US, UK, Germany and France, either moving production to cheaper locations abroad or through automation. The result is that the interests of corporations and their employees are no longer aligned.

The corollary to the squeeze by companies on labour costs has been the dwindling slice of the pie paid to labour. Again, US data graphically charts the deteriorating trend (Figure 3.3).

A similar trend is clear in the UK, following the change in economic policy which transformed the balance of power between organised labour and employers after 1979's so-called winter of discontent and the election of Margaret Thatcher (Figure 3.4).

Figure 3.3: Share of labour compensation in GDP in the US 1950–2015

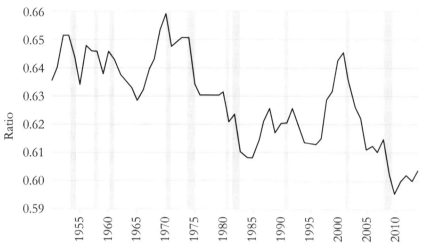

Shaded areas indicate U.S. recessions

Figure 3.4: Share of labour compensation in GDP in the UK 1856–2006

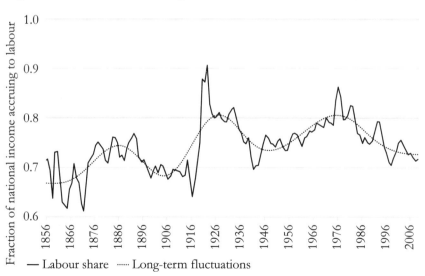

— Labour share ⋯⋯ Long-term fluctuations

This decline holds, with some variation, pretty much across the developed countries, and has been well documented by economists such at Thomas Piketty.[4]

THE INVISIBLE HAND IS BLIND

Under the economic system in force until the 1980s gains from increases in productivity were shared out between profits and wages, thus providing employees with the purchasing power to buy the fruits of their production. This created a virtuous circle of rising revenues begetting further wage and profit growth (see Minsky). Rising profits were also partly recycled into new investments that would in turn generate demand in the economy and increase productivity in a second virtuous circle.

In contrast, during the 'recovery' since the GFC of 2008 company chiefs have grown corporate earnings in spite of lacklustre revenue growth by cutting all costs. This has meant not only labour costs, but also skimping on reinvestment in productive capacity – capital expenditure. In what has now turned into a vicious circle, every round of labour cost-cutting undermines the purchasing power of consumers. This weakening demand has prompted management to engage in further cuts and dissuaded them from capital expenditure, given the visibly weak demand trend. This is partly responsible for what has become an entrenched deflationary pressure in major developed countries, in stark contrast to the great industrialist Henry Ford's benign paternalism: 'I will build a motor car for the great multitude ... constructed of the best materials, by the best men to be hired, after the simplest designs that modern engineering can devise ... so low in price that no man making a good salary will be unable to own one and enjoy with his family the blessing of hours of pleasure in God's great open spaces.' The millennial generation's questioning of the need for car ownership is a poignant reminder of the principle that you reap what you sow.

In a more modern version of the story, a company executive proudly showed off to visitors his newly automated factory. The visitors politely enquired how the robots would buy the product.

RATIONALITY AND THE GENERALISATION PRINCIPLE

This tacit recognition by companies of the need to pay workers enough so they can buy their own output both constrained the profit-seeking behaviour of companies and was consistent with acting as good corporate citizens. It also made economic sense. As we saw in Chapter 1, any single company can improve its profits by cutting its own labour costs and so it is 'rational' for it to do so on its own. But this ceases to be the case if this corporate behaviour becomes generalised, since the aggregate cut in purchasing power of labour will (unless workers find ways to supplement their purchasing power in the form of government handouts, loans or reduced savings) eventually hit that company's revenues, placing those temporarily enhanced profits under pressure.

This is sometimes referred to in ethics as the generalisation principle. A simple example of this is questioning whether to vote as a single vote will apparently make no difference to the outcome of an election; instead, you might as well save your valuable time. But if this reasoning is generalised, and no one votes, then the democratic process will implode. Likewise, squeezing wages to protect profits shows that Adam Smith's invisible hand can lead to perverse consequences if that hand is so blind as to completely miss the aggregate consequences of individuals acting only according to their narrow short-term interests.

Nor is it the case that lower wages can still maintain demand growth if it means more workers being priced into jobs. The fact is, the declining slice of wages in the national cake has occurred over a long period of time, during which there have been many economic cycles, including low and high unemployment. Fluctuating employment levels have not prevented the total take of wages from shrinking as a proportion of the whole, causing a continuing downward pressure on demand.

Classical economics does recognise some special cases where, from an aggregated point of view, the price mechanism on its own leads to sub-optimal results. Pollution and the protection of the environment is a topical case, where it is clearly of benefit to everyone to tax individual polluters for the societal consequences of their selfish actions and in order to encourage socially optimal outcomes. The only issue here is the technical one of how high to set the taxes. While it might be acceptable for a single economic entity to pollute if it gains from doing so and is too small to have a noticeable impact on the planet, it is not acceptable if this behaviour is replicated by a myriad of economic agents.

Curiously, while there is a whole body of economics that addresses the conundrum of the consequences of the rational decisions of individual economic agents in the case of pollution, there is, with some notable exceptions, much less discussion of this conundrum when it comes to the sharing out of the economic pie between profits and wages. This is probably because it is a more directly political issue which raises awkward questions for free-market ideologists.

Since the short-term, profit-maximising behaviour of companies is in conflict with the concomitant growth of wages, it is equally fair to say that there has been a breakdown in the social contract. Not only is this new model of growth not sustainable, it is clearly leading to disaffection among Western populations that threatens to challenge the economic and political status quo. Henry Ford was aware of this danger when he said, 'Profits made out of the distress of the people are always much smaller than profits made out of the most lavish service of the people at the lowest prices that competent management can make possible.'[5]

THE RISE OF SHAREHOLDER VALUE

The collapse of the Soviet Union and the discrediting of the communist system opened the way for a capitalist system that has turned its back on balancing the interests of business, the managerial class, shareholders, workers and consumers to an almost unbridled anything goes – as long as it's the result of the market operating without constraint. The market may not be perfect, but, like its twin, democracy, it's the best we have. Those within government who believe they can successfully second-guess the market are doomed to failure, as demonstrated by the collapse, under its own weight of inefficiency, of the seven-decade communist experiment of social and economic organisation starved of the vital price signals generated by the free interplay of supply and demand. The counter-example of the successful Chinese state-capitalist model was not yet evident in the 1980s and 90s when the unconstrained free-market ideology rippled out from the Anglo-Saxon countries across the globe under the political leadership of Ronald Reagan, Margaret Thatcher and their successors.

If the free market was the undisputed champion of the world, then its consequences could be justified by its economic efficiency and the invocation of supporting mantras. Companies are major players in markets; they allocate scarce resources through the signals of the price mechanism. The least efficient go out of business or are eaten up by their more efficient competitors in a Darwinian struggle for survival. The share price of a company reflects its perceived success or failure and acts as currency for takeovers and mergers. A company's share price being expensive or cheap determines whether it is able to stalk the corporate jungle as a predator or struggle to avoid becoming prey.

Shareholders in a company are rewarded by owning a part share in the earnings growth of the company and through payouts such as dividends or buy-backs of shares. No wonder the exhortation that the goal of business is to maximise earnings per share over time, encapsulated in the mantra of 'shareholder value', was an easy sell.

Of course, the goals of the professional managers hired by the owning shareholders of limited-liability companies to realise this objective are not necessarily aligned with their owners. Unlike in the time of the high priest of the market, Adam Smith, when business was arranged around partnerships constituted by active partners, today's free market has separated ownership from management. The potential for conflict of interests, sometimes referred to as the agency problem, manifests itself most blatantly in the realm of pay.

Faced with thousands if not millions of shareholders who subcontract the stewardship of their ownership interests to professional investment managers (who in turn have their own commercial interests to defend), there is little to deter corporate managers from seeking to game the system. There are many ways in which this can be done, but perhaps the most effective has been to tie top company management's compensation most heavily to the simple metric of earnings per share, either in the form of the granting of options related to this number, or bonuses contingent on reaching some pre-determined earnings per share target within a set time period.

Earnings per share are the result of three factors: revenue, costs (the difference between these two being earnings) and the number of shares outstanding (being the denominator). Management can influence all three, but to different degrees. Revenue growth is a function not only of a company's products and services, but also the general economic environment, demographics and technological change. It's easier for management to control costs. This can be achieved in a number of ways, including moving production to cheaper locations, increasing automation and granting wage rises below the rate of increase of productivity.

Another strategy to flatter profitability, at least in the short term, is to minimise reinvestment in the business, for example by reducing capital expenditure. Instead of reinvesting to promote the company's profitability and survival, management often prefers to spend cash on buying back the company's own shares. This mechanically increases the key metric of earnings per share, to which is tied top management's variable remuneration, typically many multiples of fixed salary. We shall return to the subject of market manipulation by senior managers in order to game the system in Chapter 8, as it does not directly affect the overall share of labour in the national pie. Cost reduction, on the other hand, by whatever means, is a direct cause of the falling share of labour in national income.

Some might argue that stock-owning households have seen their wealth increase as a result of this focus on share price, offsetting the effects of wage stagnation. However, according to the Federal Reserve Board, only 30 per cent of the lowest paid in the USA invest in stocks, compared to 92 per cent of the richest families. In other words, it is scant consolation for many that investment portfolios have done well; all they have are stagnant incomes. And while it is true that the ageing baby boom generation, with generous pension plans, may enjoy a comfortable retirement thanks to high growth in their stock investments, it is highly unlikely younger generations will enjoy the same stock returns or generous gold-plated defined-benefit pension plans.

The inflation-adjusted annual rate of return from US stocks (with dividends reinvested) since 1946 to July 2019 was a whopping 7.1 per cent,[6] far higher than the rate of growth in real wages, a theme which also features in Thomas Piketty's work. The extraordinary asset price inflation, including property, since the early 1980s has also contributed to a huge increase in wealth inequality.

THE DECOUPLING OF WAGES FROM PRODUCTIVITY

Figure 3.5 graphically illustrates the increasing gap in the US between the growth in output per head and how much each head in the middle of the income distribution scale is paid.

Part of the explanation is that some components that make up the consumer price index – such as energy, medical and housing costs – started to rise quite sharply from the 1970s onwards. This effectively increased GDP while holding back the purchasing power of labour. But, on its own, this cannot entirely explain the growth of the gap.

In contrast to median wage levels, average wages did somewhat better because the average is skewed upwards by the outsize gains of those at the top end of the income distribution. The median (the individual in the middle of the pack) is a fairer measure of change because it is not affected by the change in the distribution of income within the labour force. If those at the top reap almost all the gains from growth, the purchasing power of the majority of the workforce stagnates.

Figure 3.5: The productivity–wage gap

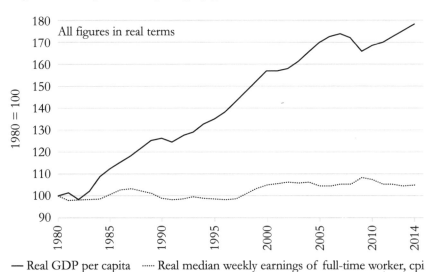

— Real GDP per capita ····· Real median weekly earnings of full-time worker, cpi

Table 3.1 shows this phenomenon with the changes in real household incomes skewed in favour of those at the top. The average household has seen modest gains, slowing sharply since 1980, and partly emanating from the increased participation of women in the labour market.

Table 3.1: Changes in real incomes per household by distributional shares, US 1945–2012

	1947–80	1980–2012
Bottom 90% =	+87%	-6%
Average =	+87%	+24%
Top 10% =	+89%	+80%
Top 1% =	+57%	+178%
Top 0.1% =	+63%	+312%
Top 0.01% =	+83%	+431%

The picture appears slightly different in other developed countries such as the UK. While real median wages in the UK seem to have progressed until the GFC struck, they fell back during the 'recovery' and are still below the pre-crisis peak.[7] Note that weekly earnings are not the same as median wages, since they are the combination of average wage rates and changes in hours worked such as overtime.

Even though UK real earnings have slowly recovered since 2015 to 101.7 in July 2018 (taking 2015 as 100), they are still substantially below the pre-crisis peak of 108.2.[8] Stephen Machin, however, believes that the stagnation of the wages of typical British workers predates this post-GFC downturn but has been masked by the gap between median wages and average wage growth inflated by faster wage growth among top earners: 'The opening of the gap between mean and median wages is because of rising wage inequality. As top

Figure 3.6: Median wages lag behind average wages and productivity in the UK between 1988 and 2013

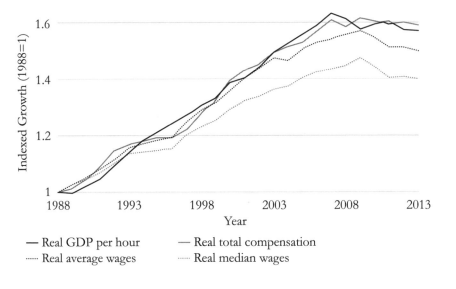

Figure 3.7: Real and nominal median wages lag in the US between 1980 and 2013

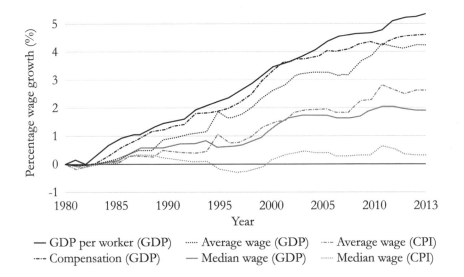

Figure 3.8: Real productivity, compensation and wage growth in Germany between 1980 and 2010

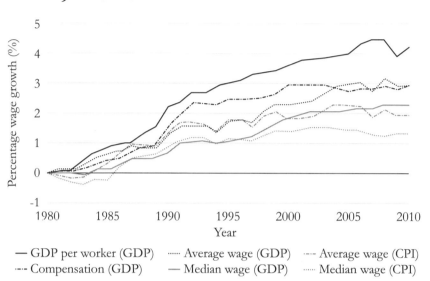

earners had faster wage growth, that pulled the average (mean) wages up at a faster rate than the median wages (of the middle or typical worker).'[9]

He also points out that similarities can be seen in other developed countries (Figures 3.7 and 3.8).[10]

In fact, in many OECD countries wage growth is lagging behind GDP growth, slowing the progress of real median incomes. With some exceptions, such as Portugal and Spain, the story is generally consistent in developed countries: workers in the middle of the income distribution scale have seen miserly income growth compared to their economies' growth per person.

CORPORATE CASH PILES
There must be consequences to this phenomenon. In fact, the decoupling of wages from GDP has coincided with the

unprecedented accumulation of cash by corporations over these same decades. This represents a greater share of retained profits in the economy, caused by two factors: a failure by company managers, as we've seen, to increase investment at a corresponding rate, and decreasing corporate tax rates tied to the effects of globalisation.

As companies have gained the freedom to divert production to low-cost, higher-growth countries, so their 'home' countries have felt the need to offer greater incentives in the form of reduced tax rates. This naturally leads to a race to the bottom, with tax authorities in the developed world leapfrogging each other to offer the best tax deals. While individual governments may reason that a lower corporate tax take is better than no tax take at all if companies were to move elsewhere, the long-term effects are pernicious, a negative-sum game between countries, with the only winners being the corporate sector. This is yet another example of the generalisation principle: what is rational for one economic unit, in this case a country, may cease to be so if it is generalised by its peers. In fact, it becomes counter-productive.

As a result, companies have built up cash mountains, often in lower-tax jurisdictions, sometimes referred to – without the slightest hint of irony – as the 'savings glut' responsible for the slow growth and deflationary pressure in the industrialised world. But company cash piles are in fact the consequence of a rising share of less taxed profits, not the cause of low growth.

TAX

The same mechanism is responsible for the growing indebtedness of governments in industrialised countries, as they are faced with the stark choice of making up for the loss of corporate tax revenue by either raising personal taxes (not exactly a vote winner) or borrowing to plug the gap.

President Obama, among others, verbally took aim at the more than $2 trillion in corporate cash parked abroad to avoid paying federal taxes of 35 per cent. However, this does not seem to have deterred companies from seeking to escape Uncle Sam's tax rates by moving their tax domicile to less onerous jurisdictions.

President Trump's Tax Cuts and Jobs Act cut federal corporate tax rates from 35 per cent to 21 per cent in December 2017, with a one-time 15.5 per cent tax on repatriated liquid assets, payable over eight years, to encourage some of that cash to return onshore. It did partially succeed in that objective, since the cash piles of the largest companies (much of it held overseas) did fall from $1.99 trillion in 2017 to $1.69 trillion at the end of 2018.[11] However, this was largely used to boost returns to shareholders in the form of share buy-backs and dividends. In 2018 share buy-backs almost doubled from 2017 to $467 billion. The tax changes overall served only to reduce the tax take over the medium term and boost the government budget deficit.

The UK has slashed taxes on companies over the years to 19 per cent (2019 rate), well below the average for developed countries of around 25 per cent, but still much higher than the Irish world-beating bargain rate of 12 per cent.

In the US in the 1950s, corporate tax represented just under 6 per cent of GDP. By 2013, this had shrunk to 1.6 per cent. In the EU, the average top corporate tax rate has fallen from 35 per cent in 1995 to 22.4 per cent in 2019. Free-market ideologists, aided and abetted by increasingly powerful and effective company lobbyists, have argued that the smaller the take of the state the better, subject to a minimum required to maintain the legal and defence infrastructure. Taxes, they say, distort the signals of the price mechanism and the efficient allocation of resources, as well as blunting the incentive to create, innovate and take productive business risks.

We will return to this in Part Three when discussing how

political systems have become an accomplice to the transfer of income and revenue from households and governments to the corporate sector, causing long-term low growth and deflation. In the meantime, we will explore the twin to labour's diminishing share of the pie: the egregious increase in income and wealth inequality over recent decades.

4

Rising inequality in developed countries

We have reached a tipping point. Inequality can no longer be treated as an afterthought. We need to focus the debate on how the benefits of growth are distributed.

Gustavo Gonzales, OECD secretary general[1]

The increasing inequality of income in many developed countries over the past several decades has roughly coincided with the decreasing aggregate share of earnings going to labour. As we discussed in Chapter 3, while the two trends are linked by structural changes in the economy and dominant political and economic beliefs, they should not be confused. It is perfectly possible for one to occur without the other, and there is evidence to suggest that their causes are distinct. At its most basic, there is no reason why a greater share of the pie taken by profits could not coexist with modest executive remuneration. In other words, the gains to capital could be reaped by millions of shareholders, not just a few hired hands. However, the effects on the living standards of the majority, as well as the growth rate of economies and inflationary or deflationary pressures are similar. Why is that so and how big a change in inequality are we talking about?

INEQUALITY AND GROWTH
One of the few plausible economic theories actually backed up by evidence is that individuals' propensity to consume (the proportion

of income spent) tends to decrease with the amount of income they earn. Those at the bottom of the ladder need to consume all they can from their modest incomes. In contrast, there is a limit to the number of meals a rich person can eat. Although the very well off can spend excess cash on property and luxury goods, this is unlikely to soak up all their income. Put another way, those further up the income distribution scale earn more than enough to cover their needs and so are able to save a greater proportion. Research by Emmanuel Saez and Gabriel Zucman shows that the savings rate of those in the bottom 90th percentile in the US was about 0 per cent in 2010, about 20 per cent for those in the top 10th percentile of income distribution, and a whopping 40 per cent for the top 1 per cent.[2] The same holds for the UK.[3]

Consequently, for any given economic pie, if income shifts from those at the lower end of the scale to those towards the top, the aggregate rate of consumption will fall. For every loss of $1 or £1 or €1 of income by the less fortunate, consumption will fall by close to $1 while the wealthy will only spend a miserly fraction of any extra $1 or £1 or €1.

An International Monetary Fund study from 2015[4] found:

> an inverse relationship between the income share accruing to the rich (top 20 per cent) and economic growth. If the income share of the top 20 per cent increases by 1 percentage point, GDP growth is actually 0.08 percentage point lower in the following five years, suggesting that the benefits do not trickle down. Instead, a similar increase in the income share of the bottom 20 per cent (the poor) is associated with 0.38 percentage point higher growth.

A similar 2015 study from the OECD concluded the same thing. Interestingly, the negative correlation between inequality and growth is found even when controlling for a country's income level. This isn't simply a case of wealthier countries growing more slowly and also being more unequal.[5]

The IMF and OECD list some channels by which inequality might actually be causing lower growth. The most important one has to do with investment. When poor people have more money, they can afford to invest more in human capital (education and skills) and nutrition. Because these investments have diminishing marginal returns – the first year of schooling matters a lot more than the twentieth – every dollar invested by the poor raises national productivity by more than if it gets invested by the rich.

The analysis by the OECD, which draws on data for 31 countries covering the period 1970–2010, found that income inequality has a sizeable impact on growth. Between 1985 and 2005, for example, inequality rose on average across 19 OECD countries, an increase estimated to have knocked 4.7 percentage points off cumulative growth between 1990 and 2010. The report also found that, as inequality rose, there were significant falls in educational attainment and skills among families in lower-income groups, implying large amounts of wasted potential and lower social mobility.

According to the Bank Credit Analyst (BCA), countries with greater inequality, such as the US, tend to have a lower variation in earnings across generations. In other words, parental income in more equal societies such as Scandinavia 'is a much less powerful predictor of income for future generations'.[6] This has been exacerbated by the runaway cost inflation of higher education in America. From 1980 to 2013, tuition and book costs rose by over 800 per cent compared to nominal median income growth of just over 200 per cent. Little wonder that graduation rates among the lower half of income families stagnated over the period, while they rose from 30 per cent to over 70 per cent for those coming from top quartile income families.

If America was once the land of opportunity, those that have made it to the top have sawn off the rungs of the ladder to ensure their descendants are more likely to maintain their position. The obvious consequences are lack of growth in human capital for large sections of the population and the rising indebtedness of students, who can only bridge the increasing gap between the cost of higher education and income through loans.

In England, since the introduction of university fees in 2006, student debt has ballooned to over £100 billion, equivalent to over £50,000 per graduating student.[7] This is even higher than in the US, where average debt on graduation is around £27,000.[8] Fees were sold to the electorate under the guise of fairness – why should the entire population subsidise the beneficiaries of a university education? In practice, this has probably backfired as students from better-off families can pay their fees up front while those from more modest backgrounds either think twice about attending university or are saddled with debts at high interest rates – hardly a social leveller. We have yet to see the full impact on demand and on graduates starting working life handicapped by hefty debts.

Continental European students (and the Scots) have escaped such huge fees by and large, on the principle that society should provide a free education (but not maintenance) to all who will benefit from it, without discrimination. Higher education is seen as a public good, just like universal healthcare.

INEFFICIENCY, FAIRNESS AND THE MISALLOCATION OF RESOURCES

Growth is also negatively impacted when corrupt or uncompetitive practices contribute to rising inequality. Phenomena like crony capitalism – where friends of the ruling classes are allowed to appropriate large amounts of wealth for themselves through government contracts or protected monopolies – lead not only to inequality of income and wealth, but also to economic inefficiency. According to economists Sutirtha Bagchi and Jan Svejnar, 'cronyism may also reduce growth by allowing the wealthy to exert greater influence on political policy, creating inefficient subsidies for themselves and unfair penalties for their rivals'.[9]

Bagchi and Svejnar found evidence for this; their research did indeed find a negative correlation between growth and inequality if, and only if, billionaires in a country acquired their fortunes through political connections. Inequality per se might not be so bad if it is the result of equal opportunity. But in the absence of fair competition through corrupt or anti-competitive practices inequality increases in a manner that is toxic economically, socially and ultimately politically.

The reduction in consumption from inequality can have knock-on effects as lower levels of demand and growth reduce companies' investment, capacity is used up more slowly, and the return on future investment is expected to drop. Over time, the cumulative effects of this slower path can be significant. In other words, increasing inequality is inefficient from a pure economic growth point of view for a number of reasons. Some of these have to do with the demand side of the economy, but others are linked to the supply side of the growth equation. Most worryingly for free marketeers is the possibility that their principles have been hijacked by a self-serving self-replicating elite at the expense of everyone else, resulting in a spectacular misallocation of resources.

Very few dominant market positions by companies have been acquired by such obviously corrupt means, but there is no denying the power of company-sponsored political lobbyists. The very existence of companies with dominant market share, however acquired, belies the original rationale of the free market: the benefits of competition in the efficient allocation of resources. Adam Smith's hand loses its invisibility cloak if it takes on the shape of a monopoly or even oligopoly that can maintain high margins and profits without the threat of erosion from competition.

The political elite, while ready to trumpet the virtues of the free market, are either in denial about the extent of uncompetitive practices in the economy or are reluctant to enforce competition by breaking up cartels or near-monopolies, for reasons we will return to in Chapter 7. Even leaving aside questions of fairness, the evidence points strongly to the conclusion that we have reached a level of inequality in most countries that is detrimental to their economies.

For example, the economic utility of an extra dollar of income per day is much greater for someone living in poverty than someone earning a comfortable living. There is therefore a case for redistributing income to reduce inequality on the utilitarian grounds of promoting the greatest happiness of the greatest number, subject perhaps to a constraint of not sacrificing overall growth too much as incentives are eroded. But even reduced incentives to become filthy rich (to coin a phrase) may not blunt growth prospects as much as some may protest. Sweden, one of the world's most egalitarian societies, also has a growth rate near the top of the developed-country league, a clear refutation of the dogma that high inequality is the necessary by-product of a system offering strong enough incentives to encourage high growth.

So much for why rising inequality is incompatible with a healthy economy. What about the facts. How much inequality is there?

MEASURES
There are many different ways of measuring inequality of income. Economists tend to use the Gini coefficient, whereby a reading of 1 represents a completely unequal society (winner takes all) and 0 a completely equal one (everyone earns the average).

Figure 4.1: The Gini coefficient

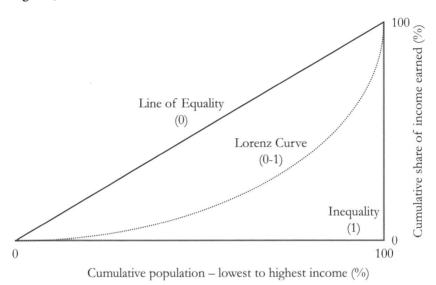

So what does the data show?

For the developed OECD-member countries for which we have data, the Gini coefficient for income rose from 0.29 to 0.32 (more unequal) from the mid-1980s to 2011, with some differences between countries. In the US it rose from around 0.34 to around 0.41 (by 2012) and a similar increase from 0.31 to 0.35 was seen in the UK. In France and Italy, never paid-up members of 'liberal' free-market ideology, there were more modest increases from around 0.30 and 0.29 respectively to 0.32 over the period.[10]

Perhaps the most important study in recent times has been Thomas Piketty's *Capital in the Twenty-First Century*, a best-selling analysis of growing inequality within countries. Piketty's hypothesis, supported by a wealth of empirical data, is that when the return on capital exceeds the economy's growth rate, this increases the share of capital in national income, and since capital is more unequally distributed than labour income, this increases inequality. Whether past history is a sufficient guide to the future is always debatable, but his argument and evidence for rising inequality remain compelling. The study is also wide-ranging, showing that the Gini coefficient has increased by 10 per cent on average between 1980 and 2010 across all OECD countries. There are a few exceptions, with France, Turkey, Greece, Hungary and Belgium experiencing little variation over the period, in stark contrast to the Anglo-Saxon countries.

Nor is rising inequality confined to developed, self-styled-capitalist countries. A report by Peking University calculated the country's Gini coefficient at 0.49 in 2012, having risen from around 0.3 in the 1980s. According to Zhou Xiaozheng, sociology professor at Renmin University in Beijing, 'To put it simply, the poor are getting poorer and the rich are getting richer.'[11] China's Statistics Bureau claimed that the coefficient had fallen to 0.46 in 2014, but other estimates have calculated it as high as 0.61 in 2010 (according to the World Bank, a coefficient above 0.40 represents severe inequality). Only two of the twenty-five countries tracked by the World Bank are higher: South Africa at 0.63 and Brazil's 0.53.

The other important vector of inequality affecting behaviour and the economy is wealth. The Bank Credit Analyst points out that inequality of wealth is greater than that of income in some countries. It registers a high 0.8 in the US, surprisingly followed by over 0.7 in France and over 0.6 in Italy. There could be many reasons for this, including the obvious one that the wealthiest disproportionately accumulate wealth through means other than current income, in the form of assets such as real estate, stocks and shares and even pension rights. Wealth has accumulated to a staggering degree at the top: one family, the Waltons, owners of Walmart stores, is said to have accumulated wealth equal to all that of the lowest 40 per cent of American families put together.[12]

According to the research by Saez, in 2013 the wealthiest 1 per cent of American households owned 42 per cent of all US wealth.[13] Put it another way, the median wealth of America's affluent families was nearly seven times that of middle-income families, up from about three and half times in 1983.[14] In China the top 1 per cent own only 33 per cent of total wealth[15] and the UK's rich appear very restrained in comparison, with the top 1 per cent only owning anywhere between 11 per cent of the total pot[16] and 23 per cent (equal with France), depending on who you ask.[17] This shows the greater difficulty in gathering reliable data on wealth, which is largely not subject to direct tax.

In 2016 a study by the charity Oxfam made quite a splash when it calculated that the global top 1 per cent own as much as the remaining 99 per cent.[18] That would imply that wealth inequality must be even greater outside the developed countries. Oxfam condemns a world where 26 people own as much as the poorest half of the world's population. This compares with 388 super-rich people in 2010.

This trend is clearly unsustainable. Renowned linguist Noam Chomsky believes that the harm and bitterness created by a generation of neoliberalism risks causing more lasting damage than the Great Depression of the 1930s, when 'despite the grim conditions, there was a sense of hopefulness, a belief that we'll get out of this together'. In contrast, today this hope has 'been largely supplanted by fear, despair, and isolation'.[19] There can be few more damning comparisons for our modern age.

OTHER MEASURES

Gini coefficients may understate the changes in inequality because they are based on the average, which may itself be distorted by changes at the extremes such as increasingly skewed distributions of income towards the very top. The measure is also particularly sensitive to what is going on around the average, where the greatest weight of the population is found. Other measures capture more dramatically the different rates of increase of incomes depending on position in the distribution, and by how much the gains from economic growth have been captured by those at the very top.

In 2014 Atkinson and Morelli looked in more detail at income inequality in the US.[20] Their data shows that the last time incomes were as unevenly distributed as now was in the 1920s. The subsequent fifty years saw a trend towards greater equality as the state grew more interventionist after the crash of 1929, the Great Depression and the Second World War. Banks and credit were tightly controlled and progressive tax rates climbed.

The pendulum then began its long swing back to historic extremes of inequality as the interventionist state was rolled back and free-market ideology took over. Back in 2006 an analysis of IRS data in the US by Emmanuel Saez and Thomas Piketty showed that the share of income earned by the top 1 per cent was as large as in 1928.[21] The share of all income before tax earned by the top 1 per cent is currently around 20 per cent of the total, similar to the peak in the 1920s, but more than double the roughly 8 per cent of the early 1970s. The top 10 per cent saw their income share rise from 25.3 per cent in 1979 to 30.6 per cent in 2016.[22] According to Jon Cowan of the centre-left think tank Third Way, 'everyone agrees what the core problem is in that we are seeing an erosion of middle-class prosperity ... where people disagree is what you do to address it'.[23] Little wonder that the recovery in the West is anaemic, weaker than past recoveries, and continuously disappointing the expectations of political and economic elites. David Madland of the Center for American Progress explains why finally the American political process is responding when he says, 'The basic reality is that the economy is not working for most Americans.'

America is far from unique in evolving towards a system where winner takes almost all. And the collateral damage is not confined to the stagnant living standards of the middle classes. Those extolling the benefits to developing nations of globalisation ignore the absolute poverty that exists at the lower end of the social spectrum even within the world's richest countries.

Italy is one of the world's richest nations, a member of the elite G7 club, yet, according to its national statistics agency, about 6.2 million Italians live in absolute poverty, twice the number compared to ten years previously. Four million are estimated to suffer from hunger, of whom 10 per cent are children under five years old. According to the think tank Censis, 60 per cent of those interviewed recently feared ending their lives in poverty as the economy falters. Lack of growth since 2000 has compounded rising inequality. The share of total income earned by those in the bottom half of the income distribution fell from 30 per cent in 1980 to 24 per cent in 2016 while the top 10 per cent progressed from 23 per cent to 29 per cent over the period. The national mood is a toxic combination of rage and resignation.[24]

In the UK real earnings fell more than 9 per cent in the six years from March 2008, the steepest and longest drop since records began in the mid-nineteenth century.

This rising inequality trend has been less pronounced in northern continental European countries that never fully embraced red-blooded free-market ideology. In Germany the income share of the top 1 per cent has hardly changed, from a little over 10 per cent, with the top 10 per cent earning around 175 per cent of the median, up a paltry amount from 150 per cent fifty years ago. Germany is widely recognised and admired as a template for commercial and economic success and strength, and yet it has preserved its own form of market economy where the interests of all stakeholders in society are balanced through governance structures at the company and industry level. It also has a much smaller financial sector, preferring traditional engineering to financial engineering.

But the picture is not all rosy there either. Markus Grabka and Carsten Schroeder of the German Institute for Economic Research in Berlin noted that while Germany enjoyed near full employment in 2017, this was thanks to a policy of low wages. Nine million workers, or 24.5 per cent of those employed (compared to 18.9 per cent for OECD countries), earned less than two thirds of the median wage of €15 per hour, which itself is lower that it was in 2003. The German economic engine runs on workers who make around €19,656 a year, less than the average wage in all OECD countries bar Mexico. Low-wage jobs are even more prevalent among workers with an immigrant background and those in the east of the country, with purchasing power often comparable to that of workers in emerging markets. Upward mobility is low with people stuck without much chance of advancement.

The French picture is even more egalitarian, with the share of the top 1 per cent not changing at all from a little below 10 per cent of the total, and the top 10 per cent actually losing ground relative to the median over the past four decades.[25]

Countries like Germany, France or Sweden show that inequality is not an inevitable consequence of the workings of a modern, efficient economy. Neither does inequality imply higher growth; quite the reverse. It is neither a necessary nor sufficient condition for success or the avoidance of crises. The truth is that inequality and its progression are a result of the political process, not of economics, a process tied to an ideology that dictates that government should keep its hands off the market and its allocation of resources and wealth, whatever the outcome.

How has this dogma expressed itself within the economic structure of the Anglo-Saxon countries? According to the distinguished economist John Kay, about one third of the top US 1 per cent income earners and an even greater proportion of the top 0.1 per cent are corporate executives. He also notes that rising

Figure 4.2: Relative proportions of public sector, service and manufacturing jobs, UK 1980–2009

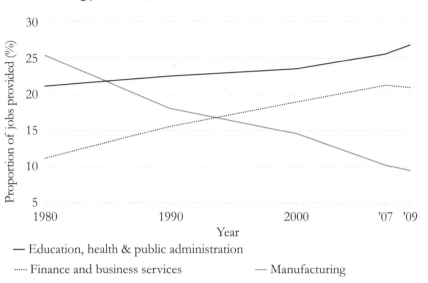

— Education, health & public administration

····· Finance and business services   — Manufacturing

inequality in some countries is mainly the result of 'the growth of the finance sector; and the explosion of the remuneration of senior executives'.[26]

In the 2017/18 tax year, median gross full-time income in the UK stood at £29,588[27] compared to average salaries in finance (excluding bonuses) of around £35,000 (2019).[28] Not only are finance professionals better paid; there are many more of them than thirty years ago. Finance has been one of the few consistently growing sectors of the UK economy over that period. Political establishments complacently bought the idea that making things, aka manufacturing, was a dispensable 'old economy' activity that could be wound down in developed countries in favour of more sophisticated, higher value-added services, of which, in the case of the UK, finance was the jewel in the crown (see Figure 4.2). This meant manufacturing could be outsourced abroad to cheaper

Figure 4.3: Average compensation: financial sector versus total private sector, US 1929–2011

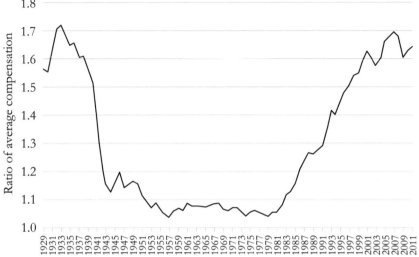

locations without risk, the second pillar of the justification for globalisation. It took the GFC for developed countries to rediscover the virtues of manufacturing and express the desire to rebalance from financial engineering to plain old-fashioned engineering.

Figure 4.3 shows the relative pay of finance employees in the US over time. Interestingly, this pay was equivalent to the levels of 1929 just before the Wall Street Crash. It was in reaction to the catastrophic consequences of finance's excesses in the 1920s that the US authorities passed the Glass-Steagall Act in 1933 to put an end to casino banking and prevent a repetition of the Great Depression. It is no coincidence that the same causes produced the same effects within less than a decade of the act's repeal under President Clinton in 1999, not because the dividing line between retail and investment banking had not become blurred, but because it signalled a no-holds-barred growth strategy to all banks.

REGIME CHANGE

One should not distort these facts into a conspiracy theory. Financiers did not set out decades ago to launch a campaign to boost pay for themselves and their employees. Rather, finance has been a passive but massive beneficiary of the extraordinary and unprecedented ski-slope of falling inflation, interest rates and government bond yields since their peak in 1981. Falling interest rates and deregulation enabled them to offer cheaper and cheaper credit to a population looking for instant gratification.

The world has changed dramatically since the early 1980s. The rejection of the post-Second World War Bretton Woods order of fixed exchange rates, gold backing the US dollar, big government spending, redistributing income from the rich through high taxation and the power of the big labour unions had already started in 1971. It took another decade of chaos, in the form of oil crises and inflation threatening to run out of control, to provoke the birth by forceps of the new regime of monetary discipline at the Fed under Paul Volcker. He squeezed interest rates higher until the inflationary pips squeaked, and the triumph of the Reagan-Thatcherite free-market, small government, anti-union ideology completed the delivery of the new free-market consensus.

The cycle turned, the bargaining power of organised labour faded with union membership and rising competition from low-cost countries, while tax rates on income and capital fell. In the short term, the retreat in labour's share of GDP and the stagnation of real wages in the lower classes could be made up through easy credit as various restrictions (such as hire purchase rules in the UK) were removed in a lending free-for-all. Not only did the supply of credit grow faster than economies, particularly in the Anglo-Saxon world, but the demand was there, all too eager to mop it up. Finance professionals thrived, and their high incomes contributed to inequality. A supposedly virtuous circle of rising productivity, falling unit costs of production, falling inflation and accommodative central banks lowering interest rates provided increasingly affordable borrowing conditions. Ever lower interest rates made consumption growth affordable for those on stagnant incomes, as debt service costs stayed under control. Until they didn't.

When the economy showed signs of overheating, the Fed and other central banks such as the Bank of England raised rates according to the old playbook, to keep inflation under control. By the late 1990s, however, enough debt had built up in the global economy, in emerging market countries or technology and telecommunication companies, that it took only modest interest rate rises (by past standards) to crash the system as debtors defaulted. Central banks were oblivious of the degree to which the build-up of debt had made parts of the economy more sensitive to interest rates.

We will return to the central role played by the build-up in debt in the next chapter. It is sufficient to say here that powerful economic forces conspired to encourage the rapid expansion of the financial sector over the last thirty-five years, aided and abetted by compliant politicians and regulators.

The Glass-Steagall Act had separated the activities of deposit-taking commercial banks from securities underwriting such as mortgage-backed securities. Its repeal in 1999 was the formal recognition that it had become toothless. Most notably, Citibank's 1998 affiliation with Salomon Smith Barney, one of the largest US securities firms, was permitted under the Federal Reserve Board's then existing interpretation of the act. Arguably, the act's repeal took the final brake off the finance industry and contributed to an historic financial bubble whose bursting still reverberates today.

TOP PAY DETACHED FROM REALITY

If the portrayal of Gordon Gekko in the 1987 movie *Wall Street* was an exaggeration, it was closer to the truth than many might like to believe. The main character's one-liner 'Greed is good' encapsulated and legitimised the new regime. The statistics on top pay are illuminating. According to the Economic Policy Institute, in 2017 'CEO compensation at the largest [350 by revenue in the US] corporations has ballooned by 979 per cent since 1978, *when adjusted for inflation* [my italics]. A typical worker's compensation grew a measly 10.2 per cent over the same period.' The average CEO total compensation was $18.9 million. The average ratio of CEO compensation to the median worker in their company stood at 312:1, up from about 58:1 in 1989 and 20:1 in 1965.[29]

This trend is not confined to the US. UK ratios may be less extreme, but the progression is still spectacular, leading to an observation from an official of the High Pay Commission of a '30-year trend of increasing top pay that has left the earnings gap between the very richest and the rest of society wider than at any point since Queen Victoria was on the throne'.[30] The report cites the example of Barclays, where top pay was 75 times that of the average worker. In 1979 the multiple was 14.5.

Stagnant shareholder returns in recent years have not prevented FTSE 100 company CEOs' pay from rising inexorably, serenely detached from reality. While the FTSE 100 is at broadly similar levels to late 1999, meaning that shareholders have received an annual return of about 2 per cent after inflation, purely from dividends, CEO pay has risen several hundred per cent over the period. The average pay of a FTSE 100 company CEO was equivalent to 129 of their employees in 2016,[31] growing almost six times faster between 2000 and 2014.[32]

A study by Robert Naess at Nordea Bank on how CEO pay affects company returns shows that from 2008 to 2018 the hundred

US companies with the *lowest* CEO compensation within the S&P 500 index outperformed the hundred with the highest-paid CEOs every year except 2013, and by a wide margin: 17.2 per cent per annum versus 8.4 per cent.[33]

If companies cannot justify top executive pay rises in terms of performance or shareholders' returns, they fall back on the defence that you need to pay enough to attract the best talent. Unfortunately, although this may be true in some cases, it fails to square with the facts in aggregate. Not everyone can hire top talent. And since company remuneration committees recommend securing the services of the best managers by paying top-quartile compensation, companies keep leapfrogging each other to demonstrate they are paying more to get the best. Turning the pay-incentives argument on its head, companies justify their high pay policies as evidence of good governance.

Even in more socially minded Germany, where pockets of resistance to the market free-for-all have survived to this day, things have got to the point where *Der Spiegel* wrote in 2013, 'Average employee wages have increased by 6.1 per cent since 2000, while the salaries of senior executives at companies traded on Germany's DAX stock exchange index have risen by almost 55 per cent during that time period.'

Elsewhere, *Der Spiegel* expressed concern that the poverty and wealth gap 'has reached disconcerting proportions in Germany. Many can no longer support themselves with the money they earn in a full-time job. Almost one in four workers earns less than 9.15 euros an hour, which translates to about 19,000 euros a year. This is less than one-seven hundredth of what the CEO of VW makes.' While this was denounced as unacceptable by Chancellor Angela Merkel at the time, little has changed since.

The increasing debate over high-end pay has prompted a belated response from governments and regulators. There has been a smattering of legislation around the developed world designed to appear to be doing something to tackle the trend. Since 2014 in the UK new rules have forced companies to seek shareholder approval for their pay policies as well as holding an *advisory* vote on the report of the committees that set top executive pay. These reports should now detail these compensation packages more clearly and compare them to pay across the company. It may seem odd that company management, who after all are the hired hands and agents for the owning shareholders, should have got away with little transparency about pay up until very recently. One can also be forgiven for speculating whether they could have got away with it longer had their egregious self-awarded pay rises not reached such extremes as to attract attention. Greed may be good, but only up to a point.

Elsewhere, in 2013 the European Union capped bonuses for investment bankers, and Switzerland approved a referendum that makes company shareholders responsible for setting the chief executive's salary. By 2018, the European Banking Authority was reporting that the number of bankers in the European Union earning a million euros ($1.2 million) or more had fallen in 2016 as the EU's cap on bonuses drove a shift towards fixed pay. The million-plus club decreased to 4,597, down by 10.6 per cent from 2015, the London-based regulator said. However, the EBA reports salary data in euros, and the decline was largely the result of the pound's depreciation against the common currency in the aftermath of the Brexit referendum in June 2016. The vast majority of high-earning European bankers worked in the UK – 3,539 of the EU total – and most were paid in pounds. Stripping out the exchange-rate effect, the decline was just 2.5 per cent.

The legislation on bonuses has been totally ineffectual: the number of high-paid bankers has actually increased, and they have simply upped their base salaries to offset bonus limits – to the detriment of shareholders since rewards are now even less tied to results.

In 2015 the US Securities and Exchange Commission (SEC) decided to require companies to publish the ratio between their chief executive officer's pay and that of their median employees from 2017. Business lobbyists were not amused, calling the move costly and meaningless. At the time, a report in the *Financial Times*, a newspaper known more for the pink colour of its paper than of its views, noted that between 1978 and 2013 American chief executives' inflation-adjusted pay had risen twice as much as US stock market returns to shareholders. It suggested that the SEC's new rule was 'a response to real public concern. The pay gap has not just resulted in anger about corporate excess. The sense that those at the top are appropriating the spoils for themselves has undermined support for the capitalist system itself.'

We are, no doubt, in the early stages of the pendulum beginning to swing back the other way. That does not mean that those who have been the biggest winners recognise the profound change in public mood which is altering the political landscape. The sense of entitlement built up over decades of inaction by governments and authorities is unlikely to dissolve overnight. There have been waves of ineffectual protest before (remember Occupy Wall Street?), so why should they worry that this time is different?

In 2014 journalist Kate Burgess pointed out that the 650 members of the UK House of Commons, responsible for legislation for over 65 million people, were each paid £67,000 for a total cost to the country of £43 million. That is how much *one CEO* at the time, Sir Martin Sorrell, then boss of WPP, an advertising company, is reported to have earned in one year. It is not hard to challenge such relative rewards in terms of societal value, and yet our elected representatives are reluctant to do so, presumably partly for fear of companies and their top executives decamping to more accommodating tax jurisdictions. Even if WPP shareholders enjoyed a return of over 170 per cent including dividends over five years, and Sorrell's pay was linked to share price performance, one may ask where are the economists' cost-benefit analyses of such a situation?

In another case of corporate chutzpah, the corporate governance of insurance claims processor Quindell came under fire for granting over £25 million worth of stock options to its new chairman, deputy chairman and existing executives.[34] Some of these options were exercisable within twelve months, disregarding the UK's Corporate Governance Code's recommendation that options 'should not be exercisable in less than three years'. The award also casually disregarded the code's recommendation that the compensation of non-executives, such as the chairman, should not include options, in the interests of providing some distance and independence from management. It seems that as long as restrictions on executive pay exist only in advisory form rather than being legally binding, many will brazenly disregard them.

In fairness, some institutional investors, such as Standard Life Investments, have exercised their shareholder powers, while in 2012 investors succeeded in unseating the CEOs of AstraZeneca, Aviva and Trinity Mirror after protests at annual meetings. However, according to the *FT*, more shareholder protests have been registered against non-binding remuneration reports than against binding votes on pay policy, suggesting that shareholders' bark may be greater than their bite.[35] By July 2018 there had been eighteen cases where at least 20 per cent of shareholders voted down the executive compensation packages, twice as many as in 2017. Nevertheless, these voters were still in a minority in almost all cases, and the votes were advisory rather than binding.

In the US, Oracle founder and CEO Larry Ellison has faced shareholder pressure on pay. It was reported that Mr Ellison enjoyed an annual package averaging $77 million over the three years to 2013 even though a majority of shareholders had voted against the company's remuneration policy in the advisory vote for two consecutive years. This did not stop him claiming $108.9 million in compensation in fiscal year 2018, although only $3.6 million was in cash, the rest being the value of a grant of stock options on Oracle.

SHARE BUY-BACKS

Perhaps the most insidious mechanism that top management has found to game the system is through the use of apparently respectable share buy-backs. The rationale is that if companies cannot find a productive and profitable use for their cash, they should maximise shareholder value by paying it out to shareholders. This can be in the form of increased dividends or by buying back company shares. Managements prefer the latter as dividends are supposed to be regular rather than one-off payments, and share buy-backs have the advantage of arithmetically boosting earnings per share (fewer outstanding shares are left as a company buys some back and cancels them). Since earnings-per-share growth is a key performance indicator used to calculate top executive compensation, this has been a popular strategy in recent years. It would be justified if companies bought back their own shares because they had good reason to view these as undervalued and cheap, thereby improving capital efficiency and shareholder value. Unfortunately, there is little evidence that this is the case.

Buy-backs in the US hit a peak in 2007, right at the peak of the housing bubble and when shares were at their most expensive. According to a Deloitte survey of North American chief financial officers in 2013, only 11 per cent thought their own stock overvalued, even while they thought that 60 per cent of US equities in general were overvalued. In other words, buy-backs tend to be poorly timed, are based on contradictory assumptions, and often destroy shareholder value. Companies should be issuing new equity at high valuations towards the end of the cycle, not buying it back.

Worse still, low interest rates have encouraged company managements to load their companies with new debt, the proceeds of which are used to buy back company shares. So managers weaken their balance sheets, making them more vulnerable to rising interest rates, in order to juice up their remuneration. In some cases, such as at Boeing, the company has been the largest buyer of its own shares in recent years, using cash it has not reinvested to design new planes or maximise quality control.

The only conclusion that can be reached is that, even if a company does not grow earnings much or at all for shareholders, it will find ways to justify handsome top executive pay rises. BP CEO Bob Dudley received a 20 per cent increase in total pay in 2015 to nearly $20 million despite the company making its worst loss ever ($5.2 billion) and BP shares falling 13 per cent in that year. The company justified this on the grounds of performance on safety, project management and cost-cutting – 5,000 jobs were cut, saving money to finance part of Dudley's pay hike.

In summary, over the last three decades those hired to run companies on behalf of their owners have seen their pay rise exorbitantly relative to the pay of the workforces and also to the returns to those owners – the shareholders. This is unlikely to be a reflection of the skill or hard work or contribution of the top executives compared with the rest of their staff; rather it is due to laissez-faire government regulation and the passivity of public equity shareholders, many of whom behave more as share renters than owners, given the short average period of time they own a company's shares. This has given carte blanche to top executives gaming the system, at least until the excesses become too egregious to ignore.

This pay explosion is the result of several trends: the growing share of profits as a proportion of national economies; the increasing valuation of those profits by the markets, in turn partly due to management buying back company shares with the company's own money in order to boost measured earnings per share under cover of 'shareholder value' slogans; and remuneration committees staffed partly by other CEOs, which encourages a game of compensation leapfrog.

While it is impossible for *everyone* to hire the best managers, it is entirely possible for the best managers to hop from job to job in a pay-for-talent auction, perpetually pulling up the average in the process. Neither the labour force that produces a company's output, nor the company's shareholders benefit from this game and yet it has been tolerated up until now.

The income elite has learned to game the system to its advantage under the theoretical cover of a free-market ideology, and in practice through the power of lobbying and contributions to politicians' election campaigns. They have also honed their skills at influencing regulators directly or through their political contacts, to maintain regimes that preserve their interests. The trouble is, they have been so successful that the masses below them, on whom they depend to consume their products, have been slowly starved of income growth. While this could be masked for some time by the addition of credit to stagnant or slowly rising wages, like all Ponzi schemes, there comes a point where not enough new money can be created to maintain demand and profits growth.

5

The debt explosion in the West

Asset price bubbles depend on the growth of credit.

Charles Kindleberger

Debt or more explicitly excessive debt and financial crises are at the very heart of our narrative. They provide the glue holding together all the pieces we have looked at so far. Banking crises caused by too much debt creation are as old as, well, banking itself, so what is so special about the most recent Great Financial Crisis (GFC) other than its scale? What exactly is the link between the build-up of debt, the GFC, long-standing trends towards greater inequality of incomes, technological change and stagnant wages for a large proportion of the working populations of developed countries?

The key is provided by the long downtrend of US Treasury bond yields from their peak of 15.8% in 1981 to their trough around 1.4% in 2016. US treasuries yields are the interest rate at which the US government borrows when it issues treasury bonds. As such, these set the benchmark for long-term borrowing costs for the entire global financial system because the US dollar serves as the world's reserve currency, with all other rates referenced relative to it. Investors assume US treasury paper to be, by definition, effectively risk free as it is backed by the most powerful economy and government in the world, which controls its own central bank.

There are no circumstances, other than some global catastrophe such as nuclear war, that would prevent investors holding such debt from getting their money back.

If push comes to shove and the government gets into trouble with its debt, the Federal Reserve Board, the US central bank, can always accommodate this by printing dollars to honour the debt. If that sets the risk-free rate, then everything else keys off that. That means that any extra return from an investment above this risk-free rate is there to compensate you for some (extra) risk. It also means that the cost of borrowing worldwide tends to move up and down with the yield on US treasury debt. If yields go down in America, they tend to follow in the UK and Germany and Australia, albeit with some variations.

After an unprecedented run up in US treasury bond yields from the end of the Second World War to 1981, there followed an equally unprecedented run back from that point, to levels that reached all-time record lows in 2016. Something started at the beginning of the 1980s to cause this inflection point and then propel this downward trend for the best part of the next four decades. The billion-dollar question (a million dollars is simply not what it used to be) is what?

Actually, something started in 1971 when US president Nixon pulled out of the post-war fixed-exchange-rate system of Bretton Woods and left the gold standard. This severed the fixed link between the world's most important currency and any other, including the oldest hard currency known to man. By no longer tying the supply of dollars to the amount of gold reserves held by the government, it removed constraints on monetary policy. America could now print as many dollars as it pleased, for example, to help pay for the Vietnam War or to bail out banks. It could set interest rates at any level it wanted, without concern for any obligations towards its trading partners or the preservation of the value of its currency.

In a world which at the time was still arranged into trading blocs with a finite supply of labour that wielded considerable bargaining power through unionisation, this produced the runaway inflation of the 1970s. The unprecedented peak in bond yields and interest rates in the early 1980s came about as the flow of US dollars was choked off when the Fed hiked rates to record levels. In subsequent years, political change led to the dismantling of the negotiating power of labour, further degraded by the massive supply shock of China entering the world trading system ten years later and technological change replacing millions of jobs. The rest is history.

THE POLITICS OF THE FREE MARKET AND DEREGULATION

In 1979 Margaret Thatcher was elected prime minister of the UK. A year later, Ronald Reagan became president of the United States. Their elections reflected a sea-change in the political mood after the failed policies of the 1970s, which had led to unemployment, strikes, oil crises, petrol shortages and high inflation; UK annual inflation hit 25 per cent in the mid-1970s, coining a new economic term: stagflation.

The Reagan and Thatcher revolution of the 1980s restored the doctrine of the free market, which had prevailed before the Great Depression and Keynesian economics briefly became the new orthodoxy. Thatcher and Reagan believed in the power of Adam Smith's invisible hand to provide the only efficient way to allocate scarce resources. The previous consensus in favour of government intervention in the economy to shore up demand if it was too weak to provide full employment – most famously represented by the work of British economist John Maynard Keynes and President Franklin Roosevelt's New Deal – was now unceremoniously dumped in favour of a return to belief in self-adjusting markets, supported by the 'monetary school' whose high priest was Milton Friedman at the University of Chicago.

Keynes had talked of a 'liquidity trap', when all the efforts of central banks to stimulate credit and aggregate demand by lowering interest rates or printing money would be ineffective if people did not want to borrow more and preferred to hoard cash rather than consume or invest. Friedman agreed that you could not manipulate growth by pressing on the monetary pedal, whose sole effect would be inflation. For Friedman, therefore, inflation was a purely monetary phenomenon, controllable through the amount of money washing around in the system.

Cue Paul Volcker, appointed chairman of the Federal Reserve Board by President Jimmy Carter in August 1979, who restored monetary discipline by hiking interest rates way above the inflation rate, culminating in the 20 per cent peak of June 1981, limiting the supply of dollars to the point where the real cost of money (inflation adjusted) became punitively high. This trickled down throughout the economy. Spending projects requiring credit got cancelled unless they were sufficiently profitable to outweigh the heavy cost of finance, and workers found it more difficult to demand high wage rises as companies found they could not pass them on in higher prices. Inflation fever began to subside. When the economy showed signs of overheating, the Fed raised rates; when it cooled down or risked stalling, it cut them.

Reagan and Thatcher came to power on platforms based on a free-market ideology and a commitment to shrink government's role. They were hostile to the use of public finance to manage the level of demand in economies, and embarked on programmes of tax cuts that brought down marginal tax rates from punitive levels of over 80 per cent to below 50 per cent. Although the immediate beneficiaries were high earners, tax cuts were sold to the electorate as 'trickle-down economics'. Lower top tax rates would release the entrepreneurial drive to create wealth. As wealth creators stood to keep a greater share of the fruits of their success, they would be more motivated and could afford to take more risks since their potential gains would be higher. This would translate into greater innovation, more investment, more growth and jobs, and money would trickle down through the system's layers and benefit everyone. Not only that, higher growth rates would result in governments collecting as many dollars or pounds in tax as they did before tax rates were cut. This was as close as it gets to the proverbial free lunch.

The Thatcher–Reagan axis denounced anti-competitive practices. In what Nobel prize-winning economist Joseph Stiglitz wittily referred to as 'market fundamentalism', a quasi-religious belief in the infinite wisdom and efficiency of markets, deregulation was the name of the game in every sector, and most crucially in finance. In the UK for example, one of the main regulatory constraints on the growth of consumer credit – controls on hire purchase – was taken out to the backyard and shot in 1982.

Back in America, Reagan showed scant gratitude to Paul Volcker (who died in December 2019), whose monetary policy discipline laid the foundations for decades of non-inflationary prosperity, by unceremoniously firing him in 1987. According to Professor Stiglitz, this was because the Reagan administration didn't believe Volcker was a committed deregulator. This was probably true, since Volcker's unparalleled integrity in modern times, and staunch defence of the common good as a public servant, would inevitably clash with the new consensus elevating the market to supreme arbiter of all things economic and financial. It was no coincidence that Volcker made a comeback under the Obama administration after the GFC, drafting the eponymous rule re-instating restrictions on banks' ability to gamble in the markets with their own capital, much to the fury of Wall Street.

LABOUR LOSES BARGAINING POWER

A political corollary of the crusade against anti-competitive practices was a drive to reduce the wage bargaining power of labour unions. And as their power faded, unsurprisingly union membership also started to fall. This trend has been extensively documented by Bruce Western, who clearly identified 'the role of unions as an equalising force in the labour market':

> From 1973 to 2007 [in the US], wage inequality in the private sector increased by more than 40 per cent among men, and by about 50 per cent among women ... de-unionisation – the decline in the percentage of the labor force that is unionised – and educational stratification each explain about 33 per cent of the rise in within-group wage inequality among men. Among women, de-unionisation explains about 20 per cent of the increase in wage inequality, whereas education explains more than 40 per cent.[1]

Western also attributed changing attitudes towards the perception of pay equity to the decline of unions, arguing that they 'helped institutionalise norms of equity'. Since the decline in the union movement of the 1970s, and (as we saw in Chapter 4) the severing of the link between worker productivity and wages, employees have had to work harder for less and less money. Even non-union workers benefit from strong unions as employers have to raise wages and increase employee benefits. Between 1980 and 2008, nationwide worker productivity grew by 75 per cent, while workers' inflation-adjusted average wages increased by only 22.6 per cent.

The middle class is also markedly stronger when workers join together in unions. As Figure 5.1 demonstrates, the sharp decline over the past forty years in the percentage of workers organised in

Figure 5.1: As union membership decreases, middle-class income shrinks, US

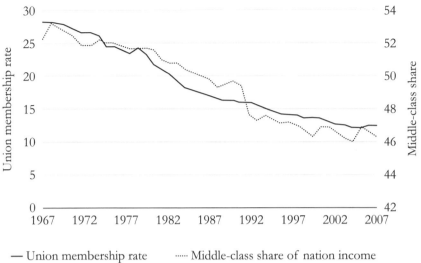

— Union membership rate   ⋯⋯ Middle-class share of nation income

unions has been associated with an equally sharp drop in the share of the USA's income going to the middle class.

When unions were stronger in the middle part of the last century, American workers' wages rose as they became increasingly more productive. But today, as union strength has decreased, this link has been broken and their wages have stagnated, while the share of income going to the top 10 per cent has soared.

Even today, unionised US workers earn significantly more than their non-union counterparts non-union workers had weekly earnings that were 82% of earnings of workers who were union members, according to a recent study by the US Bureau of Labor Statistics.[2] Among full-time wage and salary workers, union members had median usual weekly earnings of $1,051 in 2018, while those who were not union members had median weekly earnings of $860. Yet despite all the evidence that unions contribute to increased wages and benefits, a harsh legal environment and negative public perception keep unionisation rates low.

Other Western countries also saw a decrease in the unionisation of the labour force. In France less than 8 per cent of employees (less in the private sector) belong to a trade union, down from a high of about 30 per cent in the 1950s. In Britain the figure is 23 per cent compared to 58 per cent in 1979 when Thatcher became prime minister.[3] In Germany it is 18 per cent, and the USA 11 per cent.[4]

In a 2015 paper Florence Jaumotte and Carolina Osorio Buitron looked at the relationship between labour market institutions and a range of income inequality measures, including top 10 per cent income share, the Gini of gross income and the Gini of net income, focusing on twenty advanced economies between 1980 and 2010. Even allowing for other factors such as technology, globalisation and financial liberalisation, they found a strong negative link between the rate of unionisation and top earners' income shares.[5]

So labour, or at least a high proportion of labour, has been the loser from general deregulation – another factor driving wages down. In Chapters 3 and 4 we've already seen how wages have stagnated. And as wage rises shrank, so did inflation, and interest rates followed.

THE LONG DOWNTREND IN INTEREST RATES

With wages under pressure, inflation had nowhere to go but down. And falling inflation meant interest rates could decline. From a peak of 19 per cent in 1981, cash interest rates, directly controlled by the Federal Reserve Board, declined steadily to 0.15 per cent in January 2009. As Figure 5.2 shows, there were brief rises in rates, but these did not stick. Why did this huge and prolonged slide in rates, unprecedented in modern history, occur, why did it coincide with an unprecedented build-up of debt and why was this pattern echoed in most developed countries?

By the early 1980s, the free-market fundamentalists had taken total control. Paul Volcker was succeeded by Alan Greenspan as

Figure 5.2: Effective federal funds rate

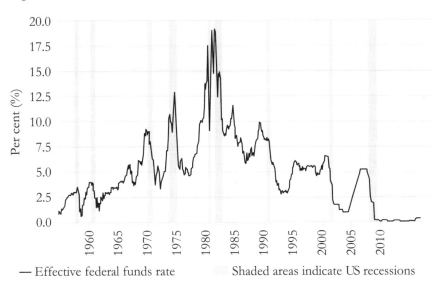

— Effective federal funds rate   Shaded areas indicate US recessions

chairman of the Fed. Greenspan, a Republican and a high priest of free-market ideology, continued the inflation-fighting crusade of his predecessor, with a succession of taps on the brakes when the party got a little too raucous, and swiftly pressing on the accelerator if the economy threatened to stall, hence the peaks and troughs shown in Figure 5.2.

But why the overall decline? In other words, why was each peak and trough lower than the previous one, until it overshot and hit zero after the GFC? Vigilance against inflation should not require that it trend down to nothing – as it has. Inflation could have stabilised around 3 per cent (the long-term average) with oscillations around that. This would probably have translated into interest rates fluctuating around a 5 per cent average. Instead, we have witnessed a remorseless downward trend in the risk-free rate down to zero, and in some countries even below that. This dragged down ten-year US treasury yields to unprecedentedly low levels, below 1.4 per

Figure 5.3 Thirty years of falling UK interest rates

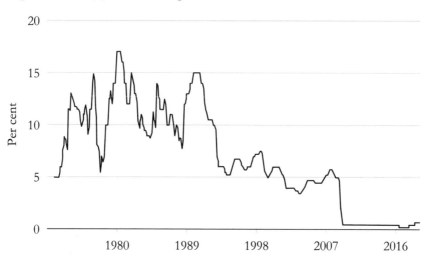

cent. Because of America's size in the global economy and similar changes taking place in the labour markets, this trend has been replicated worldwide. Even in the UK, where the inflationary record is worse than the US, interest rates have declined inexorably (see Figure 5.3).

Let us pause in passing to reflect on this Alice in Wonderland world in which serious countries such as Japan, Germany and Switzerland now oblige creditors to actually *pay* to lend them money, because interest rates are below zero. For example, if you invest your money in a ten-year German government bond, it will promise to pay you a return of around minus 0.5 per cent per annum for the privilege of lending it money. Put another way, if you buy today and hold this bond to its maturity, you will end up with less cash than you invested – you are guaranteed to lose money – and that is before any inflation is taken into account. How did we come to this, and surely something is deeply amiss?

The explanation must have something to do with a change that took place in the structure of the economy which has persisted over decades and through several economic and market cycles. Something must have occurred which meant that every time the Fed and other central banks had to raise rates to curb an uptick in inflation or an overheating economy, they did not need to raise them quite as high as the last time to achieve the desired cooling effect.

In the weak parts of the cycles, when demand sagged so far as to threaten or actually cause a recession, the central banks found they needed to slash rates even lower than in the previous trough, in order to rescue their economies from stalling. In other words, not through choice or planning, but in response to the conditions they encountered, central bankers found themselves responding to an economy whose vigour, on the upside, could be curbed more easily, and whose weakness, on the downside, needed ever lower interest rates to provide the requisite shot of adrenalin to revive the patient. Why might that have been the case?

Unlike the physical sciences, there is no such thing as proof in economics; it is simply impossible to conduct controlled experiments to observe cause and effect. Neither do we have sufficient historical data to enable statistical analysis of correlations between variables. So we have to make do with common sense, observable relationships and plausible explanations that link them.

In the developed world roughly 55–70 per cent of an economy is made up of demand from consumers. The balance consists of public-sector purchases (central and local government plus state-owned enterprises and utilities) and private-sector investment. Both public-sector demand and private-sector investment are ultimately dependent on the dominant source of demand in Western economies: private consumer demand. Businesses will invest less if they read the outlook for consumer demand as weak and vice versa (other things being equal). And governments are constrained in how much they can spend on services or infrastructure by their tax take and how much they can borrow at affordable rates – except where central banks are willing to finance some part of public-sector borrowing. This depends on the overall size of the economy and its growth, which again is mainly influenced by the consumer.

THE LONG GOODBYE TO DEVELOPED-WORLD WAGE GROWTH

Consumer purchasing power depends mainly on jobs, wages and their growth, relative to prices. Other things being equal, the faster job and wage growth are, the faster the increase in consumer demand and the greater the increase in planned investment to meet it by businesses. Of course, other factors come into play, such as fiscal and monetary policy, commodity prices and exchange rates, but if the authorities don't move the tiller significantly, the path of wages is the key factor for growth. It is also the key factor in determining inflation. It is difficult for firms to hike prices aggressively if wages are lagging behind, as consumers will simply not have the purchasing power to buy the same quantities at the new prices, unless they stretch to borrow. Again, other factors such as commodity prices and the exchange rate can also influence inflation, but probably only on a temporary basis if wages do not follow.

Therefore, if the Fed and other central banks are able to snuff out inflationary pressures earlier and at more modest levels in each cycle, and are also forced to reduce rates to ever lower levels to prevent or cure recessions, the only plausible explanation must be that the trend in wage or job growth has been pointing down *structurally, across several economic cycles*. Wage growth still waxes and wanes according to where we are in the business cycle, but around a declining long-term average. This is graphically demonstrated in Figure 5.4.

Figure 5.4: US wage and salary growth 1960–2019

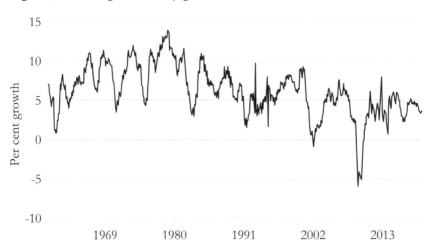

Of course, given the link between wages, demand and inflation, the downward trend in wage growth has been matched by a corresponding downward trend in inflation. And while it is true that after a weak period average real wages have, as of March 2019, recovered back to their 1973 peak of $23.24 per hour,[6] as we have seen this was achieved by the top of the income distribution scale doing very well. Even then, it equates to a paltry recovery since the 1990 lows.

Along with inflation, wage growth in the US has been on a steadily declining trend through several economic cycles. At the same time, the distribution of wage growth became skewed towards high earners, so that the dwindling gains in real wages accrued to those in the top half of the income distribution. More often than not, these are also older workers, which has exacerbated generational inequality too.

A paper by the Pew Research Center[7] notes that in the US:

- Young workers are earning significantly less than they did in 1980, but the opposite is happening with older workers. Among full-time, year-round workers, the median earnings of 16 to 24-year-olds in 1980 were $28,131. By 2015 the median had fallen 11 per cent to only $25,000. Meanwhile, the median pay of workers 65 and older rose 37 per cent, from $36,483 in 1980 to $50,000 in 2015. And workers aged 55 to 64 also earned 10 per cent more in 2015 than they did in 1980. (Earnings data in 2014 dollars.)

- Americans are putting in more time at work. The average length of a working week was 38.7 hours in 2015, slightly up from 38.1 hours in 1980. And Americans are working more weeks per year. Average weeks worked per year increased from 43 in 1980 to 46.8 in 2015. Combined, this adds up to an additional one month's worth of work in a year. So, any gains in real earnings are partly the result of having to put in more hours, with the benefits of higher productivity going largely to the employer, given the shift in relative bargaining power.

This confirms the conviction of many American parents of young adults that their children will be the first generation in modern times to be worse off than their parents.

The situation appears not as bad in the UK, where millennials' disposable income is higher than that of their boomer parents, as shown by Figure 5.5.

However, this chart fails to account for student debt, housing affordability and inferior pension rights, and does not adjust for lower tax rates. If you take all these factors into account, millenials' fears that they will end up worse off than previous generations are

Figure 5.5: UK disposable income through the generations 23 February 2018

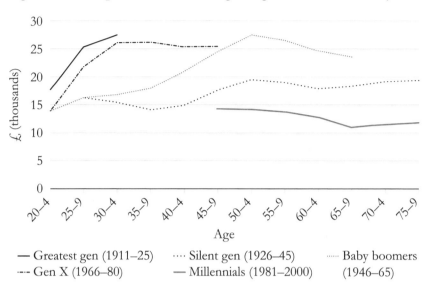

sadly realistic, especially if taxes rise back to more normal historical levels.

As we have seen in previous chapters, not only has the distribution of the productive output of the economy shifted to allocate more of the pie to the owners of capital and less to labour, but within labour the distribution of income has massively swung towards those at the very top of the pyramid. Consequently, a large part of the working population has received little or no wage increase net of inflation for decades – an unusual state of affairs in modern times.

PLUGGING INCOME GAPS: THE INCREASING RELIANCE ON BORROWING

The promise that globalisation would raise living standards for all, boosted by the availability of cheaper imported goods, has not worked out for a large section of Western society.

The deflationary impact of low-cost manufacturing countries rejoining the global trade system from the late 1990s, as well as the North American Free Trade Agreement, was significant. But unlike the Ricardian economics textbook case, where both parties gain from an exchange of trade when each specialises in what it is *relatively more efficient* at producing, (as opposed to producing more cheaply), the current form of globalisation has been an uncoordinated land-grab by those countries who are *absolutely cheaper* at producing. Labour in China has done very well out of trade with the West; the same cannot be said for Western labour.

The present system is, in practice, a travesty of Ricardian economic theory, although no one has explained this to bewildered electorates. It has resulted in millions of Western middle- and lower-class losers and a vast transfer of economic power from West to East. Of course, there has been a dramatic reduction in inequality *between countries* as developing nations have greatly benefited. However, no one asked Western electorates if they were willing to sacrifice themselves in order to reduce *global inequality*. This massive transfer of wealth came about without any democratic mandate; Western electorates were presented with a fait accompli by corporate decision makers, with little protest by the peoples' elected representatives.

The workers who have lost their relatively well-paid secure manufacturing jobs in the West have not been compensated for by balancing increases in wages in other sectors (contrary to Ricardo's thinking) or by government transfers from higher taxes paid by the winners. This is not just because globalisation has not followed Ricardo's hypothesis, but also because governments have not felt the pressure, until recently, to pay attention to the losers, let alone take from the winners enough to compensate them.

Cheaper goods imported from south-east Asia could have boosted Western living standards if purchased by households whose income growth remained steady. However, globalising free marketeers ignore the fact that jobs had moved abroad to produce those goods. In the end, you can only earn what you produce. If you produce less than you did under the old scheme of things, or add less value, your income suffers and you need to borrow more to increase consumption and maintain rising living standards.

The downward trend in interest rates over three decades has not only been the symptom of the cancer that has been eating away at workers' ability to improve their incomes, it has also provided the remedy – easy credit. This has offered, like a tranquilliser, if not a cure then at a least short-term palliative treatment of the symptoms. Unfortunately, it was not in the winners' interests to broadcast a health warning about moderation. Neither did the winners plan ahead on how the losers would eventually come off this wonder drug.

Four powerful multi-decade trends have together created a perfect storm. Job insecurity and weakening wage growth; rapid technological change; labour's declining share of the economic pie, and unequal income distribution have combined to drag down consumer purchasing power. As a result, that purchasing power has, in the main, only been able to grow through rising debt.

Even Lord Adair Turner, a pillar of the establishment, admits in his book *Between Debt and the Devil* that 'Credit therefore has to grow faster than GDP simply to maintain the demand growth which would have occurred, without growing credit intensity, if inequality had not increased .... We needed to offset the deflationary implications of richer people's high propensity to save.' [8]

THE HOLLOWING OUT OF THE WESTERN MIDDLE CLASSES

Research by the Pew Research Center on US cities shows that median household incomes, adjusted for the local cost of living, grew in only 39 out of 229 metropolitan areas in the US between

1999 and 2014. 'The share of adults who live in middle-income households (defined as those earing two thirds to double the median income), has fallen since 1971. In 2015, 50 per cent of American adults were middle income, compared with 61 per cent in 1971.'[9] Some of the steepest declines were seen in cities hit by industrial job losses, such as Springfield, Ohio, which saw incomes fall by 27 per cent over the period 2000–14 and the Detroit-Warren-Dearborn area of Michigan, which recorded an 18 per cent drop in incomes.

To compensate for the loss of income growth and to maintain rising living standards, households took on increasing amounts of debt relative to their incomes, which meant that it took smaller increases in interest rates to have an equivalent depressing effect on household finances and cash left over to spend. This explains the corresponding declining peaks and troughs in interest rates over the last three decades. Wage growth stopped at a lower level at each cyclical peak and plunged to new lows at each subsequent trough, not only because of loss of bargaining power due to technology and globalisation, but because workers made up for the shortfall in their incomes by becoming increasingly indebted.

Wage growth is also linked to productivity. If more is produced per hour of work, part of that increase in output can be shared out with workers in the form of higher wages. Unfortunately, even this driver of wage growth has begun to run out of gas. 'Among *mature economies*, the productivity slowdown in the past decade has been dramatic, as growth rates of *output per hour* halved from an average annual rate of 2.3 per cent in the period 2000–2007 to 1.2 per cent from 2010–2017. Productivity growth further slowed to 0.8 per cent in 2018, showing a small projected improvement to 1.1 per cent in 2019.'[10]

Productivity has slowed across the world in recent years, and there is a growing divide between 'frontier' businesses and the rest of the economy, with growth more concentrated in a few areas, with workers elsewhere left behind in a low-skill, low-productivity trap. While the pie may still be getting bigger, only a few of its slices are growing, rewarding the lucky ones that feed on them.

With the benefit of hindsight, we can see that the decades immediately after the Second World War were exceptional. The massive reconstruction of Europe, aided by the Marshall Plan, resulted in investment, new factories, infrastructure, and so jobs and consumer demand. America benefited through increased trade and direct investments in domestic factories, such as Ford and IBM. Manufacturing boomed. Jobs were relatively high-paying and secure.

From the 1980s onwards, this virtuous circle ground to a halt. As companies, aided and abetted by governments, began to build manufacturing capacity in cheap-labour countries, Western politicians sold this to their electorates by glibly dismissing manufacturing as archaic and trumpeting the benefits of free trade and globalisation. Back home the future lay in the higher 'value added' world of services, such as finance. The trouble was, not everyone could cast off their factory overalls to don the sharp suit or white coat of a high-powered banker, broker, lawyer, marketing executive, medical practitioner or programmer.

After the fall of the Berlin Wall and China's adoption of state-controlled capitalism, the supply of labour for Western firms jumped almost overnight. The large-scale industrialisation of the West went into a relative decline as the emerging markets snapped up the manufacturing jobs that the West appeared happy to discard. The positive dynamic of the post-war years – new jobs, rising productivity, rising purchasing power, rising consumer demand, rising investment and new jobs – ground to a halt.

This transfer of economic power and growth to emerging markets damaged not only the West but its allies, such as Japan, at one point the world's second-largest economy and a trail-blazer in terms of building up a debt-fuelled bubble from whose bursting in

1990 it has yet to recover. Since then the Japanese economy has been limping along, growing around 1 per cent per annum, with stagnant real wages, low domestic investment and public debt at stratospheric levels. The last thirty years or so have been a long war against deflation. In the 1980s Japan pioneered the hollowing out of its domestic economy by building factories in the US to quieten American protectionist rumblings. It also moved production to cheaper Asian locations to remain competitive. Coinciding with the rise of its Chinese neighbour, this has trapped what used to be one of the most dynamic and innovative nations in the world in a structural stagnation from which there appears to be no way out.

CAUSE AND EFFECT

As the engine of wage growth in the West and other developed countries sputtered to a near halt, interest rates had to fall to sustain demand growth. If half of Western households could no longer afford to buy more stuff each year because they were no longer getting paid more (after inflation), at least they could be encouraged to do so through ever-cheaper credit.

In the end, the reason interest rates entered a thirty-year downward trend had little to do with economic dogma such as the control of the money supply (hugely expanded in recent years, to little effect on inflation) or a carefully planned path by governments or central banks (consider Japan's desperate and unsuccessful attempts to nudge inflation *higher*). Instead, the decline is the consequence of globalisation and deregulation undermining labour's bargaining power, technological change effectively making millions of decently paid workers obsolete, and the resulting winner-takes-all transfer of income away from those who spend a high proportion of their pay to those who do not. While there were still cycles in the economy, the central banks had little choice but to follow the slide in wage growth.

Consumption depends on consumers' incomes and other sources of cash, namely borrowing. But unless some of that debt is written off or shrinks relative to incomes, through growth or inflation, if the borrowing is not for productive investment but simply consumption, it merely pulls forward tomorrow's demand. In economies blighted by almost static purchasing power, the only way for many consumers to keep demand growing and consume more is by borrowing more each year, giving themselves the illusion of rising living standards.

This of course is a doomed enterprise. Taking on more debt relative to income has its limits. Eventually, the cost of servicing the debt eats up so much income that either the borrower defaults or has to borrow more, a situation which then takes on the characteristics of a Ponzi scheme (named in honour of Charles Ponzi, who defrauded thousands of investors in the 1920s by taking money from new investors to pay off existing ones). Ultimately lenders will decide to cut their losses, and default becomes inevitable.

Replicated across millions of individuals, this becomes a problem for the banks, which will have to be rescued by the authorities in the form of taxpayer bail-outs, or the printing of money to inject into the system. Neither remedy can be indefinitely applied in ever greater size without increasing instability to the point where depression or hyper-inflation are all but unavoidable.

The world suffered a foretaste of the ultimate bursting of its Ponzi economy during the 2008 Great Financial Crisis, which amounted to an economic heart attack. The authorities totally overlooked the building instability generated by a booming finance industry, blinded by its apparent sophistication, which supposedly enabled it to absorb and digest more risk than in the past. While the patient has responded to gargantuan injections of monetary adrenaline and fiscal infusions by the authorities, a decade later it has yet to recover, whether in terms of debt shrinking back to pre-crash levels or interest rates moving back up from distressed levels. The need for UK government bond yields (gilts), to remain at 300-year lows is a dramatic symptom of extreme circumstances and continuing distress in the economic system.

According to Luigi Buttiglione, 'the observed acceleration in growth from the late 1990s until 2007 was supported by the build-up in global debt ... and at the same time encouraged the increase in leverage in many economies'.[11]

Achieving instant gratification through debt rather than waiting to earn what we consume has much in common with drug addiction. Once you embark on that path, it is difficult to turn back. Like any addict, we need ever-larger doses to produce the same effect, and it becomes increasingly difficult to go cold turkey. The very fact that households could borrow more relative to their incomes because interest rates were lower did not mean they *had to* borrow more. But as they did, it brought down the ceiling to which central banks could raise rates in each cycle.

A more highly geared economy based on debt taken out at low interest rates means the system is more sensitive to any rise in rates, so needs less of a rise than in past cycles to brake the economy. And it requires ever more monetary stimulus to recover from any subsequent downturn, as the appetite for re-leveraging weakens because borrowers have not fully de-leveraged from the last borrowing binge; in the later cycles, such a full de-leveraging would probably have meant a 1930s style Great Depression, something the authorities were hell-bent on avoiding at any cost. But if you have failed to repay much of your debt from the last cycle, how can you be encouraged to borrow more in the new cycle?

THE DEMAND FOR CREDIT

Not only were they able, but households positively wanted, and *needed* to borrow more. In the US, before the GFC evidence shows that mortgage credit growth rate was inversely correlated to income growth.[12] Others confirm this perverse phenomenon: Surprisingly, perhaps, during the peak of the leverage cycle in the US, people with declining incomes were the ones borrowing at a higher rate.

Most of the increase in credit in the West was related to property, which was considered safe. House prices only went one way, and that was up. Lenders saw this as good business because the mortgages were backed by the properties that were bought by the borrowers. And the flow of money into real estate, fuelled by debt, itself accelerated the rise in property prices. This meant borrowers were attracted by the prospect of making leveraged capital gains with little risk as prices went up.

Houses were no longer just homes; they became a means to speculate and become rich. Many fortunes were made riding the up escalator of the property market, with developers remortgaging existing properties to buy or build new ones. Households could borrow 100 per cent of the purchase price or could obtain interest-only mortgages, reducing the cost of servicing the debt and enabling them to stretch for the most expensive property, with the intention of 'flipping' it after a quick price gain, repaying the loan and pocketing the profit.

According to Jack M. Guttentag, the last US real estate boom was 'caused by a broad belief that house prices would keep rising – allied with strong demand created by government agencies, *under orders to boost home ownership among lower income segments* [my italics]. Lenders and the investment banks that sold their loans through securitisation had every reason to believe they were doing what the government wanted them to do.'[13]

The boost to living standards through mortgage leverage could be given a further twist. Rising house prices enabled owners to use their properties as ATM machines, withdrawing cash by doubling up on mortgages secured on rising values. Homeowners borrowed against increasing equity in their appreciating houses for home improvements, holidays, cars and everyday consumption.

This frenzy was not confined to the Anglo-Saxon countries, and, as we've seen, was preceded by a property bubble in Japan fifteen years earlier. Some European countries ramped up their finance sector to feed the property ogre, but it is true that in the Eurozone 'the build-up in household debt was more muted than in the UK and the US and, pre-crisis, at a lower level'.[14] On the other hand, the perverse consequences of the Eurozone's ideological commitment to fiscal austerity even after the bubble burst meant that the ratio of total debt to GDP is still higher today than before the crisis because GDP growth has been so anaemic. Household debt ratios have come down marginally but government debt is still much higher than pre-crisis.

You could argue that the declining trend in interest rates over thirty years was a sufficient condition for the rapid increase in demand for credit, but that is to ignore the reason why this unprecedented fall in interest rates took place. Interest rates would not have fallen as long and as far as they did had wage growth not slowed down as much as it did. The simple reason for this is that wage growth is the major factor in consumer price inflation, in contrast to asset price inflation, which hardly figures in official measures of inflation. Higher wages would have meant higher inflation and so higher rates to slow nominal growth. It is true that more leverage makes the system increasingly sensitive to higher interest rates, but leverage could not have accumulated at the same pace had interest rates not come down so far so fast; households would otherwise have gone bust earlier. Conversely, rates would not have kept falling (given stagnant incomes) if households hadn't piled on an extra level of debt during each cycle, thereby compressing the headroom for central banks to raise rates without triggering a recession. Lower interest rates made more debt affordable, and higher debt loads stopped rates rising as high as in previous cycles.

THE SUPPLY OF CREDIT

The finance industry was ready and willing to plug the gap between stagnant wages and the desire for rising living standards among the army of losers in a deregulated, globalised, technologically disrupted world. Deregulated banks' ability to create almost unlimited quantities of credit replaced the role of wage growth in supporting rising consumption. This contributed to corporate earnings growth, to which senior executives' bonuses were tied. Demand for credit was so strong that other lenders, such as investment funds, entered the fray and further expanded the supply of credit.

Government tolerance of lenders' aggressive pursuit of profit growth through faster credit creation enabled the supply of debt to rise. So did the financial industry's talent for innovation, spawning bundles of opaque 'asset-backed securities'. These were made up of a myriad of underlying loans to borrowers, whose credit worthiness was difficult to comprehend, but were snapped up by pension funds and other yield-hungry investors as they promised a better return than the yield on plain vanilla debt securities. But, as Buttiglione rightly points out, 'financial crises are more about human nature. Laws and regulations set the boundary to credit decisions, but financial innovation, charged by the prospect of capital gain, pushes out the frontier. Finance and leverage advances time and again to breaking point.'

Although the credit bubble burst in America first, it was a widespread phenomenon throughout the West in one form or another: According to Adair Turner, 'In the two decades before 2008, the typical picture in most advanced economies was that credit grew at about 10–15 per cent per year versus 5 per cent annual growth in national income. And it seemed at that time that such credit growth was required to ensure adequate economic growth. From 1970 to 2008 UK finance grew twice as fast as UK national income ... The US experience [was that] finance's share of national

Figure 5.6: Runaway US debt beats GDP growth

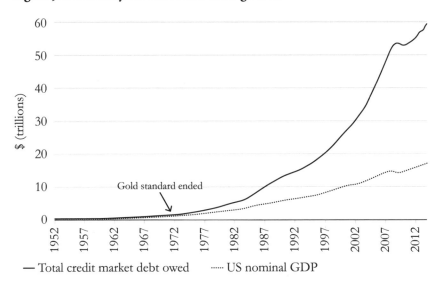

income more than doubled.' At 8 per cent, this was the highest proportion at any time since 1850, even higher than the 6 per cent of the previous peak in 1929. 'In Spain total private debt was 80 per cent of GDP in 1980 and 230 per cent by 2007.'[15]

Incidentally, we may note in passing the diminishing efficacy of new debt to boost economic growth. Put another way, each dollar of new credit contributed less and less to GDP growth. 'Between 2000 and 2007, nominal GDP growth in the US was $4.2 trillion. During the same period, total credit market debt grew by $21.3 trillion. This means that $1 debt led to just a 20 cent increase in GDP. In 1966, $1 of debt used to increase GDP by around 90 cents'.[16]

Debt growth in the US economy had a diminishing impact on GDP growth over time as the debt burden mounted. (Figure 5.6).

As usual, where America led, most of the other developed countries were happy to follow.

This is one of the reasons why this version of a Ponzi scheme is doomed: at some point adding more credit/debt simply adds to the debt servicing burden to the point where it cannot be supported by incremental growth, unless you reduce it through inflation, write-offs or bankruptcies. While the gigantic growth of the finance cuckoo within the economic nest was without precedent in modern times, the push by bankers and other credit providers to aggressively lend more could only succeed if there was demand. Demand created its own supply, as well as vice versa. As Charles Finch put it, 'The long-term decline of the upwardly mobile American middle-class created an unsustainable pull and push for debt.'[17]

BLOWING UP THE DEBT BUBBLE AND BANKRUPTING THE WEST

Figure 5.7 illustrates the dramatic increase in US household debt over many decades. It also shows that this really took off around the

Figure 5.7: US household debt to GDP 1956–2016

— US household debt to GDP

Figure 5.8: US housing bubble 1987–2012

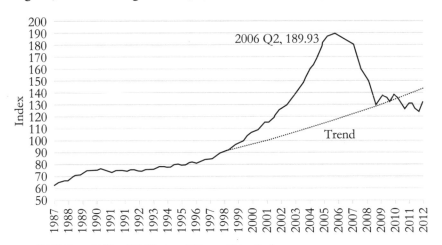

— S&P Case Shiller US National Home Price Index

······ Case Shiller Trend (3.3% Annual Growth Rate)

Figure 5.9: UK household debt to GDP 1971–2016

— UK household debt to GDP

mid-1980s as deregulation kicked in and interest rates fell. Figure 5.8 shows the concomitant house-price bubble.

The build-up of household debt was widespread throughout the Western world, with many countries such as the UK embracing the same growth model with enthusiasm (see Figure 5.9). Borrowing took off as interest rates fell and credit markets were deregulated after 1980.

As their properties appreciated in value, the 'wealth effect' meant that households also ran down their savings or neglected to put aside enough for retirement. If house prices continued to climb, why not simply downsize at retirement and use the liberated capital as a pension pot?

With all the evidence of short-term and irresponsible behaviour by lenders and consumers, it is deeply worrying that the authorities were blind to this destabilising 'virtuous' circle. Neither governments nor their central banks were prepared to take away the punch bowl, not because they did not want to bring the party to a close, but because they claimed that it was impossible to tell when the party had become too raucous.

'In April 2006, the International Monetary Fund had described in detail how financial innovation had made the global financial system more stable.'[18] In fact, officials and central bankers were often the cheerleaders for the inflating debt and housing bubble, as they praised the sophistication of modern finance in distributing risk safely across many more investors. Fed Chairman Alan Greenspan gave the green light to the industry when he claimed, 'The use of a growing array of derivatives and the related application of more-sophisticated approaches to measuring and managing risk are key factors underpinning the greater resilience of our largest financial institutions … Derivatives have permitted the unbundling of financial risks.'[19] Or again, scarily, 'Improvements in lending practices driven by information technology have enabled lenders to reach out to households with previously unrecognised borrowing capacities.'[20] And as the world approached the precipice, 'I was aware that the loosening of mortgage credit terms for sub-prime borrowers increased financial risk. But I believed then, as now, that the benefits of broadened home ownership are worth the risk.'[21]

In fact, Greenspan and politicians were keen to encourage a strong and rising housing market not only on social grounds, but also, crucially, as an antidote to the recessionary impact of the bursting of the previous asset bubble in technology, telecoms and media companies in 2002. We return to this theme later. With admirable candour, but hardly reassuringly, Greenspan claims that the onset of the financial crisis in August, 2007 left him in a 'state of shocked disbelief'.[22]

Other Western countries, such as Ireland and Spain, also went on unchecked borrowing binges that bid up real estate prices. In Spain the driver for the borrowing binge was the dramatic rise in the affordability of debt as interest rates fell after the peseta was superseded by the euro in 1999. As in the US and UK, Spanish incomes were not able to grow much, although the country was one of the winners from the globalised drive to move productive capacity to lower-wage locations. Spain and Portugal's accession to the EU on 1 January 1986 coincided perfectly with the onset of globalisation. But the fruits of globalisation, in Europe at least, did not go to the newly industrialised Spanish labour force, which enjoyed very modest real gains in spite of companies such as Volkswagen making large manufacturing investments in the country.[23] Real average Spanish wages grew from €24,543 in 1990 to €27,101 in 2007, or only about 10 per cent over 17 years (and to €27,946 in 2018). However, the adoption of the euro afforded low Germanic-style borrowing rates, of which Spanish workers could take advantage to join the property and consumption binges. Spanish house prices just about tripled in the ten years to 2008, fed by an orgy of borrowing.

Also fuelled by rising debt, Irish house prices soared to ridiculous levels by any measure, only to crash. And yet no one rang the alarm bell. Both Spain and Ireland fell into major recessions when the bubble burst. In the case of Ireland, this required a bail-out from European institutions.

To rescue the Eurozone from imploding from the consequences of the debt and real estate bubble, the European Central Bank (ECB) has had to embark on a series of extraordinary monetary measures, still in evidence to this day. These include negative interest rates on deposits and huge purchases of government and corporate debt to try and re-stimulate investment and consumption. At the same time, European governments and institutions, under the leadership of Germany, have promoted a self-defeating strategy of fiscal austerity (debt reduction by raising taxes and cutting public expenditure) thereby stunting GDP recovery prospects.

While the general tendency was to leverage up as the cost of money fell and banks pushed loans to consumers, countries with more stable traditions of financial prudence such as France and Germany did not join the credit party with quite the same abandon, and started from a position of lower debt. French household debt (see Figure 3.10 overleaf) did more than double relative to the economy, but from a very low base, and never reached the red-light levels of hard partygoers such as the US and the UK.

The temporary rise in German debt during the 1990s was probably a one-off, attributable to the reunification of the country (see Figure 5.11 overleaf). Former East Germans, suddenly liberated, with their incomes re-denominated into Western Deutschmarks at a favourable rate of exchange, could not help but binge a little after three decades of bare shelves and austerity.

This is cold comfort in an interlinked world, as the apparently more prudent Germans and French have discovered during the euro debt crisis since 2010. As creditor countries such as Germany

Figure 5.10: France household debt to GDP 1981–2016

— France household debt to GDP

Figure 5.11: Germany household debt to GDP 1971–2016

— Germany household debt to GDP

lent to the debt bingers on the periphery of Europe, when some of these went bust, creditor assets risked being wiped out; the creditors had to back the bail-outs of the debtors.

Not all debt bubbles took the same form. In Greece, for example, the debt inflation occurred in the public sector rather than among households; household debt was only around 60 per cent,[24] while public debt was already 175 per cent of GDP when the crisis hit. The Greeks were operating a modified version of the debt Ponzi scheme. Instead of the banks loading up households with credit to supplement their incomes, the Greek government supplemented the electorate's wages and employment by creating phantom or unproductive public-sector positions and a system of subsidies, none of which were financed through a corresponding and adequate collection of taxes. Because of this method of supplementing their incomes, Greeks had one of the lowest levels of household debt to GDP in Europe; the debt racked up on the government's ledger.

In stark contrast, surprisingly profligate Dutch households borrowed 126 per cent of their GDP and yet never attracted criticism from the rigorous Germans since Holland's public debt was always below 70 per cent of GDP (currently around 65 per cent). Why one form of unproductive debt should be more acceptable than another is another inconsistency of political culture.

As long as northern European banks and investors were happy to buy Greek government bonds because they yielded considerably more than German, French or Dutch bonds and were in euros so there was no currency risk, this worked out fine for everyone. Unfortunately, as in all such schemes, there comes a time where the takers of cash have taken in so much that they run out of new providers to enable them to reimburse their existing creditors and investors, at which point the game is up. With no control over its money supply or currency to bail itself out, the market woke up to the unpleasant realisation that Greece could no longer service its debt in the post-GFC world, let alone repay bondholders at maturity dates. Either European creditors would have to write off some of the debt (which they did) or Greece would have to default (which it did).

TOTAL DEBT OUT OF CONTROL

With a few exceptions, households have succeeded, in varying degrees, in de-leveraging since the GFC, thereby depressing demand and growth. However, in the Western world this has come at the cost of a corresponding increase in government debt as the authorities allowed their balance sheets to blow out to offset the consequences of households trying to get their finances under better control. Debt owed by governments rose by 40 per cent in the US, 46 per cent in the UK, and 26 per cent in the Eurozone compared to pre-crisis levels.[25]

In fact, total debt to GDP globally has inexorably continued to climb to new heights in excess of 210 per cent of world GDP. In developed markets this has now reached over 350 per cent of GDP. Only Germany has a total debt/GDP that is lower than in 2007. High corporate debt and bank leverage in the euro area, combined with an austere and unhelpful fiscal policy, has made the Eurozone crisis more severe than elsewhere. This has led to very low growth and inflation, which, combined with low productivity growth and the demographics of a shrinking native population, means the area has a lower debt-bearing capacity than the US.

The modest de-leveraging by Western households that has occurred since the crisis has mostly failed to return debt-to-income ratios to the levels that were the norm before credit was deregulated and the finance industry let off its leash. This means two things. First, governments and central banks now understand better how highly levered and fragile the system has become. They realise that they have lost the power to move real interest rates back to the 'normal' historical positive long-term levels that held before the crisis, for fear of crashing the system again. At any hint of market distress, they take their foot off the brake. Second, the ongoing weight of debt they have allowed to accumulate means that households' purchasing power can no longer be increased artificially by borrowing more, since many are close to their limits already and rates cannot drop any lower. From now on, growth will depend on growing incomes, but that is outside their immediate control. That means the West is effectively condemned to grow at a snail's pace, à la Japan after their financial crisis. We are effectively stuck on a permanently low trajectory limited by households' weak wage rise potential, unless at least one of the following occurs.

- Governments consistently spend more and/or cut taxes to juice up demand and make up the shortfall, aided or not by monetary policy – so-called modern monetary theory, or MMT.
- The West claws back good-quality jobs from cheap locations it has outsourced them to.
- Robots are taxed like labour to place them on a level playing field and the proceeds are reinvested.
- Income redistribution through taxation is increased in favour of those who have not gained from globalisation and technology and who spend more out of income.
- Productivity rises once more as labour is put to work in a more productive way (as in the 1950s and 60s), lifting all boats.

While the last solution is arguably the best and enabled the West to pay down its debt mountain accumulated from the Second World War, there are no indications that this could happen anytime soon; quite the reverse. With falling populations in many countries, and the decline of manufacturing and some clerical and administrative jobs, this avenue seems all but closed. And clearly the first option cannot be more than a temporary solution unless it is accommodated by central banks printing the requisite cash, as a country would risk public debt spinning out of control.

THE GFC – THE CLIMACTIC END TO EVER-INCREASING FINANCIAL EXCESS?

The GFC and the chain of consequences triggered by the implosion of the last great financial bubble in 2008 fully exposed the underlying malfunctioning of an economic system that had been artificially doped up on ever more easy money for decades. Having tested the system to destruction, the financial industry's business model for growth is now effectively broken. Even at close to zero rates of interest, the supply of private credit will not grow much as banks are once more hemmed in as they try to repair their balance sheets. Neither will demand. Borrowers' traumatic experiences of losing their mortgaged homes or their jobs have taught people the folly of large debt and the meaning of risk. Indeed, households have tried to de-leverage, in some cases with modest success. As a result, the demand for credit is stagnant, much to the chagrin of the West's central banks, desperate to re-ignite nominal GDP growth, as they succeeded in doing in the past by dropping rates.

Companies, on the other hand, have been willing binge borrowers at cheap rates of late – corporate debt rose from 30% of GDP in the early 1950s to over 70% by the time of the crsis – but often for 'financial engineering' rather than productive investment in capital expenditure to increase efficiency or expand capacity. For example, companies may borrow money to buy another company and so boost reported earnings per share (since they have not increased their number of shares), or simply reduce the number of their own shares by buying some back. This does not generate real output growth, as would be the case if they used the proceeds instead to invest in a new plant for example. Financial engineering was also used by the banks to package together mortgage loans of varying quality into new securities that could then be onsold to investors. As we have seen, this did temporarily boost growth by injecting more leverage, but eventually came back to bite the economy in the crisis when some of these went sour.

Since 2000 each financial crisis has been quickly swept under the carpet by cranking up the leverage machine to greater heights. But because there is a limit to this, just as there is to any Ponzi scheme, there comes a time when the rescue no longer works. We have finally reached that point as the monstrous size of the debt bubble that burst with the GFC has been reinflated. It is too big to deflate over a few years without causing a depression (à la 1930s), while our underlying weak sources of natural growth mean its sheer size will weigh on us for the long term, with all the instability that this implies. Because Western economies are saturated with debt, something snapped in 2008 that cannot be patched up one more time, and the game of masking weak wages by more easy credit is up. To the dismay and alarm of politicians, people seem to have finally noticed and are getting angry.

6

The free market, politics and the road to the Great Financial Crisis

Madmen in authority, who hear voices in the air, are distilling their frenzy from some academic scribbler of a few years back.

John Maynard Keynes

As a consequence of the latest and greatest of financial crises, the West's increasingly unstable economic and political system of the last thirty years has started to buckle. The GFC was the culmination of an ever-expanding series of crises powered by an out-of-control credit creation machine and the naive indulgence of governments and central bankers in thrall to the marvels of a growing finance industry. Instead of protecting its citizens from the school bully, the authorities behaved more like parents who refuse to discipline an unruly but bright child, overlooking and excusing its serial misbehaviour.

Within each credit cycle of the last thirty years, each individual decision may, taken in isolation, have been rational; at the macro or collective level, the aggregation of individual decisions generated credit growth far in excess of underlying economic growth and its ability to support the heavier mass of debt.

Financial crises resulting from chronic excessive debt creation are a consequence of three deadly factors.

- The problem of the 'generalisation principle' we explored in Chapter 3. The free-market-knows-best school of economics is clearly immune to the perverse functioning of a financial sector which does not limit itself, as Hyman Minsky has persuasively argued.[1]
- The self-reinforcing nature of rising asset prices is destabilising as humans are attracted to the honey pot of capital gains. In another case of perverse behaviour, and in stark contrast to economic theory's assumption that higher goods prices lead to lower demand, rising asset prices beget higher demand. But asset prices often rise under the impetus of easy liquidity and leverage. This is a recipe for overheated markets and financial crashes.
- A political and central banking establishment in denial about the inadequacies of the free market in the financial industry.

These factors escalated in importance as the authorities dared not let the market purge itself through sufficient bankruptcies and write-offs to reset the system on a sound footing for fear of the short-term pain of mass unemployment, plummeting living standards and the wrath of the electorate.

THE THREE DEADLY FACTORS

The problem engendered by the generalisation principle arises from the selfishness and self-centredness of human nature and a lack of awareness of the impact of one's own behaviour when replicated by many others. If individual bankers are motivated to grow their profits by 10 per cent per annum in a world of 4 per cent growth because, rationally, they are seeking to make their fortunes, society somewhere will become increasingly leveraged to the point of instability.

If enough debtors get into difficulty and are forced to sell assets (or their creditors are), then the entire debt structure risks collapse. Eventually, this tipping point is reached as lenders run out of safe loans they can make to sound borrowers; the virtuous circle goes into reverse; prices fall; more borrowers default; lenders cannot recoup their loans; credit conditions tighten, and cascading bankruptcies threaten.

For economists and politicians brought up with quasi-biblical reverence for Adam Smith's invisible hand and indoctrinated with belief in the collective wisdom of the market, the rational decisions of individuals translate into good rational decisions for society. As Keynes remarked, 'Capitalism is the extraordinary belief that the nastiest of men, for the nastiest of reasons, will somehow work for the benefit of us all.'

Economic textbooks are reluctant to acknowledge exceptions to Smith's model, which is intellectually satisfying, if flawed in practice. As we saw in Chapter 3, they do concede a few exceptions or special cases, such as public 'goods' (justice for example) or public 'bads' (for example pollution,) where they acknowledge the inefficiency of the market mechanism at a society level.

However, Adair Turner is one of the few establishment figures lucid and honest enough to acknowledge that the failure of markets extends to the financial industry: 'there is a negative social externality [economists' jargon for bad social effects] of debt creation: debt can be a form of economic pollution'.[2] In other words, finance, by its special nature at the centre of the economic machine, charged with recycling or creating money, if left to its own devices is incentivised to lead to perverse outcomes at the aggregate level.

The conveniently neat world at the micro level of each individual making isolated decisions that are right for him/her does not factor in the often negative consequences for society at the macro level. That is because the early economists, operating in a completely different economic system, were principally interested in the positive consequences of aggregating individual decisions through the signals of demand and supply and the price mechanism for goods. As Minsky devastatingly quips in his book, the market may be good at finding how many different flavours of ice cream to supply, but not so good at reaching a general equilibrium of demand or distribution of income, education or training. The free market has been surprisingly slow or reluctant to see its catastrophic implications when it comes to generalised, self-interested lending.

The second inconvenient anomaly in classical economic theory is presented by the behaviour of asset prices. Contrary to classical economic theory, where the higher the price of a good, the lower the demand, asset markets often behave the other way around. Rising asset prices may actually beget more demand as investors are attracted to the prospect of capital gains and reassured by the apparent enthusiasm of their peers to continue to buy, even if valuations become stretched. In a world where value is ultimately subjective and determined by the price that someone is willing to pay, the market can always justify the prices it is paying.

In this case, crowd behaviour takes over as another example of the generalisation principle: once individuals notice the price of a good or asset is rising, it is rational for them to buy in the expectation of reselling at a profit. While this is rational at the individual level, it cannot be at the aggregate level, since it is a zero-sum game. The total population cannot hope to buy to pass on to itself at a profit. In so far as a participating individual understands this, it remains rational for him/her to buy if and only if he/she assumes he/she will be able to sell before the market runs out of like-minded buyers. Of course, this assumption cannot be generalised for all buyers. The momentum-chasing tendency of human nature is unchanging and sometimes overrides a sense of good value for money. It is itself another major reason for the inherently destabilising nature of the financial industry, to the extent that it creates the credit for people to chase asset prices higher, and will always be so unless and until human nature changes.

The third factor contributing to the Great Financial Crisis of 2008 was inconsistency at the heart of monetary doctrine and policy. Ideological blind faith in the free market since Reagan and Thatcher has allowed the finance industry to ramp up its output unhindered over three decades, even though punctuated by a series of ever deeper busts. Worse, each time a debt build-up turned to bust, the authorities rushed to the rescue to mitigate the implied losses to creditors and investors, terrified of likely collateral damage to the real economy. But the very act of providing a lender-of-last-resort guarantee to the bankers has encouraged moral hazard, leading to a resumption of the lending binge with assumed impunity.

Since the 1980s central banks and governments have not dared interfere with the free market, however worrying the obvious symptoms of excess such as leverage ratios and galloping asset prices. By definition, the markets know best. But asset markets tend to crash every few years, and if left unattended, risk setting off a deep or prolonged economic recession and massive unemployment. The latter was the lesson learned from the Great Depression of the 1930s. So periodically the authorities have had to intervene after the event, to save the financial system from itself and from affecting the real economy.

Alan Greenspan famously remarked that because one could not tell when market excess had been reached, it was wrong to interfere pre-emptively. One could only know there had been a market aberration or price bubble after it had burst. Only then was it correct for the authorities to switch from being bystanders to becoming involved in mopping up the mess. This is a bit like saying that one should not get involved if someone starts experimenting with heroin as it is impossible to know if they are addicted until they are no longer able to function without constant ingestion of the drug, at which point one should try to wean them off it.

Somewhat mysteriously, the economic elite have remained wilfully blind to this self-contradiction in its system of beliefs – a perfect market needing occasional saving from itself – and have been obliged to tie themselves into intellectual knots to avoid recognising the obvious.

The combination of failing to pay any attention to the collective consequences of individual borrowing binges and refusing to allow the system to cleanse itself from the debt build-up in each cycle for fear of the consequences, has threatened to become terminal. By cutting out the ultimate downside of each burst bubble, the authorities have prioritised short-term avoidance of pain over the long-term gain that would ensue from pressing the reset button and purging the system of its excesses. Eventually, the accumulated mountain of debt became simply too big to deal with. All the king's horses and all the king's men, couldn't put Humpty together again. In a Marxian sense, the system was planting the seeds of its own destruction.

Western economies may appear to have recovered from the last crisis as unemployment has fallen and growth has resumed. However, except for the minority who are asset rich or in jobs not yet threatened by cheap international labour or technology, standards of living remain stagnant and much of our public infrastructure is old and worn. To understand how we have arrived at this unhappy state of affairs, we need to revisit the negligence of the authorities faced with ever greater financial crises that risked spilling over into the real economy. Casino capitalism was underwritten by those in positions of power who failed to exercise their social and political responsibilities.

CHEERLEADER-IN-CHIEF

Alan Greenspan, cheerleader-in-chief for the finance industry in the 1980s and 90s, serenely presided over the inflation of arguably the greatest financial bubble in history, dazzled by the industry's clever financial engineering, itself enabled by the arrival of powerful and cheap computing power. Sitting on top of the world's most powerful central bank, with access to unparalleled resources, information and a veritable army of economics PhDs, he understood the rising risks only a little better than the investors who lost fortunes buying new complicated mortgages and the other opaque assets created by the bankers.

Speaking in October 2014, Greenspan welcomed a new pool of borrowers: 'Improvements in lending practices, driven by information technology, have enabled lenders to reach out to households with previously unrecognised borrowing capabilities.' Just a few years later, these new borrowers, later known as 'sub-prime', would prove unable to pay their debts. In defence of sitting-on-the-sidelines-do-nothing fatalism, he explained in his signature tortured prose:

> But how do we know when irrational exuberance has unduly escalated asset values, which then become subject to unexpected and prolonged contractions as they have in Japan over the past decade? And how do we factor that assessment into monetary policy? We as central bankers need not be concerned if a collapsing financial asset bubble does not threaten to impair the real economy, its production, jobs, and price stability. Indeed, the sharp stock market break of 1987 had few negative consequences for the economy. But we should not underestimate or become complacent about the complexity of the interactions of asset markets and the economy. Thus, evaluating shifts in balance sheets generally,

and in asset prices particularly, must be an integral part of the development of monetary policy.

The man with his hand on the money printing press attempted to reconcile his faith in the superiority of markets with the need to mop up their mess. This fatalistic doctrine was the truly pernicious and serious error of someone endowed with enormous powers. For Greenspan, that human nature is driven by greed inevitably leading to excess from time to time did not imply that one should strive to mitigate those excesses before they become catastrophic.

'Bubbles are aspects of human nature, and you can try as hard as you like, you will not alter the path,' Greenspan told the audience at Citigroup's European credit conference via a video link from Washington.[3] 'I still hold to the general view that unless you have debts supporting the bubble, I would just let it alone because certain things about human nature cannot be changed and I've come to the conclusion this is one of them.'

Greenspan remained unapologetic about the tech bubble of the late 1990s, saying in a December 2002 speech that central banks had 'little experience' in dealing with market bubbles, and again that 'dealing aggressively with the aftermath of a bubble' was 'likely to avert long-term damage'.[4] He also suggested that history showed that taking action against a so-called bubble, such as in the stock market in 1929, could have devastating consequences in the form of triggering an economic depression.

As boss of the most powerful central bank, presiding over the world's reserve currency, Greenspan set the tone for the rest of the developed world. No one dared challenge the markets and nearly everyone hurtled over the cliff behind this monetary pied piper.

THE POLITICAL ROOTS OF THE GFC

The political roots of the GFC go back three decades to the free-market ideology and deregulation zealotry of the 1980s. As we've seen, this ideology was born from a reaction to the perceived failure of the previous system of fixed exchange rates, regulated markets, unionised labour and capital controls that culminated in the inflation of the 1970s.

Arguably, the real culprit for the problems of the 1970s was irresponsible monetary policy after the end of the Bretton Woods Agreement, contaminated by excessive spending by governments – to fund the Vietnam war in the US, for example. Whatever the pretext, it suited certain economic and political interests of the time to wrest back power by appealing to a plausible and respectable economic theory, albeit several centuries out of date, grounded in an era when the organisation of key economic units was very different.

President Reagan did not renew Paul Volcker's mandate as Fed chairman in 1987. He understood that Volcker was at heart a rules-based disciplinarian rather than a fully paid-up member of the free-market party. He appointed in his place arch free-marketeer Greenspan, a friend and disciple of the ultra-conservative writer Ayn Rand.

The ideal social system, Rand believed, is laissez-faire capitalism. Economically, this means not today's mixture of freedom and government controls but 'a complete separation of state and economics, in the same way and for the same reasons as the separation of state and church'. In laissez-faire capitalism, Rand argued, 'the government has only one function, albeit a vital one: to protect the rights of each individual by placing the retaliatory use of physical force under objective control'.[5]

There has been criticism of her ideas, especially from the political left, with critics blaming the economic crisis on her support of selfishness and free markets, particularly through her influence on Alan Greenspan.[6] For example, Greenspan has opposed tariffs against China for its refusal to let the yuan rise, suggesting instead that any American workers displaced by Chinese trade could be compensated through unemployment insurance and retraining programmes.[7]

As we now know, this ideology only contributed to the degradation of Western workers' share of national income, stagnant real wages and the massive accumulation of wealth and income in China.

THE 1987 CRASH: THE FIRST OF THE MODERN-DAY FINANCIAL CRISES

The policy template that we are still ruled by today was set only a few months into Greenspan's mandate. The Fed had raised its key Fed Funds (overnight interest) rate from around 6 per cent at the beginning of 1987 to 7.25 per cent in September. This halted a runaway speculative rally in the stock market that had jumped close to 35 per cent in the eight months to August without any fundamental justification. This asset bubble collapsed on 19 October 1987 in an unprecedented Wall Street one-day swoon of 22.6 per cent. The Greenspan Fed, in complete contradiction to Greenspan's later pronouncements above, panicked and decided to shoot first and ask questions later: 'Shortly after the crash, the Federal Reserve decided to intervene to prevent an even greater crisis. Short-term interest rates were instantly lowered *to prevent a recession and banking crisis* [my italics]. Remarkably, the markets recovered fairly quickly from the worst one-day stock market crash in history. Unlike after the stock market crash of 1929, the stock market quickly embarked on a bull run after the October crash.'[8]

This was in no small measure thanks to the Fed not only providing liquidity to the banking system and encouraging it to pass it on to stockbrokers, but also through a loosening of monetary policy in the form of cuts in interest rates. The Greenspan Fed feared the collateral damage on the real economy that the virtual financial system, represented by the stock market and the banks, could inflict.

In his semi-annual testimony to the House Banking Committee on 23 February 1988 Greenspan noted that the sudden loss in financial wealth and subsequent erosion of business and consumer confidence threatened to reduce spending. Greenspan reduced the rate again to 6.5 per cent in between the governing Federal Open Market Committee (FOMC)'s meetings in January and February 1988.

This increased liquidity, and the rapid U-turn on rate rises contributed to higher growth and inflation accelerating from 3.6 per cent in 1987 to 5.4 per cent in 1990. Of course, with the benefit of hindsight the Fed's immediate relaxation of monetary policy after the 1987 crash looks questionable given the strength of the real economy. If anyone's consumption was going to be drastically curtailed by the crash, it was that of the brokers and bankers on Wall Street rather than the shoppers on Main Street. One can attribute the Fed's febrile reaction to wanting to take out insurance against the risk of disaster. The chairman recognised the power of the financial industry to make or break the economy. This set the precedent for the Fed's rapid-response rescue of the stock market and the banks whenever these came under pressure in the ensuing busts caused by their imprudent profit-maximising behaviour.

THE US SAVINGS AND LOANS CRISIS

The re-acceleration of growth forced the Fed to once again raise rates, this time to 9.75 per cent by March 1989. This exposed what had been a simmering problem in one corner of the financial industry: savings and loans institutions (S&Ls), mortgage providers similar to UK building societies. These lenders financed the fixed long-term mortgages they granted from short-term deposits. As interest rates rose in the late 1970s and early 1980s, S&Ls started to lose money because they borrowed much of their funds at the prevailing rate but lent mainly at fixed rates. As rates rose, the need to finance themselves at the newer higher rates overtook the rates they earned on the older loans they had already made, and some became insolvent. By 1982, S&Ls were losing $4 billion a year, down from a profit of $781 million in 1980.[9] President Reagan's solution was to deregulate them in the hope they could become more profitable by lending even more, and to riskier customers, to whom they could charge higher rates. This was a strategy that would turn round to bite them.

The 1982 Garn-St. Germain Depository Institutions Act solidified the elimination of the interest rate cap. It also permitted banks to have up to 40 per cent of their assets in commercial loans and 30 per cent in consumer loans. In particular, the law removed restrictions on loan-to-value ratios. That allowed the S&Ls to use federally insured deposits to make risky loans. At the same time, budget cuts reduced the regulatory staff at the Federal Home Loan Bank Board (FHLBB), which impaired its ability to investigate bad loans. Between 1982 and 1985, S&L assets increased by 56 per cent. Legislators in California, Texas and Florida passed laws allowing their S&Ls to invest in speculative real estate, while in Texas forty S&Ls tripled in size.

But as the Fed raised rates from 5.85 per cent in October 1986 to nearly 10 per cent by March 1989, briefly interrupted by the 1987 crash (see Figure 6.1 overleaf), the trickle of bankruptcies turned into a flood, especially as many of the S&Ls had over-expanded and taken more risk. In 1988 190 S&Ls went bust, up from 59 in 1987.[10] From 1986 to 1995, the number of federally insured savings and loans in the United States declined from 3,234 to 1,645.[11] This was

Figure 6.1: Effective federal funds rate, US 1982–2016

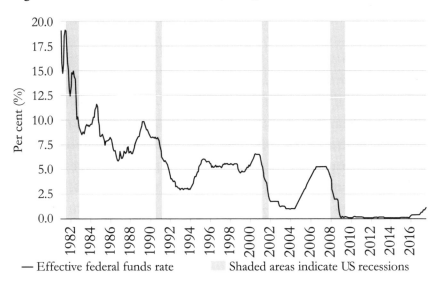

primarily, but not exclusively, due to unsound real estate lending.[12]

It must be concluded that the savings and loan crisis reflected a massive public policy failure. The final cost of resolving failed S&Ls is estimated at just over $160 billion, including $132 billion from federal taxpayers and much of this cost could have been avoided if the government had had the political will to recognise its obligation to depositors in the early 1980s, rather than viewing the situation as an industry bail-out. Believing that the marketplace would provide its own discipline, the government used rapid deregulation and forbearance instead of taking steps to protect depositors. The government guarantee of insured deposits nonetheless exposed US taxpayers to the risk of loss while the profits made possible by deregulation and forbearance would accrue to the owners and managers of the savings and loans.[13]

The ensuing slowdown in the finance industry including real estate was probably a contributing cause to the 1990–1 recession. Between 1986 and 1991 the number of housing starts more than halved from about 2 million per year to less than 1 million, at the time the lowest rate for over 25 years.[14] It is probable that this taxpayer-funded bail-out of the savings and loans institutions encouraged financial institutions to take risks in the knowledge that they would be rescued if required. The savings and loans crisis was a dress rehearsal for the real event less than two decades later.

The crisis in the S&L industry prompted the Fed to begin cutting interest rates in June 1989. This was not sufficient to avert a mild recession in 1990 (see Figure 6.1), although it is impossible to disentangle other contributory factors. The first Iraq War and the related spike in oil prices probably served to dampen sentiment in an economy that was already slowing down as the number of home loans fell and the accumulated rate rises of the last three years began to bite.

In spite of the fact that the 1990 recession was very mild, did not last long (see Figure 6.2 overleaf), and growth soon bounced back to 3 per cent in 1992, the Fed continued to aggressively slash interest rates to just under 3 per cent by December 1992 (Figure 6.1) and hold them there for over a year. No doubt the Fed was shaken by the crisis and the collapse of the home construction market and continued to ease to insure against further damage.

The massive cheapening in the cost of credit was like a red rag to the bull of Wall Street, and the banks lost little time identifying how to make the most profit from this gift, this time by channelling cheap money to the emerging markets of Mexico and south-east Asia. High growth and interest rates in these markets offered big opportunities to borrow at home at low rates and reinvest abroad at much higher rates.

Figure 6.2: US annual GDP growth

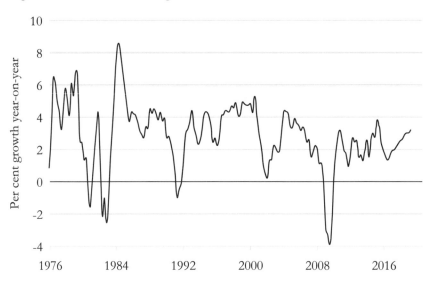

THE MEXICAN CRISIS

With US growth well on its way to 4 per cent, the Fed embarked on its next monetary tightening cycle in February 1994.

The Mexican crisis of 1994, sometimes referred to as the Tequila Crisis, is a case study in how the finance industry rushes to lend for short-term gain when conditions are good. It is also an example of how each economic unit behaves as if in a vacuum and ignores how its actions are replicated beyond the collective danger point by its peers. Each foreign loan and investment looked secure under the conditions of 1992–3, but ceased to be so if US rates rose beyond a certain threshold, with unintended consequences.

In 1992 the local interest rate in Mexico was 13.27 per cent compared to only 3.73 per cent on US treasury bills. This meant you could lock in almost 10 per cent per annum of profit by borrowing in the US and lending to Mexico. Unsurprisingly, this attracted a large flow of capital to Mexico. Joseph Whit has analysed what happened next: 'By December 1993 foreign holdings had soared to 47.7 billion pesos, 66 per cent of the amount outstanding.'[15] Clearly, this was a case of excessive and potentially destabilising lending, but no one paid any attention as short-term gains took priority.

By 1994, signs of political instability in Mexico, combined with the US Fed raising rates to 5 per cent and US bond yields rising sharply, caused a rapid reversal in the flow of funds out of Mexico, putting downward pressure on the Mexican peso's fixed exchange rate to the US dollar.

Mexico's central bank devalued the peso on 20 December 1994 to a lower band against the US dollar. However, the Mexican government's loss of credibility prompted further outflows and loss of foreign reserves. Mexico abandoned the new rate and let the peso float freely only two days later. A crisis ensued as the currency plunged nearly 40 per cent compared to prior to the devaluation by the end of December, while inflation and some interest rates soared to over 24 per cent. By early 1995, it was evident that Mexico was heading for default as foreign holders would not roll over maturing debt. President Clinton was forced to arrange a rescue loan package with the IMF and the Bank of International Settlements worth in excess of $50 billion, rather than risk the collapse of its large neighbour.[16]

The US Fed cut its key interest rate (Fed Funds) from the peak of 6 per cent in April 1995 to 5.25 per cent by January 2006, probably to alleviate pressures on the US banking system from Mexico. The cuts did not seem justified by domestic American conditions, since the economy remained in rude health with growth close to 3 per cent and no sign of it tipping into recession. The Greenspan Fed was, once again, showing its acute sensitivity to the fortunes of banks and financial markets rather than the real economy, which promptly responded to this uncalled-for loosening of monetary policy by accelerating to a 4 per cent growth rate.

With Mexico a busted flush, the banks turned their attention elsewhere, looking for a new hunting ground for quick lending profits – this time to south-east Asia.

THE ASIAN CRISIS

Undeterred by the outcome in Mexico, footloose money seeking higher rates of return poured into south-east Asia, where once again higher interest and growth rates were enticing investors to participate in the 'Asian miracle'. Thailand, Indonesia and South Korea were flooded with US dollars, pushing up local asset prices.

Increasing capital inflows were required to keep asset prices and profits rising, in national versions of a Ponzi scheme. In Indonesia gross liabilities rose from $37 billion in 1993 to $60 billion in 1997. Similarly, external liabilities in Thailand rose from $34 billion to $98 billion over the period. At the same time, several countries such as Thailand were running large current-account deficits (–6.6 per cent of GDP), which made them acutely vulnerable to any loss of foreign investor confidence. By the end of 1996 the ratio of short-term debt to foreign reserves was over 100 per cent in Thailand, Korea and Indonesia.[17]

US interest rates started to edge up again in early 1997, and with them the US dollar. The same pattern as in the Tequila Crisis began to unfold. The flows of hot money dried up and then reversed, testing the fixed exchange rates of these countries to breaking point. A vicious circle took hold as Western creditors sought to repatriate their capital, causing a shortage of credit and bankruptcies. Countries depleted foreign exchange reserves to prevent their currencies from collapsing under the sudden weight of money outflows, but it was only a matter of time before the dam burst. The situation was made worse by governments raising interest rates in attempts to stop their currencies from collapsing, causing further bankruptcies. When this proved counterproductive, the authorities stopped defending their fixed exchange rates to the US dollar, letting their currencies depreciate.

The crisis struck when Thailand broke the fixed peg with the dollar and devalued the baht on 2 July 1997. The baht lost over half its value against the US dollar and Thailand's stock market plummeted by 75 per cent. There were massive lay-offs of workers in real estate and construction. Once again countries had to go cap in hand to the IMF for assistance. In 1997 Thailand obtained a package arranged by the IMF worth about $17 billion, but the significant depreciation of its currency and the knock-on effects meant that GDP shrank by over 10 per cent in 1998.[18]

This led to regional contagion as foreign investors fled weak currencies. Even larger bail-outs had to be provided to Indonesia and South Korea, whose economies and markets were also hit and political leaders toppled. The Indonesian rupiah had fallen by 65 per cent by July 1998 compared to the end of 1997, and there was widespread social and political unrest culminating in the fall of President Suharto. Indonesia's GDP shrank 14 per cent and inflation soared to 64 per cent in 1998. International institutions spearheaded by the IMF pledged over $30 billion to stabilise the country. Malaysia, South Korea and the Philippines were also hit as speculators rushed for the exit and companies went bust, weighed down by dollar debts they could not repay. The countries fell into recession. In some cases crisis measures restricting the flow of capital remained for many years.

Reflecting on the crisis in 2013, Michael Carson and John Clark of the Federal Reserve Bank of New York concluded,

> as the crisis unfolded, it became clear that the strong growth record of these economies had masked important vulnera-
> bilities. In particular, years of rapid domestic credit growth and inadequate supervisory oversight had resulted in a significant

build-up of financial leverage and doubtful loans. Overheating domestic economies and real estate markets added to the risks and led to increased reliance on foreign savings, reflected in mounting current account deficits and a build-up in external debt … In response to the spreading crisis, the international community mobilised large loans totalling $118 billion for Thailand, Indonesia, and South Korea, and took other actions to stabilise the most affected countries. Financial support came from the International Monetary Fund, the World Bank, the Asian Development Bank, and governments in the Asia-Pacific region, Europe, and the United States.

Clearly even the most successful high-growth economies could run into serious trouble through over-leverage and excessive lending, at times to doubtful borrowers. Banks neither exercised the requisite prudence and rigorous lending standards case-by-case nor took into account the aggregation of their collective lending on the macro-economic stability of entire countries.

THE RUSSIAN CRISIS

No sooner had the Asian crisis been contained, than the ensuing weakness in demand contributed to a crash in commodity prices. This set up the next domino to fall, Russia. Western banks and money management firms had been attracted not only by 40 per cent interest rates in a currency pegged to the US dollar, but also by the value of the assets up for grabs in the aftermath of the collapse of the Soviet Union.

Money managers described Russia as an 'asset play'. There was a sense that, compared to elsewhere, assets such as barrels of oil or cubic metres of gas were significantly undervalued. Coinciding with a progressive relaxation in restrictions on foreign portfolio investment, the sense of improving economic prospects – of a short-term upside – led to a boom in foreign financial participation in 1997. Portfolio flows into the GKO (Russian government debt) market just in the first quarter of 1997 were more than three times the amount for the whole of 1996.[19] By late 1997, roughly 30 per cent of the GKO market was accounted for by non-residents.[20]

In contrast to south-east Asia, the rush to invest in Russia was not a story of high growth and profitability; quite the reverse. Since the collapse of the Soviet Union, the economy had been shrinking dramatically and the government running high budget deficits, due in part to the widespread non-payment of tax. In this case the rush of capital was partly a 'recovery story', but also a cynical short-term ploy to exploit the unsustainable anomaly of high interest rates available in a currency with a fixed exchange rate to the dollar. The assumption was that once this arrangement failed, as it was likely to, the West would bail it out. In other words, the banks were assuming that governments would pay the bill to save the system after they had milked all the profits they could.

In October 1997 the Russian government was counting on 2 per cent economic growth in 1998 to compensate for debt growth, and the economy was showing signs of turning the corner, offering some basis for the recovery rationale for investment. Unfortunately, events began to unfold that would further strain Russia's economy. The collapse of its main source of revenue, the oil price, to eleven dollars per barrel by May 1998 meant that Russia had little hope of paying the high rates of interest demanded by its creditors on the mountain of Soviet-era debt, let alone servicing more recent high-maintenance Western credits. The failure to agree an aid package with the IMF, as well as the collapse of a meeting between Lawrence Summers of the US and the Russian prime minister, rattled investor sentiment even further.

In August 1998, after recording its first year of positive economic growth since the fall of the Soviet Union, Russia was forced to default on its sovereign debt, devalue the rouble and declare a suspension of payments by commercial banks to foreign creditors. In what was by now becoming a familiar pattern, the Russian rouble collapsed from around five to the dollar to twenty-five, and the stock market gave up 75 per cent of its value. Instead of growth in 1998, real GDP declined by 4.9 per cent.

THE LONG-TERM CAPITAL MANAGEMENT CRISIS

On their own, the Asian and Russian crises could have been contained without major consequences for the rest of the world. However, by this point the financial system was globally interlinked, not only by footloose capital hungrily scouring the globe for large profit opportunities, but also indirectly in the form of speculative positions taken by leveraged investors such as hedge funds and bank trading desks, betting on the relative price movements between various instruments and investments affected by macro-economic factors such as interest and exchange rates. These positions were often partly financed with credit provided by the major Western banks, in what was beginning to resemble a global casino played with ultra-high stakes.

The next domino to fall, out of the blue and as a consequence of the Asian and Russian crises, was the comically misnamed hedge fund Long Term Capital Management (LTCM). Advised and managed by a star-studded cast of Nobel laureates and big-name traders like John Meriwether, LTCM had placed big bets that the level of risks in the debt markets would reduce. These were showing quite high readings after the Mexican and Asian crises, so they bet that these would revert to more normal, subdued levels. In other words, things would calm down in the financial markets now that the storm was over. They were so confident that normal service would resume, as it had in the past, that they bet around $30 for every $1 of real investor capital in the fund. This very high leverage meant any 1 per cent move up or down in the value of its underlying positions was magnified thirty times in terms of the fund's profit or loss.

LTCM lost 44 per cent of its capital in August 1998 when Russia defaulted on its debt, and by early September it was widely known to be in deep trouble. A collapse of its $4.6 billion fund would have caused it to default on its contracts with banks and brokers, and the ripple effect could have led to a general meltdown of the financial system. Aware of the stakes, the Fed engineered a $3.625 billion bail-out of the fund by a consortium of fourteen financial institutions, all but wiping out the original partners and investors. LTCM's positions were liquidated in an orderly fashion over the following months.

Although the Fed was careful not to contribute any of its own money to the bail-out, it did reduce its key lending rate from 5.5 per cent in September 1998 to 4.625 per cent by January 1999 even though the US was growing at over 4 per cent in real terms. In other words, it once again loosened monetary policy to protect Wall Street, even though Main Street was doing fine. When push came to shove, the American central bank's priority was to save the banks rather than follow the real economy.

THE GREENSPAN 'PUT' AND MORAL HAZARD

The cutting of interest rates and bail-out of LTCM even when the economy was healthy encouraged financial markets to think that the Fed would always intervene to safeguard the banks and brokers on Wall Street. This assumed guarantee became known as the 'Greenspan put', a term for the notion that, to prevent the entire edifice from crumbling, Wall Street would always be bailed out by the authorities if the giant banks, seen as too big to fail, placed huge bets that went wrong. Technically, a 'put' is an option to sell an asset at a predetermined price, thereby limiting an investor's loss. In this context, investors assumed that, if the market fell below a certain level, the Fed would limit their losses by taking supportive measures.

Slashing interest rates to relieve the pressure on the banks amounted to pouring kerosene onto an already roaring stock market fire. This undoubtedly contributed to the last leg of the technology stocks mania that inflated the market to unprecedented levels of speculation in late 1999, with prices that bore no relation to the reality of underlying company profits and growth rates.

Led by technology, media and telecom companies, which were seen as the vanguard of the new digital 'weightless economy', the market took off, creating the 'TMT bubble'. It was telling that the authorities could not even see it, so much were they enthralled and dazzled by the brave new world. Conventional yardsticks of market valuation, such as the price-to-earnings ratio, were dismissed as inapplicable to the new age. Cheerleaders for the market defended its ridiculously expensive levels with the mantra 'this time is different' and that old-timers simply 'didn't get it.'

As it became clear that the financial system had been saved and the economy was once more in danger of overheating, the Fed had to play catch-up once again, and raised its interest rates to a peak of 6.5 per cent in June 2000. This was enough to decisively prick the TMT bubble, which began to deflate from its March 2000 peak. The accumulation of interest rate hikes by the Fed was too much for such a speculative market built on cheap money. The stock market started to fall as rapidly as it had gone up, this time tipping the US economy into recession in March 2001. The Fed once again performed a quick U-turn, slashing interest rates down almost 3 per cent to 3.65 per cent by August 2001.

The terrorist attacks of 11 September 2001 only dampened sentiment further, and the stock market continued to plummet. By early 2002, the Fed had cut rates to below 2 per cent, the lowest since the 1960s. The real economy bottomed out a few months later. The US Labor Department estimates that around 2.25 million jobs were lost as the unemployment rate moved up from 4.2 per cent in February 2001 to 6.3 per cent by March 2003. The stock market fell further as business losses at some of the technology darlings of the market, such as Enron and WorldCom, revealed accounting fraud that could no longer be concealed by rising asset prices. By early October 2002 the US stock market had halved from its crazy highs of only thirty-one months earlier.

In spite of the stabilisation of the real economy, the Fed continued to cut interest rates to a low of 1 per cent by early 2003, as the second Iraq War, which was to topple Saddam Hussein, got under way, pressuring the stock market further. This provided further evidence of where the Fed's priorities lay. Its actions betrayed a tacit acknowledgement that the Frankenstein's monster of finance it had created was now so big as to threaten the real economy. The tail had grown large enough to wag the dog.

Ominously, Greenspan stated that the drops in rates would have the effect of leading to a surge in home sales and refinancing, adding, 'Besides sustaining the demand for new construction, mortgage markets have also been a powerful stabilising force over the past two years of economic distress by facilitating the extraction of some of the equity that homeowners have built up over the years.'[21] In other words, 'Bring on the debt!'

Greenspan's latest and most reckless brainwave to dope the US economy back to apparent health by dropping rates to historic lows, stimulating property inflation and enabling consumers to spend more by using their homes as ATM machines, contributed to the next great bubble, this time in housing. The chief financial fireman had turned serial pyromaniac.

The Federal Reserve acknowledged the connection between lower interest rates, higher home values and the increased liquidity that higher home prices bring to the overall economy: 'Like other asset prices, house prices are influenced by interest rates, and in some countries, the housing market is a key channel of monetary policy transmission.'

In a speech in February 2004 Greenspan suggested that more homeowners should consider taking out adjustable-rate mortgages (ARMs), where the interest rate adjusts itself to the current interest in the market.[22] The Fed's own funds rate was at a then all-time low of 1 per cent. A few months after his recommendation, with total disregard for those he had advised, Greenspan began raising interest rates in a series of hikes that would bring the funds rate to 5.25 per cent about two years later. A triggering factor in the 2007 sub-prime mortgage financial crisis is believed to be the many sub-prime ARMs that reset at much higher interest rates than the borrower paid during the first few years of their mortgages.

The situation was succinctly summed up by Alex J. Pollock: 'The so-called "Great Moderation," for which our fiat-currency central bankers gave themselves so much credit, turned out to be the Era of Great Bubbles. The US, in successive decades, had the Tech Stock Bubble and then the disastrous Housing Bubble. Other countries had real estate and government debt bubbles.'[23] He also questioned Alan Greenspan's role in guiding the macro-economy to a happy outcome: 'The idea that anybody, no matter how talented, could really be such a Maestro is ridiculous, just as the idea that national house prices could never fall was ridiculous – but both were widely believed and expressed nonetheless. The central bankers, working diligently for their concept of economic Moderation, presided over the Era of Great Bubbles. Is this coincidence? Or does the one cause the other?'

FINANCIAL CATCH-22
The ready availability of credit combined with inexorably declining interest rates triggered a succession of cycles of over-expansion of

credit and market speculation followed by busts and government bail-outs. Each time the financial industry picked on a different sector or region ripe for the massive lending that would satisfy its insatiable appetite for higher profits. Each time the chosen sector borrowed up to the point where it could no longer service its debt without further injections of credit. Each time, as the flow of new credit fell below the level needed to keep the show on the road, a financial crisis occurred. With banks operating with very small reserves and little capital, the imploding sector threatened a collapse of the banking system as the weakest creditors went bankrupt first, dragging down the rest through a domino effect.

While the Volcker Fed in the early 1980s was willing to let rising interest rates purge monetary excesses out of the system, even at the price of some temporary collateral damage to the economy, his successors, starting with Alan Greenspan, adopted a much more protective approach towards Wall Street and the consequences of its excesses. With little stomach for potential damage to the real economy from the implosion of over-extended creditors (and debtors), the US Fed panicked, flooring interest rates or flooding the market with money every time a bubble burst. And the more it repeated this behaviour, the more bankers and borrowers threw caution to the wind in the reassuring knowledge that the Fed would be there for them if things went wrong – thereby ensuring that things would indeed go wrong.

A credit binge (such as occurred between 1980 and 2007), during which debt increases faster than income thanks to falling interest rates, at some point becomes unsustainable because ever more monetary stimulation is needed after each cyclical bust. There is a limit to how far interest rates can fall without triggering inflation, either of the traditional kind or in assets such as equities, property, land or commodities, as everyone tries to get rid of zero- or negative-yielding (after inflation) cash by buying claims on real things that cannot be created at the click of a mouse. If the cost of money cannot fall further, then at some point credit growth relative to income has to cease, since the market runs out of Minsky's 'hedge' borrowers (those that can service their loans from income rather than from capital gains on the levered asset they have bought) at current prices.

Although the lending machine can prolong the game by extending loans to borrowers whose only hope of servicing and repaying the debt is by selling the assets they have bought at a profit (Minsky's 'speculative economy'), at this point the system becomes totally unstable and fragile. Any slight hiccup, such as a rise in interest rates which renders some borrowers insolvent, brings down the entire house of cards as these borrowers are forced to sell, thereby interrupting the rise in prices needed to keep speculative high-risk borrowers solvent.

What was a virtuous circle of new debt pushing up asset prices, thus attracting new borrowing to buy assets, turns into a vicious circle of asset sales and debt liquidation and profits turning into losses for those borrowers and creditors who do not get repaid 100 per cent on their loans. Left to its own devices, this downward spiral can have catastrophic consequences; witness the events of the Great Depression in the 1930s, when the economy shrank, people lost their jobs, poverty increased and wealth was destroyed. No wonder central bankers will do whatever it takes to avoid such an end game.

What is ominous today is that the trauma of the last crisis has altered central banks' behaviour. Alert and sensitive to the risk of raising interest rates to the point where the bloated credit structures collapse, they are now determined to hold off raising interest rates to a level that might trigger a recession, for fear of the consequences. In fact, they may never do so for a generation (as in Japan), so heavy is the debt burden and so anaemic the forces of growth. This means that debt levels continue to rise and are tolerated for fear of the consequences were the system to be reset. Global debt has climbed by $100 trillion since just before the GFC to $240 trillion.[24] So much for learning its lessons.

The received wisdom is that we cannot purge the system of excessive debt through write-offs or bankruptcies for fear of severe collateral damage to the economy. But failure to purge encourages a further accumulation of debt, creating the conditions for a final catastrophic bust. In the first stage of debt bubble inflation the commercial banks were prisoners of their clients. In the terminal stage, which we have reached, the central banks are caught in a monetary catch-22. To purge the system of debt would create a crash, but not to purge it will create a crash because of the debt. They have lost control of the debt in the system, which has become a financial Frankenstein's monster.

THE BUILD-UP TO THE GREAT FINANCIAL CRISIS

By now it should be obvious that the bursting of the US and European real estate and mortgage debt bubble in 2008 was not an isolated incident in time or geography. It was the dramatic apotheosis of a build-up of global debt over several decades and economic cycles. Japan holds the dubious distinction of leading the way, with the implosion of its real estate bubble in the 1990s, from which it has yet to recover fully. Western countries were eager to throw stones at Japan's foolishness without noticing that they were living in a glass house which duly shattered.

Finance benefited on several fronts while the going was good. Falling rates raised the value of real estate, equities and bonds, igniting a bull market in tradable assets. As the croupiers in the casino, banks and brokers profited handsomely from all manner of fees and commissions. Initial public offerings from private companies, the privatisation of public enterprises on stock exchanges, corporate mergers and acquisitions and public debt issuance were just some of the services that provided rich pickings.

The real estate bubble of the noughties was the last straw that killed off once and for all the Western model of debt-fuelled growth, but credit growth had been outstripping the economy ever since deregulation became all the rage in the 1980s and interest rates embarked on their long downward trend. If they ran out of borrowers at home, lenders found willing takers for credit abroad. The credit creation machine found new victims for its wares, in excessive numbers, in each cycle. As one client base went bankrupt, it found other eager takers to sell to. And when each successive bubble burst, Western governments and central banks were willing to pick up the tab to prevent the unsavoury knock-on consequences for their economies as a whole.

ESCALATING FINANCIAL CRISES

Underpinning everything was the dominant faith in deregulation and a market-knows-best philosophy. It is no coincidence that the first market earthquake since 1929 – the Wall Street crash of 1987 – occurred so soon after the red-blooded no-holds-barred free market ideology had taken hold, nor that it was followed in 1990 by the US Savings and Loan crisis, when the authorities were forced to bail out the financial system for the first time in generations. Far from the market disciplining itself, as it should have done according to idealised economic theory, the demand for credit tested the market's resilience to destruction every few years in a series of rolling credit crises triggered by repeating cycles of credit expansion, albeit targeted at different areas each time.

While there was nothing new about credit crises, the frequency of the crises, their increasing severity and the ever more desperate and extreme measures taken to prevent the consequences of them was of an entirely different order. Moreover, in complete contradiction to the market fundamentalism of the times, governments cut off the downside of each crisis by pouring huge sums of money into the system to shore up both debtors and creditors when defaults threatened to plunge the real economy into depression. This encouraged massive and irresponsible risk-taking by creditors and investors, who knew that 'Heads I win, tails you lose.' The building into the economy of such complacency, politely termed 'moral hazard', or more cynically 'the Greenspan put', sowed the seeds of the next crisis. More importantly, it was the transmission mechanism for a reverse Robin Hood effect: robbing the poor to give to the rich.

The simple fact is this: financial markets have no track record of exercising self-restraint. Once they latch on to a profit opportunity, they will pursue it to destruction.

THE GFC

The Great Financial Crisis (GFC) of 2008 was the financial crisis to end all financial crises, or so it seemed. The financial equivalent of the First World War, it nearly blew up the world economy. Just as the assassination of Archduke Ferdinand in Sarajevo is often referred to as the spark that led to the conflagration of the First World War, a small, apparently localised financial accident set off a chain reaction that led to the effective bankruptcy of the global financial system. Only a massive taxpayer-led bail-out of banks and the printing of gargantuan sums of money by the major central banks saved the global economy from disaster.

As we have seen, after the technology bubble burst in 2002, the Greenspan Fed was desperate to avert an economic downside by slashing interest rates to 1 per cent and encouraging a re-leveraging of the economy. Having all but blown up the corporate sector, banks switched their attention to households and the housing market. With interest rates at new lows, they easily found eager borrowers who could now afford mortgages to get on to the property ladder. The phrase 'as safe as houses' did not exist for nothing, and it was well known that house prices always rise, at least in nominal terms.

Finance for house purchases was deemed safe given increasing property prices brought about by more freely available credit. While each mortgage decision may have been carefully considered in the early days of the expansion, credit growth that far exceeded economic growth necessarily meant that the quality of loans had to deteriorate at some point. But to each lender this was not obvious: the collective effect of ever more credit was house price inflation that validated the creditworthiness of even marginal borrowers. But for house prices to continue to rise at a rate required to justify the solvency of the related debt, ever more borrowers had to be found.

For Hyman Minsky, pro-cyclical behaviour is characteristic of lenders and borrowers, such that instability is baked into the free market system.

> Whenever full employment is achieved and sustained, businessmen and bankers, heartened by success, tend to accept larger doses of debt financing ... profit seeking financial institutions invent and reinvent 'new' forms of money ... and financing techniques ... this results in higher prices of assets, which, in turn, raises the demand price for current investment, and increases the finance available for investment ... An investment boom leads to a financial structure that is conducive to financial crises.[25]

As we've already seen, this infernal mechanism in effect turned into a giant Ponzi scheme in several countries. New buyers on credit had to be sucked into the housing market by the promise of capital gains in order to validate the assumptions of the rising prices needed to support the creditworthiness of many existing debtors and support the prices of mortgage-backed securities that had been sold to investors. Doped on debt, new home sales in the US rocketed from around 600,000 per year on average to more than double that after 2000.

At some point all this was bound to blow up, either because the market ran out of buyers and borrowers, because rising bad loans started to impact lenders and investors in mortgage-related securities, or because interest rates rose.

Home ownership peaked in the US at 69 per cent in 2006.[26] Interest rates had been rising slowly since the last cyclical low in 2003. Oblivious of the dangers and the mounting instability of the system it had condoned, the Fed continued to raise interest rates into 2007. Rising rates cause a triple whammy on the property market by increasing the cost of purchase, reducing demand and damaging the creditworthiness of existing marginal borrowers who had come into the market at lower rates and needed to refinance themselves at higher rates.

The system reached a tipping point in 2007, surprising everyone, as interest rates had topped out just over 5 per cent, lower than the peak of the previous cycle, and the credit creation machine abruptly went into reverse. Delinquent borrowers and their creditors were forced to sell the properties held as security. Property prices fell, forcing the next layer of borrowers into distress as the value of their debts exceeded that of their assets.

In July 2007 Wall Street investment bank Bear Stearns announced that two of its hedge funds had imploded because of the fall in the value of their investments in mortgage-backed securities – securities sold to investors which consist of bundles of mortgages offloaded by the banks. Economist Mark Zandi wrote that this 2007 event was arguably 'the proximate catalyst' for the financial market disruption that followed.[27]

The news had a ripple effect through the financial system. The price of similar securities fell, which in turn impacted lenders unable to refinance their holdings of such securities. House prices tumbled as cheap mortgage finance packaged into securities dried up through lack of buyers. Lower property values in turn affected the collateral value of other mortgages, reducing their credit quality and hence the ability of leveraged investors to refinance their positions, causing another downward turn in the financial death spiral. This was the mirror image of the upward spiral of credit creation that had been prescribed to save the economy from the bursting of the technology bubble.

Unlike previous financial crises, which had been largely confined to the banks of a few countries, the shock waves of the imploding US housing market not only threatened to drag the US banking system into insolvency, but quickly spread to Europe and Asia. Not only had financial globalisation reached such an advanced stage that banks and insurance companies across the globe had become intertwined, financing and guaranteeing each other's assets, but many had also participated in the rapid creation of credit in their respective countries. The high degree of leverage that had built up across the global financial system eroded any margin of safety that would have previously existed in regions with lower leverage. As investors saw how interdependent the banks and the loans they had made to households for house purchases were, confidence eroded. One by one, banks failed, and with no end in sight to this dynamic, panic set in.

Out of the blue, in September 2007 Northern Rock, a second-tier UK mortgage bank, suffered a run, as it could no longer finance its mortgage book in the wholesale money markets. It was taken over by the British government.

The chain reaction of failures in the financial markets gathered pace as money market funds, essentially pooled cash funds that retail investors thought were safe, 'broke the buck' – fell below 100 per cent of the value of the cash paid in. These funds held securities of banks or finance houses that had exposure to some of the mortgage-related securities falling in value. As nervous investors in these funds tried to get their cash out, the funds could not buy any more mortgage-backed securities, so fewer new mortgages could be created. House prices came under more pressure, and marginal debtors were unable to service their debts or refinance because the value of their properties had fallen below the value of their loans. The dominoes were falling.

By March 2008, the crisis has found its way back to its origins, Bear Stearns, as rumours spread about its inability to fund a balance sheet that was leveraged thirty-six times with many unsaleable illiquid assets. Banks are a confidence trick. Lack of confidence becomes self-fulfilling. The New York Fed arranged for the bank to be sold for $10 a share (down from $172 in January 2007) to JPMorgan. Famously, Bear Stearns CEO James Cayne was at a bridge tournament during the final days of the bank, clearly failing to grasp the enormity of the situation.

Other banks began to eye each other, wondering what suspect securities they might own. In a classic case of the pernicious effects of the generalisation principle in markets, what appeared a rational decision by each bank individually – to reduce risk by reducing its credit exposure to other banks – became catastrophic when all the banks made the same decision, as no banks could finance themselves adequately. The system was on the edge of collapse with the real danger over the weekend of 18 September 2008 that customers in the UK would not be able to take cash out of ATMs.

The finance industry had manufactured an inordinate amount of credit. It had also transformed part of this into complicated and opaque structures that could be bought, sold and distributed across the world to every type of investor. From retail savers in money market funds to large insurance companies such as AIG in the US, who 'guaranteed' the creditworthiness of these securities for other financial institutions, nearly everyone stood to lose once the weakest link snapped and the music stopped as investors tried to pass the parcel. The contagion was inevitable and unprecedented. This was a truly global crisis, whose repercussions continue to constrain the global economy and undermine faith in democracy and its institutions to this very day.

THE INFERNAL TRIANGLE

The seeds of the GFC were planted by an uncritical espousal of the deregulated market – including the finance industry, with all its perverse incentives and destabilising tendencies – by the central banks and the political elite. But it was the impunity with which bankers and brokers operated – in the knowledge that the authorities would bail them out – coupled with the refusal to limit credit creation, that was a major cause of the disaster. The political system of the West had malfunctioned because its power had been usurped by the finance industry.

The implicit social contract of democracy, whereby the people freely elect a government that will represent their interests *nationally*, no longer held. In thrall to the markets, governments and central bankers failed to check changes that undermined their citizens' incomes and welfare. Not only were good jobs lost, but national infrastructure was eroded as public bodies ran short of funds. This became glaringly obvious in the case of public services: underfunded and stretched health services, relegation down international league tables of educational attainment, the inability to fund university education or maintain a good road and bridge network. The list goes on.

The second cause of the crisis was collateral damage resulting from the massive transfer of good-quality manufacturing capacity and jobs to low-cost developing countries such as Mexico, Thailand

and above all China. This is globalisation under cover of the free market principle, and was sold to a population not well schooled in the principles of economics as a means to benefit from the availability of cheaper goods. However, as the growth in real wages of Western labour was eaten away, even cheap goods were not enough to sustain a rising standard of living for many, leading to a growing demand for credit.

The bottom line was a massive transfer of wealth from West to East and a considerable widening in the US and UK trade deficits, as consumers had to buy goods now made abroad on credit provided by industrious and thrifty workers in developing countries. Putting it more crudely, the Chinese (principally) embarked on a massive vendor-financing scheme, reinvesting their trade surplus and savings from their new-found industrial jobs into Western financial markets, thereby providing money for their impoverished customers to borrow to buy their goods.

Last but not least, none of this would have occurred had elected governments not been seduced by business. Instead of protecting the long-term interests of constituents and consumers, politicians were lobbied by, and accepted campaign funds from, companies. In many cases corporations pushed for unregulated globalisation in order to maximise their profits – manufacturing cheaply abroad and selling this output expensively back home. As usual, where the US led, others were happy to follow. Corporate titans stuffed each other's remuneration committees with their executives who awarded themselves generous stock options and bonuses tied to company earnings per share. Globalisation turbocharged company earnings growth, top executive income sky-rocketed relative to that of their workers, and inequality widened to levels not seen since the 1920s.

While this functioned for a while, it was doomed to collapse under the basic contradiction that domestic consumers could not continue to buy goods at expensive Western prices if they were no longer earning high wages from Western-based production. Plugging the gap with debt could only work for so long.

THE COST

The GFC was no isolated accident, but the latest, and greatest, in a series of crises that have recurred every five to eight years with the threat of increasingly dire consequences for the global economy. It was the culmination of a prolonged and inexorable build-up of debt in Western countries through several economic cycles. This excessive debt created bubbles of overvalued assets and liabilities that could no longer be serviced when the interest rate cycle turned up. That these bubbles were allowed to inflate time after time reflected the free-market fundamentalism of the epoch, famously expressed by Fed chairman Greenspan's extraordinary dogma that bubbles could not be spotted in advance.

Even today it is impossible to quantify the cost of the GFC, not only in money but in human suffering, of hopes and lives wrecked. In the US the cost of just one of several government assistance programmes – the Troubled Assets Relief Program (TARP) – amounted to $700 billion. The government also bailed out General Motors and the giant insurer AIG. Central banks spent trillions of dollars buying government and other bonds to provide cash for the system and lower the cost of credit by reducing bond yields.

While the US government claims that it has recouped more money than it provided under TARP and so made a profit for taxpayers, this is a misleading picture of the current state of affairs.[28] According to a study published in August 2018 by the Federal Reserve Bank of San Francisco, the GFC will have cost the average American around $70,000 in lifetime income. In the UK, according to the National Audit Office, total support for the banks during the GFC amounted to over half of the size of one year's production by the economy (GNP) – over £1 trillion. In the UK, as we have seen, the average worker has suffered years of lower real earnings.

What we do know is that the cost of saving the economic and political system can be measured in terms of the vast transfer of debt from the private to the public sector (taxpayers present and future). In other words, most Western governments took on massive amounts of debt as they spent to bail out banks and other large companies that would have gone under, and on unemployment benefits and other safety nets for those who lost their jobs or homes due to the crisis.

US public debt ballooned from around 31 per cent of GDP in the early 1980s to an estimated 106 per cent of GDP in 2017 with a leap of 30 per cent during the crisis years of 2007–10.[29] A similar pattern occurred in the UK, with national debt rising from less than 40 per cent of GDP in 2007 to nearly 90 per cent by 2018. Although UK public debt was higher relative to the economy after the Second World War, this was quickly brought under control by decent growth in the 1950s and 1960s. Today, this does not appear likely to recur.[30]

The massive rise in government debt has mortgaged the future of entire nations. Not only are the UK and US governments so much in debt they will not be able to help out should another crisis come along, but the debt inhibits them from investing in education, public services and infrastructure.

But government bail-outs were not enough on their own to prevent a collapse of the system. Central banks also had to print money and spend it on buying government and private-sector bonds. As a consequence, the Bank of England's balance sheet, bloated by the purchase of debt, rocketed from around £77 billion in 2007 to £359.3 billion in October 2018. This is paltry compared to the Eurozone and the US, where central bankers have printed around €3.6 trillion and $3.7 trillion respectively since 2007.[31]

These are colossal sums disbursed by public institutions to save the banks, and in so doing have jacked up the value of stock markets and property.

The winners in the West have been the well-to-do, who only suffered a brief flutter of anxiety. Everyone else remains trapped in a web of low or no-growth wages, decaying public services and rising social and political disenchantment and violence. Political institutions have fallen into disrepute, unable to quell growing disaffection with current economic and political systems. It is to politics that we now turn in Part Three.

Dysfunctional Politics and the Decline of the West

7

The challenge to democracy

A system is corrupt when it is strictly profit-driven, not driven
to serve the best interests of its people.

Suzy Kassem

Most government is by the rich for the rich. Government
comprises a large part of the organised injustice in any society,
ancient or modern. Civil government, insofar as it is instituted
for the security of property, is in reality instituted for the
defence of the rich against the poor, and for the defence of
those who have property against those who have none.

Adam Smith

Experience demands that man is the only animal which
devours his own kind, for I can apply no milder term to the
general prey of the rich on the poor.

Thomas Jefferson

THE REVENGE OF LAISSEZ-FAIRE CAPITALISM

The election of Margaret Thatcher in Britain in 1979 and Ronald
Reagan in the US in 1981 were watersheds. They marked the
beginning of a political backlash against post-Second World War
regulated capitalism with Keynesian 'pump priming' enshrined in
the benign intervention of the state in the economy.

This hitherto successful framework was blamed for the perniciously high inflation of the 1970s, bringing to a close the three decades of high growth in living standards that followed the Second World War. Budget deficits became anathema since they would lead to unsustainable levels of government debt and crowd out more productive private investment. Margaret Thatcher likened the country's finances to those of the corner shop where she had grown up, meaning that you had to balance the books. Reagan echoed the new orthodoxy with: 'We don't have a trillion-dollar debt because we haven't taxed enough; we have a trillion-dollar debt because we spend too much.' The message was consistent; government should get out of the way of the more productive, efficient private sector, period.

In fact, Reagan did not actually practise what he preached; quite the reverse.[1] US budget deficits actually got worse in the 1980s, for two reasons. While the US was not involved in a major conflict at the time, defence spending rose to pay for the cold war with the Soviet Union. And taxes were cut, benefiting the rich, under cover of the Laffer curve economic theory.

Popularised by economist Arthur Laffer, the Laffer curve theory argues that the more money is taken from a business in the form of taxes, the less money it has to invest. In a high tax regime a business is more likely to find ways to protect its capital from taxation by relocating all or a part of its operations overseas. Investors are less likely to risk their own capital if a larger percentage of their profits are taken. Workers are demotivated when they see a larger portion of their wages taken in tax. The argument is based on the notion that for every type of tax there is a threshold rate above which the incentive to produce more diminishes, in turn reducing the amount of revenue the government receives.

The Laffer curve quickly became a cornerstone of President Ronald Reagan's economic policy, supporting the argument that tax cuts would pay for themselves and more, since this would stimulate economic activity, with the revenue lost due to lower rates more than recouped by the higher volume of income on which tax would be paid. This was part of the new consensus of encouraging the free market, known as supply-side economics, in contrast to Keynesian demand-side economics.

The Laffer curve and supply-side economics inspired what became known as Reaganomics. During the Reagan presidency the top marginal rate of tax in the United States fell from 70 per cent to 50 per cent in 1981. However, contrary to Reaganomics, later studies showed that this tax giveaway did not pay for itself, but reduced federal revenue by about 9 per cent or $129.4 billion (in 2012 dollars) over the first two years.[2] David Stockman, Ronald Reagan's budget director during his first administration and one of the early architects of Reaganomics, shocked polite society by appearing to disparage supply-side economics as a convenient cover for old Republican doctrine and the objective of reducing taxes on the most affluent, which was related to the old notion of trickle-down economics. Give tax cuts to the rich and their increased spending and investment would trickle down and benefit the rest of society. 'It's kind of hard to sell "trickle down",' he explained, 'so the supply-side formula was the only way to get a tax policy that was really "trickle down". Supply-side is trickle-down theory.'[3]

During Reagan's presidency, the US national debt grew from $997 billion to $2.85 trillion. This led to the US transforming itself from the world's largest international creditor to the world's largest debtor nation.[4] During the same time the after-tax income of the top 1 per cent nearly doubled, while the incomes of those lower down either increased marginally, or in the case of the bottom 20 per cent, actually declined.[5]

In reality, America had developed a debt addiction since it went off the gold standard – the US dollar being convertible to gold at a fixed price of $35 per ounce – in August 1971. This decision was taken under pressure from inflation rising to over 5 per cent, as the Fed maintained an easy money policy to help pay for the Vietnam War and to appease President Nixon. While it is probably true that the build-up of inflation in the 1970s was due to misguided policies by governments and central banks, this was in part because of the breakdown of the post-war system of fixed exchange rates to the dollar, which in turn was anchored by the fixed conversion rate to gold. Suddenly the global monetary system was cut loose and the inflationary genie soon escaped out of the bottle.

The Nixon tapes prove that Nixon pressured the Fed chairman, Arthur Burns, to ease monetary policy ahead of the 1972 presidential election, even though the economy was already growing at a healthy clip of around 3 per cent. The discount rate was lowered from 6 to 4.5 per cent between 1970 and 1972, while the Fed Funds rate dropped by a whopping 4 per cent. Moreover the data shows that the inflation of the 1970s was hardly due to massive government spending or tax cuts (i.e. big government) since budget deficits were relatively contained before Reagan (see Figure 7.1), so laying the blame for high inflation at the feet of big government was simply wrong. Inflation was more likely the result of loose monetary policy, the formation of the Organization of the Petroleum Exporting Countries (OPEC), which caused two spikes in the price of oil, and the ability of organised labour to push up wages to keep up with rising prices. Nevertheless, it suited the counter-revolution to pin the blame on big government.

For all the talk of the importance of fiscal discipline, in the 1980s President Reagan singularly failed to walk the walk even if he talked it. And yet, as we saw in Chapter 4, inflation came down as the Fed tightened policy under Volcker and labour union power was dismantled. So much for the much-touted errors of Keynesianism and the deleterious consequences of government deficits.

Figure 7.1 Annual US federal deficit from FY 1900 to FY 2020

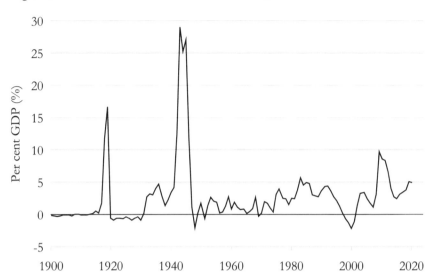

The US conservative backlash against the liberal 1960s and the consumer activist movement spearheaded by Ralph Nader arguably began with the infamous memo by Supreme Court Justice Powell to the American Chamber of Commerce in 1971. This warned that business was losing control of society – 'business and the enterprise system are in deep trouble'– and complained of the failure of schools and institutions in 'the indoctrination of the young'.[6] His vision was the restoration of a pro-business America as it was before Roosevelt's New Deal, with a minimalist government and little regulation. Powell called for business to become more aggressive in moulding society's thinking through the funding of various foundations and efforts to influence the federal government through lobbying.

Equally important were a number of judicial decisions protecting business influence in politics. Powell's memo foreshadowed a number of his Supreme Court opinions, especially *First National Bank of Boston v. Bellotti*, which shifted the direction of First Amendment law by declaring that corporate financial influence of elections by independent expenditures (for example on advertising), should be protected with the same vigour as individual speech. Many future court decisions made reference to this landmark ruling.

These rulings essentially defanged any attempt to keep big money out of politics in America. That they were inspired by a lawyer who spent time as a director of Philip Morris, championed the tobacco industry and attacked the growing evidence linking smoking with cancer only underscores the moral bankruptcy and deep corruption at the core of the American political system. As Noam Chomsky said, 'businesses need to shape ideology'. Any criticism of free enterprise was labelled anti-American. For Chomsky, the second step in the counter-revolution against the interests of workers and consumers involved a redesign of the economy by increasing the role of financial institutions. This was carried out over the ensuing decades. Financial institutions represented 40 per cent of profits in 2007, up from 11 per cent in 1990. At the same time, manufacturing shrank from 28 per cent of profits to around 10 per cent. The offshoring of jobs through globalisation reduced the share of income of American workers, not only within the US, but globally (see Chapter 3).

Ideas originating in America, the leading global economy, quickly crossed the pond to its European mini-me, the UK. There, Thatcher was in thrall to the teachings of monetarist guru Patrick Minford, and embarked on a similar crusade to cut taxes, reduce regulation and join the growing chorus of praise for the free market. Manufacturing was seen as old hat, with the future spearheaded by the gleaming new service sector. UK manufacturing output fell from 16.7 per cent to 10.1 per cent of the economy between 1992 and 2017.[7] Jobs in manufacturing fell even more steeply, from 15 per cent to 8 per cent of all jobs, as mechanisation displaced thousands. At the same time, UK manufacturing exports grew sluggishly while the country found itself having to import more and more of the manufactured goods that it used to produce. This worsened the UK's chronic trade deficit, which even the expanded services sector could not fully offset. Many industrial cities in England were left to decay as good jobs vanished for ever. The folly of relying on the absurdly volatile financial sector to drive an economy was cruelly exposed during the GFC. While some British politicians subsequently championed the need for conventional rather than financial engineering, there has been zero follow-through in policy or practice.

Even state-interventionist France under socialist president François Mitterrand could not swim against the tide for long. He performed a spectacular policy U-turn by embracing the free market within a few years of being elected in 1981. The simple truth was that any country not playing by the new rules would be left out of global economic growth, since capital was free to leave relatively highly taxed and regulated countries for low-tax, low-regulation jurisdictions. Once the capital controls of the post-war era had been dismantled, everyone had to fall in line.

The die was cast, Western governments following a laissez-faire policy of non-intervention in markets. Even when competition – an important condition for a self-adjusting market – was not present because one or a few players in an industry had become dominant (most obviously in the technology sector), regulators either turned a blind eye or were ineffective at breaking up monopolies. That this obvious contradiction between stated ideology and what was tolerated in practice by the political establishment and all mainstream political parties can only be plausibly explained by the capture of the political system by the interests of big corporations, top income earners and capital accumulators. We shall return to this central theme later.

Before we do so, we need to examine two more crucial factors: how the political systems of the advanced developed countries drove a complete change in their guiding model of what was good economic policy and the role of government; and the consequences of this new economic orthodoxy for the way democratic systems worked, or, more accurately, how they ceased to function in the interests of the majority.

The assumptions under which Western democracy found its legitimacy as a mechanism for making political choices is in danger of no longer holding. Its increasingly obvious failure to deliver the goods it promises is exposing some of its fundamental flaws and weaknesses. We need to take this stuttering mechanism apart in order to see if it can be repaired and saved, or whether we should even attempt to do so. Perhaps it is simply time to move on to a newer model and scrap the old one as no longer fit for purpose.

TWO CENTURIES OF WESTERN ECONOMIC DOMINANCE AND DEMOCRACY

We had a good run, there's no denying it. From the Industrial Revolution in the nineteenth century until 2007 the West was dominant economically, militarily, technologically, culturally and some might add morally. We have shown the way, and the rest of the world's people have aspired to follow in order to catch up with our enviable quality of life and standard of living. We have also been trailblazers in the realm of personal freedom. The French and English revolutions liberated individuals from the arbitrary rule of hereditary monarchs and state policy designed to preserve and enhance the wealth and power of a minority. The last two centuries have been an unprecedented success for the West, with the developed nations most likely creating more wealth in the last century and a half than in the whole of history before then.

This all came about parallel with the evolution of a political system of democratically elected representative government and the empowerment of the individual. Freedom to take risks independently of a landowner or feudal lord, and to keep the fruits of one's risk-taking and labour lifted the lid on economic development. No wonder this inspired the first economists to construct elegant theories 'proving' the superiority of the free market.

While the coincidence of change in political system with an economy that took off is almost perfect, one should remain wary of the old trap of assuming that correlation is causation. Nevertheless, the West's success under these twin regime changes has deeply anchored the belief that the two systems – the free-market and democracy – go hand in hand.

The new system worked because everyone was free and equal before the law. The transition from decrees by the ruler to the rule of law to which everyone has equal access guaranteed property rights and the enforcement of contract, which in turn enabled commerce and industry to take off. Equality eventually also meant one person one vote in free elections for representatives and heads of government or state. Each individual's vote counted, and it counted equally. This promoted fairness in decision-making, and, by giving everyone an equal stake in the political process, it ensured widespread buy-in to the system. A new moral basis for organising society was born, superseding the religion that had anchored the divine right of kings.

The direction of causality also ran both ways, or so it appears. The rise of merchants and those engaged in commerce created the pressure for political change. Armed with wealth created outside feudal land ownership, they demanded a slice of the political pie to protect and further their interests. While early forms of Western democracy were only partial – not everyone was eligible to vote and some decision-making bodies such as the American Senate or the British House of Lords were made up of the rich, landowners, the aristocracy and the religious elite – it was only a matter of time before universal suffrage became the norm.

Democratic takeover of the political system not only provided an apparently elegant and moral solution to the problem of how to govern a society and arrive at decisions other than through the dictatorship of an individual or group, but was also a necessary and sufficient condition for a transformative leap in economic growth and rising living standards. What was there not to like? No wonder Westerners believed it was the best and only legitimate way of organising society and zealously exported our template with quasi-religious fervour. Witness our intervention in Japan, imposing a Western-style constitution and democratic system down the barrel of the gun, or in India, now the most populous democracy on earth, where democracy was introduced by decades of colonisation and by example. If it worked for us, it was an easy sell to others, especially as these societies aspired to follow in our economic footsteps. Not surprisingly, the occasional failure of this policy, as in the Middle East, not only stung, but proved utterly baffling.

THEORY AND PRACTICE

The West's conviction of the superiority and inevitable global triumph of its political-economic system was based not only on its economic success, but also its moral attributes, efficient decision-making processes and guarantees of dignity and freedom to individuals. In other words, democracy not only proved superior in practice, it was also the best *theoretical* solution to the problem of collective decision-making. The fact that this was not necessarily true was no impediment to its adoption, as we shall see.

Political philosophy has struggled with the problem of deciding on a justifiable and workable solution to political organisation and societal decision-making between competing options. The most obvious of the choices has to do with the distribution of income and wealth (and work) in society and the capacity for deriving satisfaction from either consumption or accumulation of capital. There are a number of competing alternatives. The problem is, no one has found the formula to determine how this should be done in a way that is not arbitrary and subjective. There is simply no generally accepted solution. There is no theoretical proof of the superiority of democracy over other political systems, because there is no proof of its superiority at producing the best outcomes for society. We may like it as a system because that is the culture we have been brought up in, but its moral and economic superiority is neither demonstrated in theory nor, more recently, in practice; consider the economic success of Chinese autocratic capitalism, for example.

The American founding fathers actually limited democracy in the Constitution in order to protect the wealthy minority, giving power to a Senate comprised of the unelected wealthy to enable them to protect their property from the masses. In ancient Greece, Aristotle had seen the flaw in democracy: that the poor would get together and take away the property of the rich. Arguments over how to divide up the cake and organise society swing from periods of democratisation, like the 1960s, back to regression towards concentration of power and wealth.

John Stuart Mill attempted to construct a formula by stipulating that each individual will derive levels of 'utility' (satisfaction) from each of the various outcomes that result from different decisions.[8] He assumed that each individual has a combination of outcomes that maximises his or her utility, thereby enjoying the greatest happiness possible. He also assumed that each individual's utility could be aggregated to society's utility. If that is true, he concluded that the best state of society is one where decisions are made to 'maximise the happiness of the greatest number'.

Unfortunately, this is fraught with obstacles. Even if one accepts that individuals can rationally choose the best option from all the permutations of possible outcomes that might affect them, the system still needs a way of measuring or calibrating all the different outcomes for each individual to determine which add up to the greatest total societal happiness. What is better, a society arranged to maximise total satisfaction but where satisfaction is skewed to say the top 10 per cent of the population, or one which produces less total satisfaction but provides more to the bottom 90 per cent? And how can you measure one individual's satisfaction compared to another's? If you can't, how can you combine them? It is not as if satisfaction/utility can be objectively measured like temperature or weight.

Faced with these insurmountable flaws, the branch of study known as welfare economics moved on from utilitarianism and cardinal measures of welfare to a theory based on the principles of choice based on order of preferences. This sidesteps the need to measure satisfaction/utility/happiness. Instead, we can order our preferences between various combinations of outcomes and even make trade-offs between various 'goods' that provide us with satisfaction, although we may be indifferent to some combinations. For example, you may be happy to trade $100 less income per week for an extra four hours of leisure (you prefer the latter) but may be indifferent between $100 less income and an extra three hours of leisure.

This attempt to solve the problem of collective decision-making and social choice using an ordinal system of ranking preferences remains problematic since a mechanism is needed to aggregate individuals' orders of preferences. The democratic process of one person, one vote fails miserably on this count, as proved by the simple example commonly known as the paradox of voting.[9]

Let A, B and C be three possible outcomes for three people 1, 2 and 3, and assume people are rational.

Individual 1 prefers A to B and B to C

Individual 2 prefers B to C and C to A

Individual 3 prefers C to A and A to B

So a majority prefers A to B and a majority prefers B to C, therefore a majority prefers A to C.

But a majority also prefers C to A, so what to do?

If this approach breaks down with only a tiny number of people and choices, imagine the even smaller likelihood of obtaining a clear, consistent outcome for millions of people and multiple choices. And if it is theoretically impossible to ensure a rational choice between outcomes for people, as demonstrated above, how can the democratic process in the form of one person, one vote, electing representatives who will have to deal with a myriad of choices and possible outcomes, realistically hope to produce socially rational choices, let alone the 'best' results?

Worse, economic theory positively demonstrates that popular democracy is inherently dysfunctional. Why? Voter ignorance.

According to Anthony Downs, 'it is irrational to be politically well informed because low returns from data simply do not justify their cost in time and other resources'.[10] For any one individual voter, it is mad to spend lots of time educating himself or herself on political issues in order to vote in elections or referendums, since the expenditure of time and effort is huge compared to that individual's likely gain from making a better-informed choice. That is because a single person's vote is extremely unlikely to make any difference to the outcome: it will probably not be the casting vote. In other words, 'If time is money, acquiring political information takes time, and the expected benefit of voting is roughly zero, a rational selfish individual chooses to be ignorant.'

This, however, is a classic case of the generalisation principle – my walking on the grass makes no difference but I must not because if everyone did there would be no grass left. In fact, this could be an argument for making sure all citizens take the time to inform themselves on key issues that will come up in votes, rather than an apology for selfish laziness (all must get informed = do not walk on the grass). It is not acceptable to be a free rider in the democratic process if one attaches value to it as a political system. In fact, it is inconsistent to believe in democracy and not do the work.

However, this still does not solve the problem of aggregating individuals' preferences in a justifiable way to derive justified political decisions.

If there is no theoretical basis for choosing democracy as a political system other than its simple appeal to a sense of justice through equality – one citizen, one vote – on what basis can it be chosen? To answer 'a common sense of justice' is unfortunately subjective and dependent on an unprovable assumption of what is just. Who is to say that a choice imposed on 49 per cent of the population by 51 per cent is just if it oppresses the 49 per cent? A referendum where 51 per cent of the population voted to confiscate the wealth of the bottom 49 per cent, and so return society to a more feudal state, would pass the democracy smell test, if not an ethical or economic one.

If we reject such an outcome, this means we do not believe in the absolute and unconditional validity of majority rule through the democratic process. To some, the tyranny of the ruler has simply been replaced by the tyranny of the majority, with no guarantee of a socially optimal outcome; far from it. History is stuffed full of examples of injudicious decisions democratically arrived at, not least of which was the election of Adolf Hitler as German chancellor.

HORSES FOR COURSES

Perhaps more convincing is the empirical link between political systems and the underlying technological and economic reality of the times. If we can't justify democracy on theoretical or moral grounds, perhaps the fact that it has worked to deliver the greatest increase in living standards in human history is sufficient. If there is no rational solution to the problem of decision-making by society, the next best hope might be to find the system that demonstrably works best in practice. That may be so, but what happens when this ceases to be the case, as in the last few decades? We will return to this question.

In prehistoric times man was a hunter-gatherer. Gradually, it made sense to join together in groups for protection and more effective hunting. This economic mode went hand in hand with the birth of tribal societies. Without delving too deeply into sociology or anthropology, there is a Marxian sense in which we can explain the organisation of society according to what best serves its economic, technological and security model at the time.

Similarly, as man evolved and learned to cultivate the earth and breed and control certain animal species, the notion of land ownership within clear boundaries gave birth to feudalism – society based on ownership by landowners or rentiers, tenant farmers and serfs around city states, followed by nations and empires. This coincided with the rise of organised religions, such as Christianity, which provided legitimacy to the rule of the king or emperor at the top of the pyramid, anchoring the ruler's political power and the use of force. To make it in feudal society, one had to be either a landowner or rise through the ranks of the church or the army.

Western religion legitimised only the family unit and monogamous sex in order to clearly delineate ownership of land and wealth and to facilitate its orderly and efficient transmission from one generation to the next. One can be forgiven for thinking that if Christ did not exist, he would have had to be invented anyway. Indeed, it is the rigidity and simplicity of this structure that gave the West a leg up in transforming essentially agricultural wealth into the next phase of the economy, based on commerce and industry, and, eventually, finance.

There is of course no sharp frontier in time separating one social system from the next. Political assemblies providing checks and balances on the power of the leader came into existence during feudal times in Europe, and democracy was invented as far back as ancient Greece.

In Greece's 'golden age' (starting around the fifth century BC), the political units were cities such as Athens, where the citizens were sufficiently few and local that the assembly could be attended by all of them. This was direct democracy in action rather than representative government through elections. However even this system did not insulate Athens from capture by certain interests. It has been estimated that only 3,000 or so people actively participated in politics. Of this group, perhaps as few as a hundred citizens – the wealthiest, most influential, and the best speakers – dominated the political arena both in front of the assembly and behind the scenes in private political meetings.[11] Direct mass participation may appear to be the fairest version of democracy, but in practice probably only about 10 per cent of the citizenry participated. And there was no guarantee that this would yield good decisions: 'Critics of democracy, such as Thucydides and Aristophanes, pointed out that not only were proceedings dominated by an elite, but that the *demos* could be too often swayed by a good orator or popular leaders (the demagogues), get carried away with their emotions, or lack the necessary knowledge to make informed decisions.'

This sounds depressingly familiar even 2,500 years later, proving that not much has changed.

Fast-forward two thousand years, and European nations such as England and France were wresting political power from absolute monarchs in favour of elected assemblies of representatives. These states were too big geographically to operate direct democracy as in ancient Greece, so the only solution to the puzzle of how to empower citizens, to deliberate over issues and make decisions, was for them to elect representatives to meet in one central location for that purpose on their behalf.

Seen in this light, it is almost surprising that the mechanics of the political system have not evolved with the enormous changes to the economic structure of society and the rise of technology. Frozen for centuries, political sovereignty still rests, wholly or in part, in national assemblies such as the House of Commons in the UK, Congress in the US or the Bundestag in Germany. In an age of smartphones, artificial intelligence, instant messaging and information, the principle of electing representatives on our behalf sticks out as an anachronism, at least from a technological point of view. If modern communications empower us to involve all citizens in direct political debate and decisions, just like the ancient Athenians, why would we not switch to this form of democracy?

Irrespective of our answer to this question, we should also ask: what is so sacrosanct about democracy? Should we always prefer it to another political system, whatever the outcomes in practice? Are its moral foundations strong enough to support it even if it fails to deliver the goods that its citizens expect? And how absolute and unconditional is our belief in the principle of one citizen, one vote?

THE POLITICAL CANCER AT THE HEART OF WESTERN SOCIETY

These are real and pressing questions, because as we move from an industrial society with high-paying manufacturing jobs to a service society dominated by finance and technology, history suggests a corresponding political regime change is in order and probably overdue. This is a huge issue because our system of representative democracy is manifestly under stress, no longer delivering the goods that have justified its existence. In the UK the chaos that has engulfed government and parliament in trying to deal with Brexit has cruelly demonstrated how these institutions are no longer fit for purpose and are falling into disrespect.

The recent rise of populist and nationalist forces, the decline of the established political parties and platforms and the election of mavericks such as Donald Trump in America, and the Five Star movement and Northern League in Italy, have real causes that have been allowed to fester and grow for too long. Some of these causes, such as stagnant real wages, record inequality and job insecurity in the West, we have already discussed, but we need to link the discussion to the working of our democracies. How have the rich and the large corporations succeeded in capturing political systems to their sole advantage, including persuading politicians to alter tax and regulatory systems for their benefit and pursue other policies that have cumulatively favoured the minority at the top of the income ladder?

At the global level, Western governments' abetting of the enormous transfer of economic weight and relative income from the West to China must stem either from negligence, corruption or both. This transfer has been achieved via an international trading system that handicaps Western companies and workers through forced knowledge and technology transfers to the Chinese and has failed to gain access to the Chinese market equal to that provided to them. In other words, it has not even met the basic criteria required for free trade to be mutually beneficial. We will discuss this in more detail in Chapter 10.

Why and how this has come about shows how our democracies have been captured by the principal beneficiaries of the international trading system. When did Western electorates vote on and acquiesce to a massive transfer of income and wealth from them to the East? Clearly never, and the casualties of this transfer are becoming increasingly unhappy.

The debasement of Western political discourse, manifested in the increasingly shrill and angry intolerance of others' rights to express conflicting opinions, is symptomatic of societies slipping closer to the edge of the political cliff. We are morphing from a culture of political consensus, openness to debate, tolerance and non-violence to a society composed of groups living with closed minds in the silos of their beliefs, aggressive and prepared for violence towards others. In short, we are turning into a nasty ragbag of tribes that our grandparents would not recognise.

Western voters are finally waking up to the fact that the precariousness of their jobs and the poor prospects for their children are not the temporary cyclical effects of the GFC, but are entrenched and structural aspects of our economies which they have endorsed over decades without understanding the consequences. The realisation that they have been sold a pup has rightly ignited people's indignation and anger. No surprise that a growing proportion of the electorate is prepared to tear down a political system which is too weak to change course and incapable of offering solutions let alone hope.

The clear conflicts of interest between elected representatives and those who elected them have burst into the open and decimated respect for authority. If our lawmakers are really on the take or only in it for their own career interests, why should we respect their laws? Underfunded health, education and other public services, poverty and exclusion, and cuts in policing resources have all conspired to create areas and types of crime where the law can no longer effectively be enforced.

We will now explore the multiple and interrelated dimensions in which this growing political cancer risks killing Western society and democracy, unless a dramatic course change is undertaken soon. For those of us who still care, understanding must go hand in hand with action.

THE AGENCY PROBLEM 1: CONFLICTS OF INTEREST BETWEEN THE PEOPLE AND THEIR REPRESENTATIVES

It is easier to define the interests of politicians than those they represent. Why? Because it is the job of the political process to work out and discover what the citizens' interests are – as we have seen, a problematic task. If the test is through the ballot box, we don't know specifically what the majority has voted for, given that the alternatives presented by candidates include a long menu of policies. And as we have seen above (see page 190), even if the choice is only between three choices, there is no guarantee that a clear winner will emerge. Even with a seemingly simple single issue and binary question, the majority that voted for one side of the question may have done so for several incompatible reasons. For example, in the 2016 UK Brexit vote, some leavers voted because they wished to restrict immigration but wanted to preserve the UK's access to the single market – in reality two mutually exclusive outcomes.

We won't discuss areas of social policy which are not directly relevant to our case, which is one of political economy. Nevertheless, in spite of the difficulties of pinning down what is in society's interests, we can express certain high-level principles in economic terms, subject to constraints about environmental sustainability and work conditions. For example, we could agree that it is in the interests of society to raise the standard of living of all its citizens over time, subject to preserving the environment. In order to build in an intuitive sense of fairness, we could add that it is unacceptable for any significant section of society (by income band) to suffer stagnant or declining living standards over the medium to long term, if not all sections of society suffer the same. This is to prevent some parts of society making out like bandits at the expense, in absolute terms, of others.

A political test of such a consensus could indeed be the

restoration of social peace, respect for laws, tolerant, respectful debate, and freedom of expression without intimidation. We can argue about the finer details, but let us agree that this is how we imagine some of the interests of society and so the electorate.

As for the interests of the political class – our elected representatives – it is not hard to see that these are specific to them. We can approximate their interests as centring around their careers. These can be defined in terms of getting elected and re-elected, implementing their beliefs and leaving a positive legacy. Politicians may be conflicted within their career objectives. For example, they may seek office and power in order to do good, but may find that the policies needed to achieve this conflict with the need to be elected or re-elected. This is because the policies that are necessary to promote society's interests over time may require a sacrifice in short-term income growth for example. In concrete terms, mending public services that have suffered decades of underfunding relative to their needs probably requires the courage to be unpopular and raise taxes, taking money out of private pockets. But this may be a vote loser, so not a career-enhancing move.

Time horizons
The fact of the matter is that politicians are constrained by the rhythm of the electoral calendar, which is too short (four or five years) for desirable policies that work in the long term to show their benefits. We should not lay the blame entirely at the feet of politicians either. The electorate is also short term in its thinking, or at least politicians assume it is, and is likely to be swayed by promises of instant gratification, like tax cuts. Since getting elected is an intensely competitive business, it is difficult to avoid being dragged down to the lowest common denominator in terms of policies in the absence of strong, principled leadership. Recent political discourse in Britain, including on climate change, more

responsible business and spending on health and education, suggests that the pendulum is starting to swing back from the free-market-small-government ideology that has dominated for so long. The UK Labour Party's 2019 general election rout had more to do with poor leadership and the party's indecisive and insincere stance on Brexit, since its main policies of renationalising the railways and utilities polled as popular. Even Boris Johnson's victorious Conservatives have promised to open the spending taps on infrastructure and health, sensing the need to tackle the causes of the anger and frustration felt by whole swathes of the British population. Failure to grasp the extent of the task, act to rebalance key economic relationships and upgrade the economy for the twenty-first century will bring back disappointment with a vengeance, perhaps irretrievably deepening the divide between citizens and their elected representatives.

The conflict of interest between voters and their elected representatives is most harmful in the area of education. The better educated children and young adults are, the more they can aspire to fulfilling and well-compensated jobs and compete in the world. The educational capital acquired by citizens determines a country's competitiveness and ability to grow in a globalised world. It is therefore crucial to make the necessary investment to raise and maintain educational standards and universal access to top-quality education. To promote a globalised system of trade and not do this is to condemn a country not endowed with the advantage of plentiful natural resources to disappointment and relative decline.

Unfortunately, it takes a generation for an upgrade in educational standards and resources to show through in economic terms. Needless to say, by the time a politician has climbed the greasy pole to be in a position of power, their time horizon is seldom that long. Why should they take money from short-term needs to invest in projects that will take years to put in place and decades to bear fruit, only for their successors' successors to claim the credit? In a globalised world where technology is rapidly superseding human labour in multiple tasks, failure to make this investment must logically condemn increasing swathes of society to low-pay jobs or unemployment. Politicians have opted for free trade and competition but neglected to equip their populations with the skills to compete with countries that, while they may not be democratic, do have long-term plans and prioritise education.

THE BREAKDOWN OF THE SOCIAL CONTRACT

As the saying goes, when the tide goes out, it reveals who was swimming naked. Since the GFC, the social contract which tolerated some inequalities resulting from capitalism in exchange for generally rising real incomes and job security has been broken in the West. This in turn undermines the legitimacy of democracies which are clearly no longer delivering the goods.

Living standards have been held back by austerity and underlying feeble real wage growth. In many countries the baby boom generation is seeing its children struggle to secure good stable employment and reliable pension rights of the kind they themselves enjoyed. According to Federal Reserve data, millennials in the US earn 20 per cent less than boomers did at the same stage of life, despite being better educated.[12] Another report estimates that only 60 per cent of the cohort born in 1960 was better off in 1990 than their parents were at thirty. For those born in 1940, 90 per cent were better off at thirty than their parents had been at the same age.[13]

The damage has been greatest in southern European countries such as Spain and Greece, where youth unemployment remains persistently high. Even in the UK, opinion polls consistently reveal the pessimism younger people feel at their economic prospects. Half of respondents to a poll conducted by Ipsos in late 2016 said they thought today's youth would fare worse than their parents, compared to 22 per cent who thought young people would fare better.[14] This broadly reflects the feeling in many Western countries. In the UK, the so-called silent generation (born 1928–45) and baby boomers both enjoyed considerably higher real incomes than their predecessors at each age. This progress has all but disappeared for generation X (1966–80) and millennials (1981–2000) in spite of the fact that many more of them are university graduates.[15] In fact, generation Xers who have reached the 45–49 age bracket appear to be earning no more in the UK than the boomer generation before them did at the same age. The 2019 audit of political engagement by the UK's Hansard Society shows that opinions of the country's system of government are at their lowest in the fifteen years the survey has been running and that 54 per cent of Britons say the UK needs 'a strong leader who is willing to break the rules'.[16]

As Bernie Sanders has tried to hammer home, given record wealth and inequality, people all over the world are losing faith in democracy as they recognise that the global economy has been rigged to reward those at the top over everyone else. This is fuelling anger which is turning destructive. There are signs that this breaking down of the social contract in the West is being recognised. As far back as 2012, the *FT*'s John Plender noted:[17]

> Such resentment is not completely new. It bears some resemblance to the hostility towards profiteers after the First World War which prompted Keynes to remark; 'to convert the business man into the profiteer is to strike a blow at capitalism, because it destroys the psychological equilibrium which permits the perpetuance of unequal rewards ... the businessman is only tolerable so long as his gains can be held to bear some relation to what, roughly and in some sense, his activities have contributed to society'.[18]

What is new, according to Plender, is the aggressive way companies shed labour now that executive pay is linked to short-term performance targets: 'In effect, the American worker has gone from being regarded as human capital to a mere cost.'

As for the free-market model of maximising international trade, even the more sentient members of the establishment are beginning to recognise its shortcomings. For Harvard's Lawrence Summers, 'international agreements [should] be judged not by how much is harmonised … but whether citizens are empowered'.[19] John Nelson, ex-chairman of the very international Lloyds of London insurance market, has gone on record as saying, 'capitalism must demonstrate that it is an engine of economic growth for all; not for an exclusive minority'.[20] But for all the talk, virtually nothing has been done to try to stop let alone reverse the trend.

The social contract underpinning Western democracy was not just about rising living standards for all, but also about hope. It is now failing us to the point that we are giving up hope. Even the great American dream – that in the land of opportunity anyone can make it – ceased to be true some time ago. In the US today a child's life chances are more dependent on the income of his or her parents than in Europe or any of the other advanced industrial countries for which there are data.[21] Waking up to the fact that the American dream is now a myth is proving a shock to many US citizens. Well before President Trump took power, years of declining trust in public institutions led the Economist Intelligence Unit to demote the US from a full democracy to a flawed democracy – a nation it defines as having free elections but weighed down by weak governance.[22] Like many so-called democracies across the globe, once-proud Western exemplars have morphed into grubby plutocracies.

No longer delivering the goods or compensating the losers

Another crucial part of the social contract underpinning the legitimacy of our democracies was the understanding that, if there were losers along the way, the system would compensate them so that they did not become disaffected. The deal was that capitalism would deliver the goods. This has ceased to be the case. A fundamental change since the free marketeers took over in the early 1980s in the West has been the capture of the system by a minority of winners who don't feel the need to share out their gains and don't bother to look out for the losers.

For market ideologues, deregulating finance and trade, promoting unfettered global competition and weakening the power of trade unions was the sure-fire way to turbocharge growth for everyone. The opposite has been the case. The economic principle that more redistribution would be needed to compensate those on the losing side of this new economic deal has simply not happened. Instead, the free marketeers have got away with maintaining that the rest of the population would catch some of the crumbs falling off the high table – better than nothing. In practice, the trickle-down effect, if it ever operated, has hardly compensated for the lack of growth and the concentration of wealth into fewer and fewer hands.

The crowning hypocrisy of the free marketeers is their ultimate theoretical defence: that governments must refrain from intervening in markets and their outcomes because doing so restricts the growth of the economic pie. They admit that inequality is a by-product of an unfettered free-market system, but interference to reduce inequality should be avoided as entrepreneurs' spirits would be dampened by the resulting loss of incentives. Even if the pie's slices are unequal, in absolute terms there will be more for everyone.

In the US, the facts flatly contradict this. In the decades when income inequality was low, the 1940s, 50s and 60s, average real growth rates were robust, around 4 per cent per year. In contrast, the 2000s and 2010s, the most unequal since the 1920s, have only managed growth rates averaging around 2 per cent. Far more egalitarian societies such as Sweden have produced higher average rates than the very unequal US or UK. So much for this self-serving myth.

The negative social and health impacts of inequality are alarming. In the US a growing section of the population is falling victim to drugs, legal or not. And, after decades of improvement, mortality rates among white middle-aged men and women in the US ceased declining around the turn of the century and began to rise. Research by Princeton's Anne Case and Angus Deaton shows that 'the story is rooted in the labor market ... nor can those in mid-life today be expected to do as well after age 65 as do the current elderly'.[23] The deterioration is particularly marked among the less well educated (high school degree or less), and, when analysed in more detail, Case and Deaton's findings show that the rise in the death rate is driven by drugs, alcohol and suicide – what the authors grimly term 'deaths of despair' – which more than offset decreases in deaths from heart disease and cancer.

As they dug deeper to understand the causes of this phenomenon, it became apparent that slow-burning sociological trends, such as declining employment-to-population ratio and the drop in marriage rates had effected a long-term process of decline. Since the early 1970s, the steady deterioration in job opportunities for the less well educated meant that

> Traditional structures of social and economic support slowly weakened; no longer was it possible for a man to follow his father and grandfather into a manufacturing job, or to join the union ... people moved away from the security of legacy religions ...[to] less structure to choose their careers, their religion, and the nature of their family lives. When ... such choices ... fail, the individual can only hold him or herself

responsible. It is not low wages by themselves that explain the rising death rates, but the broad social and sexual consequences.

Low wages and bleak prospects also made men less marriageable. Less stable and more temporary partnerships formed, divorce and separation rates soared, often adversely impacting the children.[24] In 2016, 40 per cent of children were born to unmarried mothers across OECD countries, up from 7.2 per cent in 1970.[25]

Case and Deaton's conclusion makes for grim reading: 'we can see globalisation and automation as the underlying deep causes. Ultimately, we see our story as about the collapse of the white, high school educated, working class after its heyday in the early 1970s, and the pathologies that accompany that decline.'

THE PARALLELS WITH THE 1930S

In an interview in January 2018, billionaire investor Ray Dalio revealed that his analysts had calculated that the proportion of the vote captured by populist candidates in the West had risen from about 7 per cent in 2010 to 35 per cent in 2017. The last time this happened was just before the Second World War. He could not, though, see what would reverse the trend, partly because digital technology is exacerbating inequality by eliminating jobs. 'We're heading for a world where you're either going to be able to write algorithms and speak that language or be replaced by algorithms.'[26]

The election of the anti-establishment League and Five Star Movement in Italy in 2018 is just one example of a desperate electorate turning as a last resort to 'anything but the usual bunch'. This was perhaps inevitable in a country where real GDP per head in 2018 was still a whopping 13 per cent below its high-water mark a decade earlier.[27] Since 1999, the Italian economy has been caught in a Japanese-like zombie state of near zero growth.

Unfortunately, the administrations swept into office by the

swelling current of discontent remain hemmed in by the system they have inherited. In the US the political process is controlled by the financial and corporate elite, while in the Eurozone the German-led orthodoxy of one-size-fits-all monetary policy without corresponding centralised fiscal control is bound to lead to further disappointment. With interest rates already as low as they can go in the Eurozone, and Mario do-whatever-it-takes Draghi retiring in November 2019, the European Central Bank is effectively out of ammunition should the next crisis come any time soon, in which case, it is questionable whether the EU's institutions could survive.

The historian Fritz Stern warned, before his death in 2016, that there were signs of resurgent fascism including in the US. These included 'the corruption of public discourse and a world in which everything has become opinion'.[28] There has been a sharp degradation in public discourse, including hitherto-unthinkable attacks worthy of the worst fascist demagogues on institutions of democratic government. When three UK judges ruled that the government would need the approval of parliament to trigger Brexit, the *Daily Mail* ran a banner headline calling them 'enemies of the people'. Members of parliament expressing the view that the UK should remain closely tied to the EU have allegedly received death threats. This, in a country that was the global template for civilised behaviour, respect for rules, courtesy, politeness, tolerance of different views and above all fairness and integrity in politics. The British were not liars, cheaters or violent – until now.

It seems that nature hates a vacuum in human affairs as well as in physics. Columbia University's Mark Mazower has argued that the rise of fascism in the 1930s was underpinned by a profound crisis of liberal democracy. People blamed legislatures for their woes and saw a solution in concentrating more power in a 'strong' leader: 'Parliaments were written off as facades that rubberstamped what unaccountable lobbies and elites demanded.'[29] Politics moved to the extremes and parties denied each other's legitimacy. Judges and police lost their neutrality and became politicised. Mazower notes that the hollowing-out of institutions and the extremism and violence of political discourse that enable dictators to take power are well under way today. Ominously, he reminds us that history is no one-way street of progress; democracy has turned authoritarian before.

Our societies are falling apart before our very eyes, and our politicians have no answer. At best they are still blinkered and constrained by a free-market ideology that is not fit for purpose in the modern world; at worst, as we'll see in Chapter 8, they are in the pockets of special-interest groups which are sucking our societies dry. Instead of delivering to their citizens the promised sunny uplands of prosperity via the best allocation of resources delivered by free global markets, the political class has steered the ship of democracy to within sight of the rocks. Corporate greed has run amok, hamstringing the West's ability to grow and generating stratospheric rewards for those at the top that cannot be considered fair by any measure. Those who have missed out are becoming very restless; one more serious jolt and the mood could suddenly turn very nasty indeed.

It has been a completely different story for the other winner of the last three decades: China. Just as the rise in Western median living standards has ground to a halt, so China's leap in income and wealth has been breathtaking. Playing a long game, the Chinese have correctly identified the venality and short-term horizons of our leaders, both corporate and political, and effected an unprecedented transfer of income and wealth from West to East. It is worth dwelling on this central aspect of the West's decline in more detail, since the symbiotic relationship between the Western money elites and China is a central cause of our plight. We will come back to China in Chapter 10. For now, we will look at another factor in the breakdown of the social contract: the capture of the political system by private interest groups.

8

The capture of the political system by private interest groups

> The central point that emerges from our research is that economic elites and organized groups representing business interests have substantial independent impacts on U.S. government policy, while mass-based interest groups and average citizens have little or no independent influence.
>
> Martin Gilens and Benjamin Page

Perhaps the most sinister and damaging aspects of the growing conflict of interest between electors and elected over the last thirty years have been the growing cost of campaigning, the rise of the lobbying industry and the attack on the regulatory frameworks put in place to defend the interests of the many against the few.

These three changes have led to the effective capture of the political system by well-resourced special-interest groups. We have gradually moved from one citizen, one vote to one dollar, pound or euro, one vote. In some cases it is difficult to distinguish between a company or industry seeking to influence political outcomes that will affect them and outright corruption, especially if there is an implied link between the cooperation of politicians and promises of campaign funds. While the extent of this phenomenon varies from country to country, and is widest in the US, the effects have been felt throughout the West.

CAMPAIGN FUNDING IN THE US

Bernie Sanders remarked during the 2016 US presidential campaign that nothing that was said would make any difference unless the influence of 'millionaires and billionaires' was ended. In 2018, according to Oxfam, twenty-six people owned as much as the poorest half of humanity – 3.8 billion people. Further, the top 1 per cent now have more money than the bottom 99 per cent.[1] Although there has been some progress, 10 per cent of the world's population still lives in extreme poverty – an income of less than $1.90 per day.[2] People all over the world are losing their faith in democracy – government by the people, for the people and of the people. 'They increasingly recognise that the global economy has been rigged to reward those at the top at the expense of everyone else, and they are angry.'[3]

One of Sanders' solution is the reform of US campaign funding. Not surprisingly, the system has never pursued this with any vigour, preferring the status quo. Rules limiting direct campaign contributions from individuals have been in place in the US since 1972's Watergate scandal, when President Richard Nixon took secret corporate donations in exchange for 'accommodating government treatment', but these are not watertight.[4] Individuals can still aggregate and channel individual contributions through 'bundlers', who are not legally required to disclose their activities if they are not registered lobbyists and often collect money in exchange for political favours; then there are the more recent 'super PACs' (political action committees), which can spend without limit as long as they act independently of a candidate's official campaign.

The system is supported by the US Supreme Court's ruling that paying to advertise your political views is a form of freedom of speech. In April 2014 the court also ruled that aggregate limits on campaign contributions were unconstitutional under the First Amendment.[5] Unlike in other democracies (French presidential candidates are limited to a paltry $30 million spend for example), money has always been big in American politics. Even back in 1895 Senator Mark Hanna acknowledged, 'There are two things that are important in politics. One is money and I can't remember what the other one is.'

The 2016 elections revealed that both Democratic and Republican campaigns were bankrolled by billionaires with big stakes in the outcome. Bloomberg reported,

> They include Republican casino owner Sheldon Adelson, who has opposed proposals to legalise online gambling, and Democratic investor Tom Steyer, who advocates for clean energy. Some wealthy players, notably industrialists David and Charles Koch, whose company lobbies to loosen regulations on oil and gas, run their own political operations. All this has pushed up the costs of campaigns. The amount spent on the 2016 Senate race in Pennsylvania alone was at least $139 million.'[6]

It is clear that as the cost of getting elected continues to spiral, so politicians are increasingly dependent on financing from private sources. This provides large donors with powerful direct or indirect influence. The money for campaigns for federal office comes from four broad categories:

- small contributors (individuals who contribute $200 or less)
- large contributors (individuals who contribute more than $200)
- political action committees (PACs)
- candidate's own money

The sources of campaign contributions in the 2018 Congressional races are broken down in Table 8.2 overleaf.

Table 8.1: Campaign spending in US elections 1998–2018

Cycle	Total Cost of Election	Congressional Races	Presidential Race
2018	$5,725,183,133	$5,725,183,133	N/A
2016*	$6,511,181,587	$4,124,304,874	$2,386,876,712
2014	$3,845,393,700	$3,845,393,700	N/A
2012*	$6,285,557,223	$3,664,141,430	$2,621,415,792
2010	$3,631,712,836	$3,631,712,836	N/A
2008*	$5,285,680,883	$2,485,952,737	$2,799,728,146
2006	$2,852,658,140	$2,852,658,140	N/A
2004*	$4,147,304,003	$2,237,073,141	$1,910,230,862
2002	$2,181,682,066	$2,181,682,066	N/A
2000*	$3,082,340,937	$1,669,224,553	$1,413,116,384
1998	$1,618,936,265	$1,618,936,265	N/A

*Presidential election cycle

Table 8.2. Donations by range ($ millions)

	Count	Total*	To Dems*	To Repubs*	To PACs*	% Dems	% Repubs
Donors giving $200–$2,699	1,304,490	$941.0	$387.4	$216.3	$328.9	41%	23%
$2,700+	225,043	$3,084.8	$1,008.9	$778.3	$528.0	33%	25%
$2,700–$9,999	181,206	$844.7	$341.9	$230.0	$276.0	40%	27%
$10,000+	43,837	$2,240.0	$667.0	$548.3	$252.0	30%	24%
$100,000+	2,547	$1,347.5	$248.3	$245.6	$81.3	18%	18%

*Millions of dollars

The figures clearly show that the biggest share of campaign contributions comes from predominantly large donors i.e. the wealthy, who have more at stake and more to lose from the threat of a change to the system. Around 0.47 per cent (1.3 million) of the population contributed 71 per cent of campaign funds, with the lion's share coming from about 46,000 large donors of $10,000 and above. The 2018 Congressional elections managed to burn nearly 50 per cent more money than in 2014. A total of $6.5 billion was spent on the 2016 elections, of which the presidential election alone accounted for $2.4 billion.

THE IMPACT OF FINANCE ON RESULTS

The jury is out when it comes to the extent to which campaign funding affects election results, although the Center for Responsive Politics reports, 'Candidates with most financial support generally win,' as shown in Figure 8.1.

Figure 8.1: Candidates with most financial support generally win, US elections 2000–16*

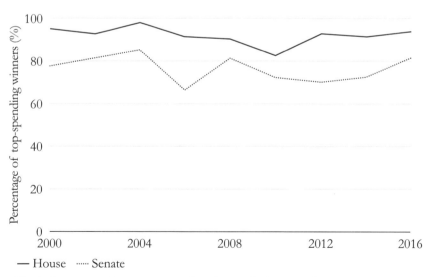

— House ····· Senate

*Excludes races with no opponent, but does include races where opponent spent nothing.

They noted however that the presidential race appeared to be an exception to this rule. Rather than financial support increasing candidates' chances of winning, it may be that better candidates attract more financial support.

Certainly, Donald Trump won in 2016 having only raised $350 million (including $66 million of his own money) directly, about a third of Obama's 2012 re-election campaign, and considerably less than his opponent Hillary Clinton's $585 million, as reported by the Federal Election Commission. This equates to about $5 spent per vote. In total, including joint party raised funds and super Political Action Committees (PACs), Trump raised a modest $647 million compared to Clinton's $1,191 million. According to Bloomberg, 'She spent heavily on television advertising and her get-out-the-vote operation, but in the end, her fundraising edge wasn't enough to overcome Trump's ability to dominate headlines and the airwaves.'[7]

The fact remains, however, that it requires large sums of money to campaign with a chance of success in the US, and that campaign funding, as we saw in Table 8.2, continues to come primarily from large donors. Unsurprisingly, a 2016 experimental study reported in the *American Journal of Political Science* found that politicians made themselves more available for meetings with individuals when they believed the people had donated to their campaign.[8]

In 2011 another study found that 'even after controlling for past contracts and other factors, companies that contributed more money to federal candidates subsequently received more contracts'.[9] And a 2016 study in the *Journal of Politics* found that industries overseen by committees decreased their contributions to Congresspeople who recently departed from the committees and that they immediately increase their contributions to new members of the committees, 'evidence that corporations and business PACs use donations to acquire immediate access – suggesting they at least anticipate that the donations will influence policy'.[10]

Other research, by Anthony Fowler, Haritz Garro and Jörg L. Spenkuch, found no evidence that corporations that donated to a candidate received any monetary benefits from the candidate winning an election.[11] Of course, this depends on how and over what period of time one measures benefits. One benefit may simply be the preservation of the status quo. A somewhat counter-intuitive 2017 study found that relatively unpopular industries provide larger contributions to candidates. The authors of the study argue that this is because candidates lose voter support when they are associated with unpopular industries and that the industries therefore provide larger contributions to compensate for this.[12]

While the data does not conclusively prove that quantity of money automatically determines electoral success, nor that those elected craft policies that benefit their donors, it stretches credibility that wealthy individuals and corporations would donate as they do if they did not obtain some financial benefits or influence for their investments over time.

Michael Traugott, a political science professor at the University of Michigan, has claimed that the traditional US model for picking presidents might seem odd to people in other nations, where campaigns are shorter and require less cash. 'The system is clearly broken,' Traugott said.[13]

Perhaps one of the most hotly contested special interest groups in America recently is the National Rifle Association (NRA). While it is not one of the big spenders, it has consistently contributed to predominantly Republican lawmakers as well as paid for advertising defending the constitution's Second Amendment, the right to bear arms. With every mass shooting, a cry to change the law or tighten regulations is left unheeded by the political class, in spite of the outrage.

In the 2016 election the NRA spent $11,438,118 to support Donald Trump and another $19,756,346 to oppose Hillary

Clinton, a total of more than $31 million on one presidential race.[14]

The sheer breadth of campaign support provided by the NRA over the years helps explain just how deeply the organisation is ingrained in the election universe. Among the 535 members of Congress in 2018 in both the House and the Senate, 307 have received either direct campaign contributions from the NRA and its affiliates or benefited from independent NRA spending like advertising supporting their campaigns. Eight lawmakers have been on the receiving end of at least $1 million over their careers, 39 have seen $100,000 or more in NRA money flow their way, while 128 lawmakers have received $25,000 or more. Only six current Republican members of Congress have not received NRA contributions.[15]

Florida Senator Marco Rubio is one of those who has received over $1 million from the NRA. When asked by a student at a school in Florida where a mass shooting had taken place whether he would now refuse to take further campaign donations from the NRA, he said no.

The NRA's influence also derives from the negative advertising campaigns it runs which can quickly destroy a political career. In 2014 one of these ads targeted US Senator Mary Landrieu, who supported a bill to expand federal background checks to include gun purchases made at gun shows and over the Internet. The NRA ad showed a mother putting her daughter to bed while her husband was away from home. An intruder enters; the police don't arrive in time, and suddenly the house is a crime scene. The message was clear. 'Mary Landrieu voted to take away your gun rights.' She lost the election.[16]

According to Vox, the NRA disbursed $144 million on advertising between 1998 and 2017, ten times its direct political contributions. US politicians know not to cross the National Rifle Association.

THE REST OF THE WEST

Expenditure by parties and candidates on elections is generally lower in other Western democracies. For example, since 2000 in the UK rules require transparency from donors: political parties must report all permissible donations above £7,500. There are also rules limiting expenditure. For the 2015 general election, total expenditure by political parties was £37.3 million, including £22.6 million by candidates and £2.8 million by registered non-party campaigners. The conservatives won and outspent Labour by around £15.5 million to £12 million. In total, this is equivalent to less than $90 million for a population around one fifth of that of the United States, and so seems more than proportionately modest, although it is true that UK election campaigns are shorter than in the US. Total donations to UK political parties over the 12-month period leading up to the 2015 election were about £90 million (around $130 million), still much lower than the US on a per-elector basis. Two years later, total spend was £41.6 million for the 2017 general election, of which over £18 million was spent by the governing Conservative Party, which still managed to lose seats to its Labour opponents.

In France, spending was limited in the 2017 presidential election to €22,509,000 for the two presidential election finalists, Emmanuel Macron and Marine Le Pen. In the event, they spent around €16.7 million and €12.4 million respectively, or around $35.5 million combined, which seems like a bargain. Individual donations are capped at €4,600, and companies or legal entities other than political parties are barred from contributing, precisely to avoid pressure from commercial donors.

In Germany in the 2012 election the expenditure by the two main political parties, the SPD and CDU, amounted to less than €30 million each. As in other European countries, the formal campaigns run for a short time. This, and their relative cheapness, means that politicians don't have to spend much of their time fund-raising for the next campaign and so have more time for the job in hand. There are no limits on individual or corporate contributions to politicians' campaigns but self-restraint seems to be exercised. There are a few officially sanctioned TV and radio slots for each party, and a large slice of campaign financing comes from public funds roughly based on the number of votes gathered at the last election. In 2006 it is estimated that around 30 per cent of parties' income came from public funds, 28 per cent from membership dues, 10 per cent from individual donations and only around 4 per cent from corporate contributions. The balance came from elected officials' donations and income from investments and commercial interests.[17] However, political parties do not have to declare immediately contributions below €50,000, so companies can game the system by contributing below-threshold amounts regularly throughout the electoral cycle.

But while the direct power of money in election campaigns is less evident in Europe, there are two other methods through which business seeks to influence or modify the laws and regulations affecting them for their financial benefit: lobbying and regulatory capture.

LOBBYING

Lobbying takes its name from the tradition of meeting British parliamentarians in the lobbies or corridors of the Palace of Westminster. It is not a new activity; however, its growth and professionalisation since the 1970s has been rapid. In essence, lobbying is a paid activity in which special interests – business, groups like the NRA, even foreign nations – hire well-connected professional advocates to plead their case with politicians, with the aim of influencing policy, legislation and regulation. Lobbying has become big business, and its effect on politics has been significant.

For example, in 2016 Taiwanese officials hired American senator-turned-lobbyist Bob Dole to set up a controversial phone call between president-elect Donald Trump and Taiwanese President Tsai Ing-Wen, resulting in a shift in US foreign policy.

In 2014 Martin Gilens and Benjamin Page suggested that special-interest lobbying enhanced the power of elite groups and was a factor shifting the USA's political structure towards an oligarchy in which average citizens have 'little or no independent influence'. In fact, even when a substantial majority wants policy change, they generally do not get it if it clashes with the elite or organised interests. Gillen and Page term this 'economic elite domination'.[18]

US lobbyists have taken the art to its highest level. They are well connected with the Washington political elite, well versed in the issues of the day and in it for the long term, patiently cultivating networks and contacts, building trust and confidence. Many will get directly involved in campaign finance by fundraising, assembling PACs and seeking donations from other clients.

Brian Ballard, a Florida fundraiser with ties to Donald Trump, reported receiving $9.8 million in federal lobbying fees in 2017. This was the most successful debut by a new lobbying firm in Washington, trumping the $8.1 million first-year income earned by Breaux-Lott, the firm set up by ex-Senators John Breaux and Trent Lott in 2008. Despite Trump's promise to 'drain the [Washington] swamp', spending on lobbyists increased to $3.4 billion in 2018, up from $3.15 billion in 2016.[19]

WALL STREET LOBBYING

Given the legal and regulatory framework within which finance operates, it's unsurprising that the sector is one of the big employers of lobbyists. Influencing how law and regulation is written and interpreted can set the rules of the game and transform their profitability. With so much at stake, it is no surprise that the financial industry has been one of the top spenders on lobbying in recent times: 'The financial industry reported spending a total of $897,949,264 on lobbying in 2015 and 2016. This puts the sector in – close – third place, behind the Healthcare sector, which spent $1,022,907,176, and a category of "Miscellaneous Business," a sector that itself probably includes some Wall Street lobbying by business groups with a broader focus than only finance.' Big banks such as Wells Fargo, Citigroup and Goldman Sachs each spent over $10 million.[20] Although the pharmaceutical and healthcare sector appeared to top the lobbying spend in 2018 at $283 million, adding up the insurance, real estate, securities and investment and commercial banking industries that comprise 'finance' reveals a record-breaking spend of $443 million that year.[21] These sums do not include 'dark money' – contributions to non-profit groups which are not directly linked to a candidate, do not have to disclose their donors and which do not have limits on donation sizes

An article in *Bloomberg Businessweek* exposed the work of ex-Undersecretary of State James Glassman, who works for a public relations firm called DCI Group on behalf of the hedge fund industry.[22] He was part of a decade-long 'influence campaign' aimed at reshaping public opinion in Washington and around the world of Argentina's government. He ultimately helped DCI client Elliott Management to turn a $2 billion profit on its holdings of Argentinian bonds. The magazine hailed the practice as yet 'another way in which skyrocketing inequality is giving a few individuals an outsize role in public life'.

Crucially, it was political donations and the lobbying power of the finance industry that succeeded in emasculating the 1933 Glass-Steagall Act, which, as we saw in Chapter 4, separated investment banks from commercial banks following the 1929 crash. Lobbying pressure succeeded in provoking its repeal by President Clinton and Congress in 1999. We now know to our cost the effects of allowing retail banks to indulge in a bit of casino banking on the side, although the merger of Citicorp with Traveller's to form Citigroup in 1998 showed how Glass-Steagall had already become a paper tiger.

The influence of lobbyists on the repeal of Glass-Steagall – with everything this unleashed – is another facet of the pervasive moral hazard built into the system since the Greenspan era at the Fed, prioritising the welfare of Wall Street over Main Street. Quite apart from the reigning ideology, any attempt to curb the banks' freewheeling habits was smothered by their constant efforts to influence the political process.

Lobbying by the financial industry has recently borne fruit with Congress approving Trump's push to pare back the regulations imposed on the sector post-GFC, embodied in the 2010 Dodd-Frank legislation. In March 2018, less than a decade after the crisis, Congress watered down the law, freeing thousands of small to medium-sized banks from the stricter federal oversight and regulatory burden that had been introduced. White House officials called it 'an important step toward ridding the economy of regulations that have held back growth'.[23]

In 2019 the Fed announced the watering-down of its stress tests on major banks, thereby freeing up more capital for them to pay higher dividends to shareholders or conduct share buy-backs.[24]

In their 2014 book *Fragile by Design* Charles Calomiris and Stephen Haber characterise banking as a rent-seeking racket between bankers and the political establishment, extracting wealth from those outside this partnership and dividing it between them.[25] They certainly have a symbiotic relationship: governments need banks to keep deposits and make loans; banks need governments and central banks to act as lenders of last resort and to enforce contracts. That basic relationship leaves plenty of room for governments to constrain what banks do. However, if governments and politicians want to ensure decent growth in order to satisfy the electorate and maximise their chances of re-election, being permissive with the banks – allowing them to create credit, especially at times of recession or low growth in underlying incomes – creates a win-win situation for both. Banks lobbying governments to unshackle them has been like pushing against an open door.

YOU REAP WHAT YOU SOW: FINANCE, LOBBYING AND THE GFC

It may seem surprising that in 2009, the year banks nearly crashed the system, New York mayor Andrew Cuomo reported 'that nine financial institutions that received a combined $175 billion in federal money [to save them from bankruptcy] handed out almost $33 billion in bonuses'.[26] Two of the banks, Citigroup and Merrill Lynch, lost $54 billion in 2008, received $55 billion of government bail-out money, and yet paid out bonuses of $9 billion.

Although fiscal and monetary action during 2008–9 may have prevented a full-blown depression, direct government support for the US financial sector totalled approximately $12.6 trillion, more than 80 per cent of 2007 GDP.[27]

UK government support for banks, including guarantees, rose to £1.162 trillion at its peak in 2009 of which around £1 trillion was in the form of guarantees, in a bail-out that began with the collapse of Northern Rock in 2007.[28] This was equal to over £20,000 for every UK resident. Meanwhile, the government's budget deficit ballooned to 12.4 per cent of GDP, crippling its finances and ensuring a massive squeeze on public spending and services for the next decade. Although the Office of Budget Responsibility has calculated that the bail-out costs have come down to only £23 billion as of January 2018, principally due to a loss on the rescue of RBS, the government's debt position has remained nearly twice as high as before the crisis due to social security outlays to support incomes and falling tax revenues during the crisis.

This was replicated across the Western world. The authorities spent whatever money it took to bail out the banks while at the same time squeezing their populations through reduced welfare, infrastructure and public services spending, higher taxes and reduced pensions in order to repair government finances. In the Eurozone this was imposed on deeply indebted countries such as Greece, whose biggest creditors were German bankers and investors, as the price of remaining part of the club. Robert Strauss expressed concern that it seemed to be more 'moral' to save German bankers than Greek pensioners; German policy in relation to the Greek bail-out was 'no more morally just than letting bankers off scot-free for causing the financial crisis'. Eighty per cent of the hundreds of billions of euros lent to Greece after 2009 was actually used to repay those very German bankers.[29]

The big winners were the owners of capital. Not only were they saved once again from the consequences of their own folly, but they subsequently made even more money as central banks printed money furiously to help governments fund their whopping deficits and bring down interest rates and borrowing costs.

As we have seen, the Bank of England printed £375 billion of fresh money to keep bond yields, and so borrowing costs, close to zero. In the US, the Fed more than quadrupled the size of its balance sheet to $4.5 trillion by purchasing treasuries and mortgage-backed securities. By 2017 the Bank of Japan had accumulated an extra 400 trillion yen (about $4 trillion or 96 per cent of GDP) of assets it had purchased by printing money since 2011. In the Eurozone the ECB embarked on a money-printing programme to buy €60 billion of assets a month from March 2015, temporarily increased to €80 billion per month from March 2016 to March 2017, since scaled back from 2018 to a monthly €30 billion. Faced with renewed economic weakness, the ECB announced in October 2019 a resumption of its bond buying programme. The ECB and Eurozone national central banks had accumulated assets of over €4.5 trillion by the end of 2018 from printing money and pinning Eurozone government bond yields close to zero, while imposing negative interest rates on bank deposits.[30]

These extraordinary measures had to be taken to save a market economy from a catastrophe of its own making. So much for the ideological purity of the free market, unfettered from government intervention.

Stock market speculators made a killing as the markets rose again on a sea of central bank liquidity. Not only were interest rates cut to historic lows, in some countries to previously inconceivable negative rates, but the major central banks embarked on a policy of creating money with which to buy assets such as bonds in the open markets, thereby raising prices and bringing down yields. This was a direct infusion of cash into the financial markets, rather than into stretched households. This policy, dubbed quantitative easing or QE (a more respectable term than printing money), meant that the central banks' own balance sheets greatly expanded with the purchase of trillions of dollars, euros, pounds and Japanese yen assets.

The world's biggest and dominant stock market, as measured by the S&P 500 index in the US, at the time of writing has returned over 400 per cent since the crisis.[31] While once again correlation does not prove causation, the depressing effect of this policy on interest rates would by itself support asset prices and funnel capital into equities as savers avoided the non-existent yields from cash and bonds. Real estate owners' wealth reinflated, as almost free money catapulted some property prices back beyond the 2007 bubble peaks, placing them out of reach for much of the younger generation.

Nevertheless, most politicians have been reluctant to abandon the free market and accept that the GFC has exposed its limitations. Hedge fund manager Paul Marshall was a brave lone voice when he acknowledged that anyone with assets – banks, hedge funds, property owners – 'made out like bandits' from quantitative easing. 'If the increased money supply had been distributed evenly, it might have been used for consumption rather than making rich people richer and bailing out the banks ... QE had clear wealth effects, which could have been offset by fiscal measures [ie tax the rich]. All political parties should acknowledge this. So should those of us who want free markets to retain their legitimacy.'[32]

As we saw in Chapter 6, the bail-out and QE system was a prolongation of a policy in place since the Greenspan Fed in 1987: every time the market overdosed on credit, threatening an economic meltdown, the money tap was opened even further, thereby inflating the next even bigger excess. And, according to economist Heinz Blasnik,[33]

the irony is the propping up of a deeply, intrinsically pathological and destructive financial system is not saving the economy, it's the reason the economy is imploding ... the truth is that keeping the zombie system from expiring and covering up the corruption with propaganda is what's actually destroying the world as we know it ... the Fed not only enabled, financed and corrupted the financial sector, but also provided it with the opportunity (through monetary inflation) to make outsized profits at the expense of the rest of the economy.

He goes on, darkly: 'I believe American democracy is doomed, and that it will be replaced by fascism or a military dictatorship and that the financial system will sooner or later implode.'

That is a very determinist view of the world, but it could happen unless the political establishment is prepared to put aside its almost religious belief in unfettered free markets, (fake) free trade and finance.

It was not just the banks that needed rescuing from the financial heart attack they caused. Insurance companies playing in the financial casino that had lost their shirts, such as AIG, had to be bailed out to the tune of dozens of billions of dollars, and iconic American car companies had their customer finance divisions' tails wagging the manufacturing dog. As credit markets dried up and business plummeted, the federal government bailed out Chrysler and General Motors to avoid bankruptcy and the loss of a million jobs. The US treasury spent $80.7 billion buying shares in the two companies as well as lending them money.

However, the finance industry's millions spent on politicians through campaign funding and lobbying proved a shrewd investment. It was repaid in spades, with few of its executives suffering punishment for their recklessness or even having to return their bonuses, while society remains crippled by public debt and austerity policies.

CORPORATE LOBBYING

Lobbying is not of course the exclusive preserve of the finance industry. Boeing, for example, is a big spender on lobbying, averaging around $20 million per year in the US. Disclosures filed with the federal government show that the US Chamber of Commerce, the National Association of Realtors (real estate), and the Business Roundtable spent more than $56 million lobbying Congress in the last quarter of 2017 in order to influence the changes to the American tax code passed at the end of the year.[34]

Technology is a big lobbyist. In Spring 2017 lobbying by Internet service providers such as Comcast and AT&T, and tech firms such as Google and Facebook succeeded in influencing a narrow vote to undo regulations protecting consumer privacy by barring ISPs from selling people's browsing history. Republican senator Jeff Flake and Republican representative Marsha Blackburn raked in thousands of dollars in donations from these trade groups to sponsor the legislation to dismantle Internet privacy rules passed by the Obama administration just a year before.[35]

A Bloomberg article revealed that Google parent company Alphabet outspent its rivals in lobbying, investing $18 million, compared to $11 million by Facebook, 'as lawmakers scrutinised the companies over questions including Russia's use of their platforms to try and influence the 2016 election'.[36] Apple spent $7 million lobbying that year and was a major beneficiary of the change in tax law passed by Congress at President Trump's behest. The company had accumulated profits of around $252 billion outside the US by 2017, on which it would be liable to pay 35 per cent tax if it brought them back to the US under the old system. Under the new tax regime proposed by Trump and passed by Congress just before the end of 2017, Apple (and other US corporations with cash stashed abroad in low-tax jurisdictions) obtained a sweetheart deal enabling it to repatriate this cash upon a much reduced payment of $38 billion, still huge, but an effective one-off low rate of 15.5 per cent payable over eight years. Given the time elapsed between the generation of the profits and the tax payment, the effective tax rate is much lower in nominal terms and positively minuscule in inflation-adjusted money.

More recently, the ending of so-called net neutrality means several of the big cable companies such as Comcast and AT&T, which provide the infrastructure for the Internet, stand to make millions of dollars in extra profits from their new-found ability to fast-track more profitable traffic at the expense of that of private individuals, thereby destroying the democratic principle of the web. Unsurprisingly, Comcast, the largest broadband provider, was the second-biggest lobbying spender among single companies in the fourth quarter of 2017 (after Google), laying out more than $4.3 million.[37]

Just as sinister are efforts by food and drink manufacturing industries to protect practices that actually harm people. Take, for example, the battles between the food industry and healthcare lobbyists over school lunches in the US. Congressional representatives from potato-growing states worked quickly to block a new rule that would reduce the amount of starchy vegetables that could be served to school children in a single week. The industry also baulked at a recommended reduction in sodium. And lobbyists working on behalf of ConAgra Foods and the Schwan Food Company, both huge suppliers to schools of frozen pizza, are seeking to block changes to school food rules that would end the current practice of counting pizza as a vegetable.

The money–power relationship works both ways. Some accuse the US Congress of deliberately structuring certain laws, such as tax exemptions, so that they expire unless renewed. This keeps the campaign donations flowing. Harvard Law School Professor Lawrence Lessig has suggested that the complexities of the tax system are in part designed to make it easier for candidates to raise money to get back to Congress. 'All sorts of special exceptions which expire after a limited period of time are just a reason to pick up the phone and call somebody and say "Your exception is about to expire, here's a good reason for you to help us fight to get it to extend." And that gives them the opportunity to practice what is really a type of extortion – shaking the trees of money in the private sector into their campaign coffers so that they can run for Congress again.'[38]

THE REVOLVING DOOR

The representatives of the people are milking the system while in power, but are also getting ready to milk it from the lobbies once they leave politics. A steady stream of ex-congressmen finds its way to lobbying firms to exploit their experience and connections for large salaries – the famous revolving door between public service and private gain. A 2005 Public Citizen report found that 43 per cent of the 198 members of Congress who had left government since 1998 registered to lobby.

Various scandals have prompted attempts at transparency and formulating rules to limit the excesses of lobbying, but these appear to be ineffectual as it is in the interests of neither party to make them work. This is perhaps the most acute example of a conflict of interest between elected representatives and those they represent. Lobbyist and convicted fraudster Jack Abramoff bragged on television that his colleagues could 'find a way around just about any reform Congress enacted' and gave an example. You can't take a congressman to lunch for twenty-five dollars and buy him a hamburger or a steak, but you can take him to a fundraising lunch and not only buy him that steak, but give him $25,000 as well, call it fundraising and have the same access and all the same interactions with that congressman.[39]

THE REST OF THE WEST

In the EU there are at the time of writing only seven countries out of the twenty-eight members (the UK, Ireland, France, Austria, Lithuania, Poland and Slovenia) where there is legislation covering lobbying, including legal codes of conduct and the registration of lobbyists. Although the situation is gradually improving, with more countries becoming aware of the need for transparency and rules, lobbying is a largely unregulated and opaque activity. A report from the non-profit group Transparency International suggests that the lack of transparency with respect to contacts between lobbyists and public or elected officials means that it is almost impossible for citizens to gauge lobbyists' effect on policy. Furthermore, while the seven countries have instituted registers of lobbyists, and in some cases a code of conduct governing contacts, there is little enforcement as the registers provide minimal information and detail concerning the interactions between officials and lobbyists. And although a majority of the nineteen EU countries surveyed had some sort of revolving-door policy, restricting how quickly ex-public officials could move into lobbying, the level of oversight and enforcement was feeble. Only one country (Slovenia) has firm rules governing ex-politicians.

REGULATORY CAPTURE AND THE STOCKHOLM SYNDROME

The third lever business employs to bend the rules to its liking involves influencing the regulators that are supposed to safeguard the public interest, while the Stockholm syndrome is the phenomenon whereby hostages become accomplices of their captors, defending them against accusations. A similar phenomenon occurs when regulators set up by governments to safeguard the public interest get too close to the industries they regulate and get turned. In effect they start working to protect the interests of these industries to the detriment of society.

This is private interests' last line of defence. If you can't buy the right electoral outcome and your lobbying does not succeed in preventing unfriendly and restrictive legislation, then you can at least ensure those charged with enforcing the rules interpret them in your favour or simply look the other way. Regulatory capture is most notorious in the areas of food, medicine (the Food and Drug Administration in the US) and of course, once again, finance.

Public regulators targeted by the finance industry have included institutions set up to protect the public from some of its predatory practices, such as, in the USA, the Consumer Financial Protection Bureau (CFPB), created in the aftermath of the GFC. This agency sought to ban the forced arbitration provisions in the small print of credit agreements that effectively deprived debtors of the ability to go to court. It also worked to rein in so-called payday lenders, requiring them to verify a borrower's ability to repay a loan. 'Since 2011, Republicans have introduced 135 bills and resolutions aimed at killing or weakening the CFPB in the House and Senate.' The Consumer Bankers Association spent $3.2 million on lobbying in 2016, but was outspent by 'the American Bankers' Association which spent $9.8 million that year on the services of 58 lobbyists that same year'.[40]

In 2016 Wall Street found an ally in newly elected President Donald Trump, who promised to 'do a number' on financial regulations. Trump appointed ex-Goldman Sachs top executives Steve Mnuchin and Gary Cohn (since resigned) as treasury secretary and chief economic adviser and has replaced most regulatory agency heads, often with former finance industry executives. In May 2017 the administration appointed Keith Noreika, a lawyer who built a 'career protecting banks', as acting head of the Office of Comptroller of the Currency (OCC).

According to Bloomberg News,

> The Office of the Comptroller of the Currency (OCC) recently circulated a blueprint to other regulators for making the [Volcker] rule more friendly to banks … Wall Street critics will take exception with the fact that the architect of the OCC proposal was Keith Noreika, a long time bank lawyer who served as the regulator's acting head in 2017 … Named for former Fed Chairman Paul Volcker, the controversial regulation was meant to prevent banks from triggering another

financial meltdown by prohibiting them from making speculative bets with their own capital.[41]

In 2018 Federal Reserve Vice Chairman Randal Quarles said US financial regulators are working quickly to make 'material changes' to the Volcker rule, one of Wall Street's 'most hated post-crisis restrictions'.[42] In May 2018 the Fed voted to ease the restrictions imposed on banks by the rule, and another barrier set up to protect society from the insatiable appetite for profit of the finance industry came down.

At the CFPB itself in late 2017 Trump had appointed as acting director his budget director Mick Mulvaney, a self-described 'right wing nut job'. While still in Congress, Mulvaney had gone on record with 'I don't like the fact that the CFPB exists.' Less than a decade after the banks nearly blew up the world economy, in January 2018 Mulvaney wrote in the *Wall Street Journal* that the CFPB would no longer assume that 'the bad guys' are the financial services firm it supervises. He pledged to tone down the agency's aggressive regulatory and enforcement stance.

Unsurprisingly, it did not take long for the agency to perform a spectacular U-turn. On 6 June 2019, under new director Kathy Kraninger, the CFPB proposed to rescind some of the new requirements on lenders due to take effect that August, announcing that it would delay compliance with new regulatory rules for short-term, high-interest loans (payday loans) to 2020.[43] The reassessment was presented as part of a broader push to rescind the bureau's most aggressive regulations and refocus the agency's work on promoting consumer freedom.

'The CFPB's decision to revisit its small-dollar rule is welcome news for the millions of American consumers experiencing financial hardship and in need of small-dollar credit,' said Richard Hunt, president and CEO of the Consumer Bankers Association.

The last bulwark against regulatory capture by the finance industry and the Trumpian push to reduce bank regulation was Martin Gruenberg, head of the Federal Deposit Insurance Corporation (FDIC), responsible for guaranteeing bank deposits and one of three federal bank regulators in the US. The Trump administration had not altered regulation as much as Wall Street had hoped until now, as the *FT* made clear with its headline FRUSTRATED LOBBYISTS PIN SOME OF THE BLAME ON MR GRUENBERG.[44] Gruenberg was replaced by bank lawyer Jelena McWilliams in June 2018.

THE US FOOD AND DRUG ADMINISTRATION

The independence of other US regulatory bodies is also questionable, including the Food and Drug Administration. In a damning 2013 article, researchers Donald Light, Joel Lexchin and Jonathan Darrow confronted the corruption they saw at the heart of the FDA:

> It is our thesis that institutional corruption has occurred at three levels. First, through large-scale lobbying and political contributions, the pharmaceutical industry has influenced Congress to pass legislation that has compromised the mission of the Food and Drug Administration (FDA). Second, largely as a result of industry pressure, Congress has underfunded FDA enforcement capacities since 1906, and turning to industry-paid 'user fees' since 1992 has biased funding to limit the FDA's ability to protect the public from serious adverse reactions to drugs that have few offsetting advantages. Finally, industry has commercialised the role of physicians and undermined their position as independent, trusted advisers to patients.[45]

In other words, contributions to Congressmen have resulted in the squeezing of the public funds available to the FDA, which has had to switch to earning fees from the very drug companies it is supposed to be regulating.

Writing from the Edmond J. Safra Center for Ethics at Harvard University, Donald Light suggests that the overfamiliar relationship between companies and FDA officials also affects the agency's assessments of what makes a drug safe or effective, and how these are communicated: 'The ... corruption of medical knowledge through company-funded teams that craft the published literature to overstate benefits and understate harms, unmonitored by the FDA, leaves good physicians with corrupted knowledge.'[46] This results in his damning conclusion: 'about 90 per cent of all new drugs approved by the FDA over the past 30 years are little or no more effective for patients than existing drugs'.

Worse, while the approval of new, expensive but useless drugs is an economic cost to the rest of society extorted by the drug companies, Light also believes that over the past thirty years the bar for drug safety has come to be set too low, with approved drugs causing serious harm even when properly prescribed. 'Every week, about 53,000 excess hospitalisations and about 2400 excess deaths occur in the United States among people taking properly prescribed drugs to be healthier. One in every five drugs approved ends up causing serious harm.'

The FDA has also come under criticism for its tolerance of certain practices by the food industry the safety of which has not been proven. For example, it permits meat manufacturers to use certain gas mixtures during packaging to prevent discolouration of the meat; these may conceal signs of spoilage. It also allows the use of bovine growth hormone in dairy cows; these have then tested for high levels of a factor in their milk which may sustain the growth of certain tumours. The FDA justified its approval on the grounds that humans are unlikely to ingest sufficient quantities of the hormone to be dangerous. An EU scientific opinion maintains that there is a potential risk to humans from the use of six hormones in cattle, including growth hormone, which has been banned in Europe.[47]

Finally, the FDA has been criticised for permitting the routine use of antibiotics in healthy animals on a preventative basis, which may give rise to evolution-resistant strains of bacteria. So, the foxes have been let into several hen coops by the farmer. No wonder the animals are getting suspicious.

EUROPE IS FAR FROM PERFECT
Dieselgate and beyond

America does not have the monopoly on anti-social lobbying or the corruption of regulators. In Europe a powerful lobbying industry has grown up in Brussels to influence the drafting of rules and regulations and, perhaps more sinisterly, promote their lax implementation. An infamous example is Dieselgate, which exposed how the European car manufacturing industry successfully subverted the application of emissions tests on European cars, resulting in on-the-road nitrous oxide emission levels from diesel engines five to ten times higher than the legal limits, thus exposing citizens to dangerous levels of pollution.

A paper published by the Corporate Europe Observatory and Friends of the Earth investigated the European Parliament's inquiry into Dieselgate and revealed a culture of regulators looking the other way.[48] The scandal came to light in 2015 when investigations in the US showed that European car manufacturers had been gaming the system, using 'defeat device' software in diesel engines to reduced observed emissions during testing.

Back in 2005 the European Commission's Better Regulation Agenda had set out to ensure that the 'regulatory burdens on business ... are kept to a minimum'. A subgroup of the newly created Competitive Automotive Regulatory System for the 21st Century (CARS21) group, comprising industry and government representatives, was tasked with simplifying the regulatory framework.

EU-wide car lobby group the European Automobile Manufacturers Association (ACEA) saw an opportunity to cut costs to help global competitiveness and called for self-testing to be introduced for certain emission and safety tests, along with EU-wide approval superseding national monitoring. This was finally approved by the EU's Council of Ministers in 2010. On behalf of Germany, Chancellor Angela Merkel lobbied the European Commission to support the car industry's demands. Leaked papers also show that the European Commission's Directorate General for Enterprise intervened to delay the implementation of more realistic Real Driving Emissions (RDE) tests to 2019. The car lobby managed to persuade the authorities that tighter regulation would cost jobs and decrease the competitiveness of the European car industry, arguments that appeared weighty to lightweight European politicians.

In short, companies' commercial interests were placed above public interests. Despite the Commission and EU states knowing since 2004 that there were discrepancies between emission test results for diesel cars and emissions in real-world driving (which exceeded legal limits), they delayed the introduction of RDE. Even after the cheating was exposed, member states were slow to apply penalties on car manufacturers.

Food safety
Although food standards in terms of artificial additives and drugs administered to animals are relatively strict in Europe, lobbying by the chemical industry and farmers has no doubt contributed to the

renewal by the EU of permission to use glyphosate (contained in the well-known weedkiller Roundup) in November 2017, in spite of controversial studies such as a 2016 report from the International Agency for Research on Cancer which stated categorically, 'There is sufficient evidence in experimental animals for the carcinogenicity of glyphosate' and, 'Glyphosate … is probably carcinogenic to humans.'[49]

Use of this weedkiller has exploded, particularly in the US, where crops have been genetically modified so that they are not affected by it. This ability to target only undesirable plants has made glyphosate an easy sell to farmers and a huge cash cow for its producer, Monsanto (now part of Bayer). While the US Environmental Protection Agency, the European Food Safety Authority (EFSA) and the European Chemicals Agency have all ruled that glyphosate is safe, a court in California upheld a verdict that Roundup caused a school groundskeeper's cancer in 2017. Since then, other juries have awarded large punitive damages to plaintiffs, noting that Monsanto failed to warn of the cancer risks.[50]

Whether or not the evidence in this specific case is conclusive one way or another, the fact is that regulators on both sides of the Atlantic appear quick to approve foods and chemicals on the basis of flimsy evidence, in some cases partly provided by the corporate sponsor. In 2017 the *Guardian* newspaper revealed that EFSA's recommendations on glyphosate included pasted-in analyses from Monsanto's own study.[51] Alarmingly, research has found that the weedkiller is

> so pervasive that its residues were recently found in 45 per cent of Europe's topsoil – and in the urine of three quarters of Germans tested, at five times the legal limit for drinking water. Since 1974, almost enough of the enzyme-blocking herbicide has been sprayed to cover every cultivable acre on

the planet. Its residues have been found in biscuits, crackers, crisps, breakfast cereals and in 60 per cent of bread sold in the UK ... But industry officials warn of farmers in open revolt, environmental degradation and crops rotting in the fields if glyphosate is banned.[52]

Diane Coyle, professor of economics at UK's Manchester University, is unequivocal about the failure of regulation and competition policy in the UK in recent decades, citing for example privately owned water companies focusing on profits for shareholders rather than reinvesting in infrastructure.[53] In transportation, after years of safety problems on the railways, the UK government was obliged to take back control of the track network and its maintenance after the private sector skimped on maintenance, resulting in a spate of accidents.

The 2019 crashes of two nearly new Boeing 737 MAX aircraft in very similar circumstances has shone a spotlight on the US Federal Aviation Authority (FAA), an organisation that used to set the global standard for the certification of new aircraft. The disasters have uncovered the dirty reality of an agency starved of funds, understaffed, run by a temporary head and delegating a high percentage of its certification work to the manufacturer itself.

There are plenty of other examples of the problems caused by privatising infrastructure and natural monopolies and then appointing a weak regulator. Private interests are maximising short-term profits rather than long-term benefits to society and customers. As Professor Coyle says, it is hard to make natural monopolies competitive. Hence the suspicion that capitalists are doing too well from them. The fact is that private companies running industries where there is little genuine competition maximise their profits through high prices or, if they cannot persuade a soft regulator to acquiesce, through minimising investment and capital expenditure, thereby degrading the long-term quality of the service delivered.

Even in industries which are not monopolies, such as the provision of gas and electricity, competition has not been a success, with prices to the consumer often bearing little relation to changes in wholesale market prices and clearly manipulated between a few dominant providers. Prices ratchet up with the market but rarely come down significantly when the market does.

Nobel laureate Jean Tirole argues that the asymmetry of information between regulator and provider can never be wholly overcome. Providers simply know more about demand, supply and the technicalities, and will always be able to game the system. That is not to say that state-run railways and utilities necessarily function much better. But the touted benefits of privatisation and competition have been greatly exaggerated in practice (they were never robust in theory) or have simply not materialised in the form of better service and lower prices. In fact, since some popular British services such as the speaking clock and Yellow Pages were privatised for no good reason other than fashion and lobbying, they have been rejected by the public and have effectively gone out of use.

Probably the best option for natural monopolies is to be in public ownership with a long-term strategy including adequate investment to cater for demographic trends (one shudders to imagine how, given the attrition of transport services in rural areas, ageing baby boomers retiring to the countryside will cope once they can no longer drive). Unfortunately, this presupposes strong enough public finances to support such an enlightened policy. Indeed, part of the reason for privatising large swathes of the state's economic activity was to raise money to compensate for the weakening of its revenue base as a result of ideologically driven tax cuts and weaker wage growth due to globalisation. It is to the issue of taxation that we now turn.

9

Declining taxes and the pauperisation of the nation state

Can it possibly make sense that at this moment, as I speak to you, the share of public investment in GDP, adjusting for depreciation, so that's net share, is zero. Zero. We're not net investing at all, nor is Western Europe.

Lawrence Summers

Business interests have been very successful in employing all the levers we've described in earlier chapters to alter the rules of the economic game in their favour. Nowhere has this been more marked than in the domain of taxation, with catastrophic consequences for public services. In a globalised world with free movement of capital, nation states have lost control of the source of their strength: the ability to raise revenue. Large multinational companies have become the new unit of power, employing hundreds of thousands of employees across the world and able to shift resources and capital to maximise profits. President Trump's December 2017 tax cut mostly benefited corporations, which were already earning record profits and stashing colossal sums outside the US in low-tax jurisdictions rather than repatriating them and paying tax to Uncle Sam. All over the world governments have been competing in a race to cut corporate taxation,

Figure 9.1: US corporate tax rate 1909–2018

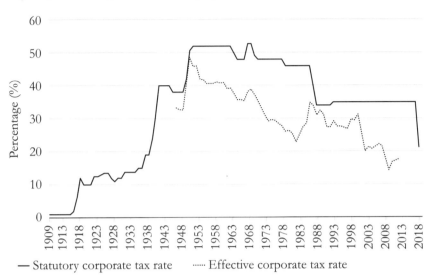

— Statutory corporate tax rate   ····· Effective corporate tax rate

leapfrogging each other in desperate attempts to prevent their tax base jumping ship.

Figure 9.1 shows how corporate taxes have varied in the US since their inception in 1894. Notice that the effective tax rate has invariably been below the official rate, as companies have arranged their affairs to minimise their actual tax liabilities through deductions and exemptions, as well as carefully choosing where their profits are booked. It is probably no coincidence that the great period of infrastructure spending by the USA in the 1940s to 1960s coincided with government coffers swelled by substantial tax revenues. Since then, the story has been one of steady erosion as companies have repeatedly nudged the political system in their favour. US taxes on corporations are now the lowest since before the Second World War.

Figure 9.2 (overleaf) shows how American corporate profits have rocketed since 1990 and the beginning of the dominance of

Figure 9.2: Declining tax on profits

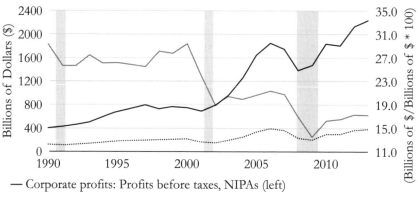

— Corporate profits: Profits before taxes, NIPAs (left)

···· Federal government: Tax receipts on corporate income (left)

— Federal government: Tax receipts on corporate income/
Corporate profits: Profits before taxes, NIPAs * 100 (right)

Shaded areas indicate U.S. recessions

free-market ideology. The absolute increase in tax revenue to the US government has been modest over the whole period and virtually non-existent since before the GFC. The government's take from corporate taxes in the US has fallen steeply from around 30 per cent of its total in the 1950s.[1]

After the Trump tax cuts, the Office of Management and Budget forecast that in the 2019 financial year, while income tax revenue would rise to $1.688 trillion, corporations would see their taxes decrease to $225 billion – only 7 per cent of the total, compared to about 15 per cent in 1978.[2] Meanwhile the budget deficit would increase by nearly half to $985 billion. All this assumes real growth of 3.2 per cent, a rate not achieved this side of the GFC and highly unlikely in a recovery now getting long in the tooth. Any shortfall in growth would make these figures look worse. Interest to be paid on the debt generated by cumulative deficits, including during the GFC, is estimated at $263 billion.

In the UK the main corporation tax rate has fallen from 52 per cent between 1973 and 1981 to 30 per cent in 2008 and 19 per cent in 2017. It is planned to decline to 17 per cent by 2020. According to the UK's Institute for Fiscal Studies,

> Cuts to corporation tax rates announced between 2010 and 2016 are estimated to reduce revenues by at least £16.5 billion a year in the short to medium run … In 2017–18 we were forecast to raise £53.2 billion from corporation tax. This represents 7.8 per cent of total tax receipts and 2.6 per cent of national income. This has fallen from the pre-recession high of 3.2 per cent of national income and is forecast to fall to 2.3 per cent by 2021–22 … Her Majesty's Revenue and Custom (HMRC)'s most recent estimates suggest that a 1 percentage point increase in corporation tax for all companies would raise £3.2 billion in 2020–21.

Putting this in perspective, this means a 3 per cent increase in corporation tax back to 22 per cent would generate revenue that would cover the net contribution of the UK to the EU of slightly under £10 billion per annum. An 11 per cent increase back to 2008 levels would pay for this plus the extra £20–£23 billion per annum pledged for the NHS by the government by 2023.

In contrast, income tax receipts increased from £151 billion in the fiscal year 2011/12 to £177 million in 2016/17. It is true that corporation tax revenue also rose during this period in spite of the rate cuts, but more modestly, from around £43 billion to around £49 billion, as profits rose rapidly, partly boosted by falls in the value of the pound after the Brexit referendum.

CHANGES IN TAX STRUCTURE

Data in the OECD annual *Revenue Statistics* shows that tax revenues as a percentage of GDP have continued to increase since the low point experienced in almost all countries in 2008 and 2009 as a result of the financial and economic crisis. The average tax-to-GDP ratio in OECD countries was 34.2 per cent in 2017 compared with 34.0 per cent in 2015 and 33.9 per cent in 2014. The 2017 figure is the highest recorded OECD average tax-to-GDP ratio since records began in 1965.[3] That year was the peak of the post-war economic golden era which lasted almost thirty years until the first oil crisis.

But the picture has not been uniform across developed countries. The UK has maintained a remarkably steady tax take of around 35 per cent of GDP, plus or minus a few percentage points, since 1965 (though it was only 10 per cent in 1900). In the late 1960s income tax rose, reaching 13.75 per cent of GDP by 1970 and then bobbing along for four decades between 12 and 14 per cent of GDP, peaking at 14.9 per cent in 2008.[4]

This stability is surprising in the face of the basic rate of income tax being cut from 35 per cent in 1976 to 20 per cent by 2007. At the same time the top rate of income tax was cut from 83 per cent in 1974 to 40 per cent in 1988 – it is currently 45 per cent. Was Laffer right after all, and cutting taxes actually pays for itself by stimulating growth? In fact, the figures are even better than Laffer predicted, since the tax take not only went up in absolute terms, but did not fall relative to GDP. However, the tax take has more likely held up due to a combination of reduced evasion and rising inequalities in income, which skews the take towards high earners who pay higher rates and whose share of total tax paid has shot up with their gross incomes.

Britain's richest 1 per cent now pay nearly three times as much, relatively, as they did in the high-tax 1970s, and over twice what the bottom 50 per cent of taxpayers hand over collectively. Similarly, the top 10 per cent of taxpayers pay 59 per cent of total income tax, compared to 35 per cent in 1976. This is remarkable given the falls in tax rates over the period, including for top earners. However, the fall in income tax rates for high earners since 1975 was partly offset by rises in their National Insurance contributions (a tax to fund benefits) from 5.5 to 12 per cent on earnings up to £50,000 (2019 tax year), whereas NI is zero for the income band below £8,632.[5] Complications also arise due to varying definitions of what counts as tax.

The Office of National Statistics (ONS) has reported that the average proportion of UK household income taken in direct taxation has generally fallen since 1977, declining from 21.4 per cent of gross income in 2007/8 to 18.8 per cent in 2014/15.[6] This measure includes National Insurance contributions and Council Tax, a local tax on domestic property.

The rising share of tax paid by high earners implies either that the rich's relative tax rates have fallen less than the poor's, which clearly is not the case, or that their pre-tax incomes have risen more, which we know to be true. According to the ONS paper, the Gini coefficient of *gross* income inequality in the UK was 50 in 2014/15, up from 42.9 in 1977 (the higher the number, the more unequal, 100 representing a state where one person has all the income and 0 is perfect equality). And after taxes and transfers, *disposable* income inequality increased over the period with the Gini coefficient rising from 27.2 to 32.6. In other words, even though the rich now contribute a higher share of the total income tax take than they did the 1970s, this increased redistribution has not closed the growing inequality gap by much at all. That's not surprising given what we know about the rich taking the lion's share of the rise in incomes (see Chapter 4).

What has also changed over the last four decades is the composition of the government's total tax take, as indirect taxes such as VAT and so-called stealth income taxes such as social security contributions have made up a larger proportion of revenue. Sales-related taxes such as VAT are clearly regressive, since they hit rich and poor equally, so the relative lightening of the income tax burden on lower earners has been partly countered by higher taxes elsewhere. Corporations have been the only clear winners.

In the US the skew is even sharper. In 2017 the share of reported income earned from the top 1 per cent of taxpayers fell slightly to 19.7 per cent in 2016, while their share of federal individual income taxes fell slightly to 37.3 per cent. In 2016 the top 50 per cent of taxpayers paid 97 per cent of all individual income taxes, while the bottom 50 per cent paid the remaining 3 per cent. The top 1 per cent paid a greater share of individual income taxes (37.3 per cent) than the bottom 90 per cent combined (30.5 per cent). The top 1 per cent of taxpayers paid an individual income tax rate of 26.9 per cent, which is more than seven times higher than the 3.7 per cent rate for taxpayers in the bottom 50 per cent.[7]

This suggests that the American tax system was, until the changes enacted by President Trump, more redistributive than the UK's, with the rich paying proportionately more. In fact the figures reflect the outsize gains in income share by the rich. Frank Samartino of the Tax Policy Center has reported, 'Much of the gain [between 1979 and 2013] in the top income share went to the top 1 per cent of the population. In 1979, they received 9 per cent of all income. By 2013, their share grew to 15 per cent, more than all the income received by the bottom 40 per cent'.[8]

In the US the tax system had become more progressive since the 1970s, with tax rates decreasing for lower-income groups. For high earners however, in contrast to the UK, tax rates remained steady at around 35 per cent. Nevertheless, the increasing progressivity of the tax system has not been enough to offset large pre-tax inequality. Samartino again: 'Because high-income people pay higher average tax rates than others, federal taxes reduce inequality. But the mitigating effect of taxes is about the same today as before 1980. Thus, after-tax income inequality has increased about as much as before-tax inequality. Taxes have not exacerbated increasing income inequality, but have not done much to offset it.'

This conclusion is important because it means that, in spite of a progressive tax system, the after-tax slice of the income pie taken home by lower earners went down. That is why they had to borrow. The rich also borrowed more, but had less need to do so and used the money to turbocharge their returns on investments, not for consumption.

WHAT ABOUT OTHER DEVELOPED COUNTRIES?

The OECD has reported that the share of total pre-tax income of the richest 1 per cent has increased in most OECD countries in the past three decades, particularly in some English-speaking countries, but also in some Nordic (from low levels) and southern European countries. This share ranges between 7 per cent in Denmark and the Netherlands up to almost 20 per cent in the US, and the increase is the result of the top 1 per cent capturing a disproportionate share of overall income growth over the past three decades. This explains why the majority of the population cannot reconcile aggregate income growth figures with the performance of their own incomes.[9]

In the US, Canada and the UK the bottom 90 per cent of the population captured only around 18 per cent, 34 per cent and 45 per cent respectively of the growth in total income from 1975 to 2007, compared to 90 per cent in Denmark. The top 1 per cent meanwhile, secured 47 per cent, 37 per cent and 25 per cent of the total income growth in those three English-speaking countries. Looking at it more broadly and more recently, the top 1 per cent in the US, Canada and western Europe captured 28 per cent of the total growth in incomes from 1980 to 2016, equal to the total growth in incomes of the bottom 81 per cent. Globally, the top 0.1 per cent of the population has captured as much income growth as the bottom 50 per cent over the period.[10]

Interestingly, countries such as France, Spain, Denmark, New Zealand and the Netherlands saw very little increase in income inequality as a result of rising shares taken by the top 1 per cent, with their top earners remaining well below 10 per cent of total incomes. This did not save Spain from suffering one of the worst crises from private individuals over-borrowing for property purchases in the run-up to the GFC. So the debt blow-outs were not exclusively an Anglo-Saxon phenomenon powered by the less well-off being forced to supplement their stagnant incomes through credit. The common denominator for all the disasters was the deregulation and encouragement of limitless finance. Spaniards went on a borrowing binge not because the middle class had been left behind, but simply because they could. Liberation from decades of repression under General Franco and the sudden drop in the cost of credit after joining the euro were simply too much to resist. The French, on the other hand, culturally closer to their conservative agrarian roots, never indulged in death by debt or a market free-for-all, and did not have much of a crisis.

AGGRESSIVE CORPORATE TAX AVOIDANCE

If the tax take from direct income taxes as a proportion of GDP has been under modest pressure over the last four decades, the fall in corporation tax take has been huge. Business has been so successful at gaming the system that the contribution to state coffers from the big economic winners of globalisation and the technology revolution – multinational corporations – has become derisory. This tightens the screws on state finances, which are at the same time under structural pressure from ageing populations and high debt levels.

At another level, the globalised economy has undermined the nation state as a political unit that can decide and control its destiny. In the UK, the Brexiters' brilliant slogan 'Take back control' touched a raw nerve in a population that senses how impotent their elected leaders have become in dealing with their primary concerns, one of which (for some) is the belief that the EU is a corrupt conspiracy to benefit big business.

The Brexit vote in the UK and the rise of populist anti-EU establishment parties in Austria, Hungary, Italy and even Germany has finally galvanised European attempts to roll back elaborate tax avoidance schemes constructed by corporations. Not only has the minimal tax paid by corporations making billions of euros of profits in the EU contributed to the budgetary problems of many countries, but the issue has also highlighted egregiously greedy pay rises financed by profits turbocharged by falling tax bills awarded to top company executives.

Take the case of McDonald's. Leaked documents from auditor PwC showed how this multinational corporation was able to reduce its tax bill by channelling revenue through Luxembourg. McDonald's set up an intellectual property company in Luxembourg in 2009 and moved its corporate headquarters for Europe from London to Geneva. This was just a year after Luxembourg introduced a generous corporate tax rate of 5.8 per cent on income generated from intellectual property. According to a report by the charity War on Want, between 2009 and 2013 McDonald's paid tax of €16 million on 'royalties' (sales) of €3.7 billion from its close-to-8,000 European outlets, but in 2013 it paid tax of only €3.3 million.[11]

The revelations forced the European Commission to investigate whether Luxembourg had engaged in a form of illegal state aid to McDonald's – and others such as Amazon – and to question similar set-ups in Ireland involving Apple, and Starbucks in the

Netherlands. As a result, the French government was rumoured to have sent a tax bill plus fines for unpaid taxes totalling €300 million to McDonald's France in a crackdown on aggressive tax structuring and avoidance.

This was not a one-off. Amazon benefited from a deal negotiated with Luxembourg in 2003, enabling it to transfer a large part of its European profits to a Luxembourg holding company that was not taxable. In October 2017 the European Commission ruled that Luxembourg had given Amazon €250 million in undue tax benefits. 'Luxembourg gave illegal tax benefits to Amazon. As a result, almost three quarters of Amazon's profits were not taxed,' Competition Commissioner Margrethe Vestager said, and ordered Amazon to pay the back taxes due.[12]

Google's arrangements have also come under pressure. Its total UK sales in 2016/17 amounted to £5.7 billion, but according to Google's accounts it earned revenue in the UK of only £1.27 billion between June 2016 and June 2017 and will pay £49.3 million in tax on £202 million of declared profits.[13] How does this work? Simple. First, it only 'makes a profit' on a small proportion of its sales outside the US because the software engineering is created in America. Second, it has set up its European headquarters in Ireland, where tax rates are much lower than in the UK. Google UK operates as a marketing and sales arm of the operation in Dublin, paying a substantial 'administration fee' to its European parent to operate across Britain. After that, there isn't much left to tax in the UK even though that's where a lot of the actual turnover is. News Corporation chief Rupert Murdoch once acidly tweeted, 'Tech tax breaks facilitated by politicians awed by [Silicon] Valley ambassadors like Google chairman Schmidt e.g., posh boys in Downing Street.'

US tech companies benefit from a tax structure and regime that was devised for another era. Taxing physical products as they crossed borders was easy and straightforward, even if the design and technology came from elsewhere, but governments have essentially allowed the Internet to become a tax-free zone. The big Internet tech companies either claim their 'production' takes place in a low-tax country such as Ireland or Luxembourg, or else is completely absent from any jurisdiction, as in the case of Apple, probably the most aggressive tax avoider of them all. That said, Mondelez International, owner of Cadbury, was revealed a few years ago to be paying no UK corporate tax at all. It is hard to claim that chocolate bars are immaterial goods whose value added is created in some offshore tax paradise.

Apple has a manufacturing and services plant in Cork, Ireland, employing around 6,000 people. It claims that 'substantially all' of its non-US international earnings are generated by its Irish subsidiaries. These amounted to $54.4 billion for the tax year to September 2013. While Ireland's low corporate tax rate of 12.5 per cent has attracted a lot of foreign direct investment, Apple has managed to pay even less than this. More recently, the company indicates the sales recorded by its operations in Hollyhill Industrial Estate, Cork, are in the region of $137.9 billion (€119.2 billion) per year.[14]

In 2017 the *Irish Times* reported that Apple had 'paid Irish corporation tax of $1.5 billion in the three years 2014 to 2016. This equates to approximately $500 million per year.'[15] How was this magic achieved? US Congressional investigators revealed a few years earlier that Apple had created offshore entities holding tens of billions of dollars while claiming to be tax resident nowhere. This included the creation of non-tax-resident subsidiaries in Ireland, through which the bulk of its profits were funnelled. The investigators found that Apple cut a deal with Ireland to apply a tax rate of less than 2 per cent, well below the 12.5 per cent Irish corporate tax rate.[16]

This is the most extreme example of a race to the bottom by

Western governments competing for globalised business where the multinationals can play one jurisdiction off against another. Not only are Western countries desperate to generate or hang on to jobs, they are also conscious that they are playing a negative sum game at best, where one's capture of a company's HQ for tax purposes is another's loss, even if success depends on further reducing a country's tax take. Despite winning the race for Apple, Ireland was forced to go cap in hand to the International Monetary Fund and its EU partners (taxpayers) for a bail-out when its banking system imploded during the GFC. It received €67.5 billion to plug the hole in its finances that, partly because of its low-tax regime, it could not take care of itself.

In 2014 Minister for Finance Michael Noonan changed Ireland's tax rules so that all of a corporation's annual profits could be written off using capital allowances. Up to then, only 80 per cent of each year's profits could be sheltered from tax in this way. Despite being invited to do so, Apple did not respond to speculation that Apple Operations Europe, tax-resident in Ireland, may have spent tens of billions of euros, and possibly well in excess of €100 billion, on intellectual property which it brought from Apple subsidiaries now based in zero-taxed Jersey. Because the 80 per cent cap had been removed, that expenditure could be used to completely write off the liability to pay tax on profits booked by Apple Operations Europe.

The European Commission then said Apple should pay €13 billion, plus interest, to Ireland on the untaxed income earned by the Irish-incorporated Apple subsidiaries that were, for a period of years, stateless for tax purposes. In 2016 Apple was ordered to pay Ireland the record-breaking sum after a ruling by the European Commission concluded that the country granted undue tax benefits to Apple.[17] This was finally handed over in 2018. The European Commission's decision sets EU law and establishes that any tax ruling allocating profits to a non-existent entity is a form of illegal state aid. Secret tax rulings by the Irish are clearly not consistent with a level playing field under EU law.

John Plender draws a parallel between the aristocrats of pre-revolutionary France, who were exempt from direct taxation, and today's large multinationals, perhaps implying a coming revolution unless privilege is reined back.

> In the early 1950s the US corporate income tax take reached 5.9 per cent of gross domestic product ... By 2013 the corporate tax take was down to 1.6 per cent of GDP. Despite a high headline tax rate, a multiplicity of tax breaks born of corporate lobbying, together with offshore avoidance schemes, wrong-footed the supposedly predatory state.
>
> In the EU the decline has been less striking. Corporate income tax revenues went from more than 3 per cent in 2000 to about 2.5 per cent in 2012, with a notably steeper decline in the UK than in Germany, France and Italy.[18]

In the UK corporate tax raised around 8 per cent of total tax take, less than the OECD average of 9 per cent.[19]

According to Plender, this decline is 'clearly unhelpful' at a time when public-sector debt in much of the developed world has risen to unsustainable levels.

> Smaller companies, which innovate and create jobs, carry an unfair share of the tax burden as they are less global and may lack the pricing power to pass on the cost of corporate tax to their customers ... to create a more robust economic recovery it would make sense in many countries to shift income from companies to households to encourage consumption ... The conclusion must be that the global corporate aristocracy will be promoting under consumption around the world for quite

a while yet – without having to fear the fiscal equivalent of the guillotine.[20]

Unfortunately prescient words given Trump's December 2017 tax changes in the US, which cut the headline top corporate tax rate from 35 to 21 per cent, to which we will return below. And although there is some discussion in Europe about reforming the corporate tax system to one based on where the revenues are generated, progress is very hesitant given the lack of consensus between countries and the need for global implementation.

The favourable tax treatment of corporations is perverse. Pascal Saint-Amans, a top OECD tax official, has remarked, 'the great majority of all tax rises seen since the crisis have fallen on individuals. This underlies the urgency to ensure that corporations pay their fair share.' Even if aggressive tax planning by companies is legal, it is hard to defend when times are hard lower down the food chain. No wonder disenchantment with the system is palpable, with the concomitant rise of populism as a political force.

On corporate tax, even the *FT* used a March 2018 leader column to remark that 'governments are trapped in a race to the bottom'. The problem is exacerbated by technology transforming economic value into more mobile and intangible forms such as software and intellectual property: 'there always seems to be another country ready to undercut whoever is offering companies the sweetest deal. The result is a steady erosion of tax rates on multinational companies at a time when revenue strapped governments are committed to austerity … or running historic deficits … or both.'[21] Companies have partly broken free of the tax regimes of nation states, with perverse consequences: 'In the ten years since the financial crisis, the reported effective tax rates at the ten biggest [UK] public companies in nine sectors fell 9 per cent (over the same period, tax rates for individuals have risen, on average). The situation is not sustainable in the long run.'

THE AGENCY PROBLEM 2: COMPANY EXECUTIVES

Perhaps things would be less serious if the increasing share of national income enjoyed by large corporations were put to good use, but regrettably much of it simply piles up as cash hoards. Governance is also a problem in the Anglosphere, with boardrooms, as we saw in Chapters 3 and 4, increasingly forgoing investment opportunities in favour of short-term earnings. Less investment leads to higher corporate savings in the form of retained profits.

Top executives have learned to game the system by creating financial reward formulae for themselves in the form of bonuses and long-term incentive plans (LTIPs) tied to growth in their companies' earnings per share and share price. Both of these rise if less income from sales is recycled into investment such as capital expenditure in new factories or developing the skills of the workforce.

In Chapter 7 we considered one of the central problems ailing our democracies: the conflicts of interest inherent in a system of representative government. From the moment the people delegate power and authority to a body of representatives, there is a risk that the representatives will prioritise the pursuit of their careers and interests at the expense of the common good. In the UK the most flagrant example of this in recent times has been around the issue of Brexit, with politicians of both major parties attempting to safeguard their careers by refusing to take principled positions in line with their personal convictions for fear of losing their seats at the next election. Although over 60 per cent of parliamentary constituencies voted to leave the EU even though only 51.9 per cent of the popular vote was for Brexit, most members of parliament were in favour of remaining in the EU. However, a large majority of MPs voted to leave the EU after the referendum, under cover of honouring the (advisory) referendum result, despite many of them privately believing it is against the interests of the UK.

The second big conflict of interest eating away at Western society is between those who run and those who own public companies. Public limited liability companies are organised such that their owners (shareholders) elect boards of directors who have responsibility for the appointment of professional managers to run the companies.

Similar to the inherent conflict of interest which exists between elected political representatives and their electors, company executives have career interests that are by definition more short term than those of their shareholders; a company is supposed to outlast many generations of executives. However, executives whose remuneration is linked to profits and share price typically over three- to five-year horizons, also have the ability to boost these metrics in the short term, even if so doing weakens the competitive position of their company in the long run. Larry Fink, the head of Blackrock, the largest asset manager in the world, has accused America's business leaders of eating their own seed corn. In a letter to S&P 500 CEOs he warned that their obsession with short termism would come at the expense of the future.

The classic method by which executives can massage up short-term profits, and so share prices, is by skimping on the reinvestment of profits and distributing more to shareholders to increase yield and short-term returns. They can use profits or issue new debt to buy back their company's own shares, or leverage up the company to acquire other companies and cut combined costs, thus raising return (profits) on equity. Never mind that increasing company debt to boost share prices can place the business under stress if interest rates start to rise.

Journalist and commentator Edward Luce wrote back in 2015 that instead of companies raising money in the stock market to finance future growth, the exact reverse is happening:

> Share buy-backs have been rising as a share of company profits for more than 30 years. Last year, the S&P 500 companies [the largest in America], spent 95 per cent of their operating margins on their own shares or in dividend payouts ... Between 2004 and 2013, IBM spent $116 billion in buy-backs, which accounted for 92 per cent of its profits, according to a Brookings paper ... Doubtless General Electric, which recently announced it would sell off its non-industrial businesses, will also be able to buy some goodwill ... its disposals will in the first instance help fund a $50 billion share buy-back.

Luce continued: 'With actions that can deliver immediate returns to shareholders ... while underinvesting in innovation, skilled workforces or essential capital expenditures necessary to sustain long term growth, why invest in your employees' skills when you can boost your earnings now?'[22]

What has happened to these companies since then? From April 2015 to 30 July 2019, IBM's share price fell from $173.62 to $150.88, during which time the S&P 500 index, representing the market, rose from 2108 to 3020. Meanwhile GE is in deep trouble, shocking the market with the rapid collapse of its profits. The share price has more than halved from around $27 at the time of Luce's 2015 article to around $10 in July 2019. This did not prevent CEO Jeff Immelt from earning $18 million in 2016, and although his pay for the last seven months of 2017 was only $5 million according to the narrow definition used by GE, he actually amassed $29.3 million, including payouts on long-term incentive plans in the form of shares, in a case study of out-of-control and undeserved executive compensation and reward for failure.[23] Among the more egregious excesses that Mr Immelt indulged in was the use of *two* business jets. GE subsequently conducted an internal review to ascertain why a spare jet accompanied its former CEO on his travels, and why no one on the board knew anything about it.[24]

As if all this wasn't enough, executives have learned to game the system by stuffing their own companies' remuneration committees with friendly executives from other companies, following the dictum 'You scratch my back and I'll scratch yours.' Companies often employ 'independent' remuneration consultants to advise them of the going rate, but this simply adds another layer to the agency problem. Rather like estate agents, who tend to outbid rivals' estimates of a property's value in order to secure the seller's mandate, consultants have an incentive to suggest overgenerous remuneration packages when they pitch for the business. Even more outrageously, consultants tend to guide their clients towards paying better than 'the average' in order to attract top talent to the company. So there ensues a game of leapfrog as each company ratchets up its top executives' pay at regular intervals in order to remain competitive, adding further impetus to the upward spiral of top executive rewards.

A few years ago, Barclays chief executive Antony Jenkins decided to boost bonuses 10 per cent in spite of falling profits and 12,000 job cuts. Even the normally pro-business Institute of Directors questioned how he could justify an executive bonus pool 'nearly three times bigger than the total dividend payout to the company's owners'. In response, Mr Jenkins said, 'We employ people from Singapore to San Francisco and need the best people in the bank to drive sustained returns to shareholders.' Over the next four years, Barclays' share price tumbled 20 per cent from around £2.50 to around £2, while the FTSE 100 index rose 15 per cent.

Measures taken by UK Business Secretary Vince Cable in 2012 gave shareholders binding votes on top executive pay, but these have thus far had little effect because of a third agency problem:

most shares are owned by institutions such as pension funds and asset managers on behalf of thousands of individuals. This bumps up against the same problem found in representative government: how to know what thousands of disparate individuals want or is in their best interests. Furthermore, an institution has little incentive to rock the corporate boat, especially if another part of the institution is doing business with the company on whose pay structure it is being asked to vote on behalf of shareholders.

According to a 2015 report by the UK's High Pay Centre, long-term incentive plans for executives should be scrapped and performance bonuses paid in cash, not shares – diminishing the incentive to manipulate share prices higher through short-term policies. According to the report, performance pay has been behind the rise in executive bonus payments between 2000 and 2013 at twice the rate of the increase of company earnings per share (returns to shareholders) and company profits. Executives have done far better than the shareholders they supposedly serve in another example of the incentivised few exploiting the passivity of the unmotivated many.[25] More recently, in a report responding to an inquiry into executive pay, the High Pay Centre wrote,

> there are still very few companies who align their bonuses with broader corporate responsibilities (relating to their social or environmental impact, for example), as opposed to financial or operational metrics. Vast Long-Term Incentive Payments (LTIPs) are still the prevailing method for paying executives, despite the growing evidence that performance-related executive pay is not particularly effective and that much smaller 'restricted share' awards would be a better form of reward.[26]

The HPC also argued that remuneration committees and

institutional investors are failing to hold companies to account over their pay practices, and recommended a greater say for workers in the pay-setting process.

With company shareholders largely passive, having delegated their rights to professional money managers and savings institutions, managers are free to run companies primarily for their own benefit on a time horizon coinciding with their career at the top, at the cost of employee remuneration and skills and the impoverishment of the public domain through the relentless pursuit of lower taxes. But companies will fail if their customers are subject to poverty, violence, job insecurity, hopelessness and wage stagnation. Unless the small band of corporate titans that have skimmed off the cream realise this very soon, it is increasingly likely that they will end up living behind high-security fences.

Everyone over the age of fifty in the West, with perhaps the exception of those living in countries that recently joined the EU, has witnessed the degradation in education and health services, transport infrastructure and policing over the last thirty years, as governments have lost corporate tax revenue. However, the capture of the political system by the wealthy and corporate interests may turn out to be a pyrrhic victory, as the impoverishment of workers and the state threaten its overthrow.

DEGRADATION OF PUBLIC SERVICES

How can we explain the perceived degradation in our public services and transport infrastructure? Answers include an ageing population demanding more expensive healthcare, large-scale net immigration not matched by a concomitant expansion in schools and hospitals, and the continuing effects of the GFC catastrophe, which holed public finances for over a decade. Japan has been an unfortunate leader in this area; it is still struggling to cope with its public debt a generation after the implosions of the 1980s.

As we saw in Chapter 6, many governments were guilty of gross negligence in letting financial bubbles inflate to the extent that their inevitable bursting destroyed the ability of states to maintain public goods and the social cohesion on which liberal democracy is built. This was due to the conflict of interest between the governed (long term) and governments happy to take in tax revenues in the short term from hot asset markets (property and finance profits), new immigrants and economic activity turbocharged by credit, but reluctant to reinvest them in new schools, hospitals, teachers, doctors and policemen or on maintaining roads and bridges.

Once the bubbles burst, government deficits ballooned as revenue fell, expenditure rose and financial companies had to be bailed out. Public debt levels soared to levels not seen since the Second World War. With growth weak, budgets had to be tightened and expenditure that could be postponed was cut.

In the UK the axe fell nearly everywhere, including on local government. Parliamentary watchdog the National Audit Office (NAO) has blamed years of cuts for putting local council finances in a perilous position, estimating that, as part of its efforts to balance the books since the financial crisis, Whitehall slashed funding for local authorities by 49 per cent in real terms between 2010/11 and 2017/18. This coincided with growing demand for public services: the number of households assessed as homeless and entitled to temporary accommodation rose by 60 per cent in the same period.[27] Spending on care for older people in England declined in real terms from £8.45 billion in 2005/06 to £8.34 billion in 2015/16, while the over-65 population grew from 8.03 million to 9.71 million.[28]

Cuts to the level of public services have been made everywhere, from less road maintenance, with a network that is now decidedly no longer worthy of a first world country, to the closure of libraries.

EDUCATION

Perhaps surprisingly, the UK scored relatively well in terms of education expenditure until recently, with an increase in government spending per full-time primary and secondary student of 36 per cent from 2005 to 2014. This is better than Germany (+33 per cent) and France (+17 per cent) and far better than the US, Italy and Spain, which registered zero real growth in spending over the period.[29] However, while schools were prioritised, universities were sacrificed as the government opted to make students pay for their tuition, which had been free up until 1998.

The picture has deteriorated since 2015. In the UK, while real spending per pupil rose for several decades, David Cameron froze budgets in 2015. The Institute for Fiscal Studies (IFS) warned that this would result in a real-terms cut in school spending per pupil due to inflation and the rising cost of wages, pensions and National Insurance contributions, and the National Audit Office estimated that schools would have to make cuts of £3 billion.[30] In its updated 2018 report on education in England, the IFS confirmed that total school spending per pupil fell by 8 per cent in real terms between 2009/10 and 2017/18.[31]

What does this mean in practical terms? A report by the Education Policy Institute think tank calculates that the cuts from 2017 to 2020 will result in 'the loss of almost two teachers in an average primary school and six in an average secondary school'.[32] Anecdotal evidence of schools unable to make ends meet is surfacing, with cases of parents being asked to pay for books or help out with lunch supervision because of staff shortages.

At the university level, the state can no longer afford to pay guaranteed pension benefits to staff. A 2018 proposal to replace this regime with a less favourable scheme under which the amount of pension received is dependent on how much an employee saves (guaranteed contribution), understandably sparked strike action.

The proposal was dropped. The latest plans by the state were presented after the Universities' Superannuation Scheme (retirement fund) asked for an extra £500 million a year in contributions from both universities and employees because of a multi-billion-pound funding hole.

On the global level, the OECD, in a 2017 report, noted that the real salaries of teachers had fallen in one third of the countries for which it had data between 2005 and 2015, and by 10 per cent in the UK, and remain low compared to those of similarly educated employees in other professions.[33] Consequently, teaching is becoming increasingly unattractive to the educated young, and the average age of the teaching profession is moving up.

In a brutally competitive globalised world, the last thing countries should be doing is skimping on their investment in education, which will arm future generations with the ability to compete. In contrast to countries like China, who have understood that education is the path to self-improvement, the West's short termism is again undermining its future.

POLICING AND CRIME

Under pressure from general lack of funds and the diversion of resources in order to contain a constant terrorist threat (itself due to dysfunctional international politics), policing has retreated in the UK. Criminals have been quick to spot this. As police numbers have been cut, so crime has gone up; the police are swamped with cases and have had to manage their shrunken resources by abandoning the investigation of many crimes: Scotland Yard has said that crimes like shoplifting and criminal damage may not be investigated in London because it is 'not practical' to do so. In the four years from 2013 to 2017 London's Metropolitan Police, the largest force in the UK, has had to make £600 million of savings and is due to lose an extra £400 million by 2020. Meanwhile, the number of recorded offences has increased, with violent crime rising by 63 per cent since May 2013 and gun crime increasing by 54 per cent in the past two years.[34]

Figures obtained by the Labour Party from the House of Commons library show that over the past six years the percentage of homicides that led to charges fell from 92 to 56 per cent. During that period, firearm offences that went to court halved to 36 per cent while robberies resulting in charges fell from 935 to 135. Soon after, in an open invitation to people to help themselves from retailers' shelves, the BBC reported that shoplifters taking under £200 worth of goods would not be pursued.[35] The Metropolitan Police commissioner has said she is 'sure' cuts to her force's budget have contributed to a rise in violent crime in the capital, a rise that is particularly marked among young people.[36]

Nequela Whittaker used to be a gang leader in south London; now she's a youth worker.

> Young people don't feel like they fit in with society and there doesn't seem to be a voice for young people so at the moment there's a bit of carnage ... Due to spending cuts there has been less policing, community centres are closing. There's been no money directed at the third sector for a while and with all these cuts and reductions we've got more young people falling out on to the streets. Young males are coming from homes with no fathers, no male role models. Many are lacking love.[37]

Rising violent crime is not peculiar to the UK. In France a January 2018 report by the Interior Ministry recorded four years of growth in violent crime up to 2017, representing a ten-year high. Unsurprisingly, such reports translate into huge insecurity. One in five people between the ages of eighteen and seventy-five reported feeling insecure in their home, their neighbourhood or their village.

Three out of ten people said they had been victims or witnesses to crime in their vicinity every year.[38]

England and France share a huge demographic problem on top of the more general Western issues of the impact on employment of globalisation and technology. Both countries have a large underclass with low skills, no culture of valuing education, whose future appears hopeless, who feel alienated and rejected by mainstream society. This problem will only get worse as job prospects shrink and the sheer number of dispossessed rises. Short of erecting high-security border fences, nothing (including Brexit) will staunch the flow of desperate people from the increasingly dysfunctional regions of Africa and the Middle East. Britain and France, both ex-colonial powers, have been too busy firefighting their internal problems to summon the vision and energy to deal with the root cause of the unrelenting conveyor belt of migrants desperate to escape poverty and death in their home countries.

As for the USA, its crime rate, especially its violent crime rate, is in a different league, partly due to American demographics, inequality and racial issues, and partly due to the successful lobbying of politicians of the National Rifle Association against gun control.

Meanwhile our current crop of political leaders has shown itself unequal to these challenges. The state is in danger of surrendering, opening the ultimate prospect of citizens taking the law and their security into their own hands by organising local militias. It is then a short step to society disintegrating into tribes with their associated territories.

We need to pull the emergency cord. Politicians need to acknowledge that the descent into anarchy cannot continue. A deep structural change in how our economies work is needed to restore some sort of balance between the wealthy globalised elite and those desperately treading water to stay alive under a system that ignores their plight. That means taxing the wealthy and diverting huge resources to education and social services, and establishing a guaranteed and decent living wage for the bottom half of society. Recent promises of big spending boosts to public services in the heat of electoral battles may, if realised, act as a necessary short-term palliative but are not sufficient to address the underlying causes of our plight

A few of the winners recognise this. Richard Branson, successful British entrepreneur and founder of the Virgin Group, weighed in on this at the Michael Milken Summit in Abu Dhabi in February 2019: 'I don't think we should throw out capitalism. But for those of us who are fortunate to have made wealth, we have a responsibility to throw that out there and tackle some of the great problems. If we don't do that, then we deserve to have very heavy taxes levelled on us.' Billionaire hedge fund veteran Ray Dalio told a panel at Davos in January 2019, 'Capitalism is basically not working for the majority of people. That's just the reality.' He said that if he were president, 'I think that you have to call that a national emergency.'

HEALTH

In spite of attempts by UK government to ring-fence the National Health Service from public spending cuts since the GFC, the experience of users has deteriorated for years with the average wait to obtain an in-hours GP appointment climbing to around two weeks.[39] Siva Anandaciva of the King's Fund charity is clear that the annual NHS budget increase of 1.1 per cent per year in real terms from 2009/10 to 2020/21 is too small to cope with the increasing demands of a larger population that is also ageing.[40]

The number of full-time-equivalent GPs (excluding locums) has been falling since 2015. After growing by 6.2 per cent between September 2010 and September 2014, the number subsequently declined by 4.9 per cent between September 2015 and June 2018 to 32,370. This is despite the government's commitment to a net increase of 5,000 GPs by 2020 (compared with 2015 figures). However, *Pulse*, a magazine on primary care, found in its annual vacancy survey in 2019 that 15.3 per cent of GP posts were vacant, compared with 11.7 per cent in 2016.[41]

Meanwhile, the morale of existing staff is low. Between 2010 and 2017 the GP Worklife Survey reported a rise in all the stress factors it surveyed and a 13 per cent drop in overall job satisfaction. The factors cited as causing the most stress were increasing workloads, insufficient time to perform work and paperwork. 'Hours of work' had the lowest mean satisfaction rating: 3.57 on a scale of 1 (lowest) to 7 (highest) – down from 4.39 in 2010.[42]

Of course, the UK health system is peculiar in being absolutely free to all, but inadequate resources results in the rationing of services, queues and long waiting times to obtain appointments or treatment. The reluctance of British politicians to tell the electorate that to fund the NHS adequately and deliver the high level of service it expects requires higher taxes is short-sighted as dissatisfaction only grows with the deterioration in service.

In the US, health spending is far higher, partly due to drug prices and partly due to the fact that healthcare is largely run as a profit-making industry.[43] Individuals need to insure themselves and then pay for treatment, making claims on their insurers. Obamacare was an attempt to cover those sections of the population that could not or would not afford the insurance needed for their health needs. So far it has resisted attacks by the Trump administration. In spite of the USA having some of the most advanced medical facilities in the world, American life expectancy, at 78.9 years, trails its peers such as France (82.6 years), the UK and Germany, both on 81.3 years, and longevity champion Japan (84.6 years). Whether the US system is value for money is open to debate.[44]

With very few exceptions, real growth in health spending per person across OECD countries has dropped since the financial crisis.[45] With the rising cost of drugs, treatment and equipment, and ageing populations, the level of service to large sections of the less well off in many developed countries, who do not have access to private medical treatment, is perceived to have fallen. While the US drop in healthcare growth has been less than for its peers, this is probably due to the one-off introduction of greater insurance coverage from Obamacare.

In France, a country that was proud of its high-quality public hospitals, times are also tough.[46] France has introduced the market to its hospitals but cut the rates at which it reimburses them for medical procedures such as operations, pushing them to increase the number of procedures they carry out, more quickly, with the same staff, to meet their revenue targets and break even. In spite of such measures, French public hospitals ran a deficit of €1 billion in 2017 in another example of the misguided substitution of the market for what should be a public service not subject to the pressures of profit and loss accounts and their consequences.

INFRASTRUCTURE

Perhaps one of presidential candidate Trump's more accurate diagnoses of what ails America was the decades of neglect of its physical infrastructure: crumbling roads, airports, sewers, tunnels and bridges. In 2017 real government infrastructure spending as a percentage of US GDP hit its lowest level since 1956.[47] This is a consequence of the dominance of free market ideology, which equates all government spending with harmful interference in the workings of that perfect economic mechanism, the market.

Even the richest countries less directly affected by the GFC have cut corners when it comes to public infrastructure maintenance. In Germany many roads and bridges are in disrepair. The authorities were obliged to close several bridges across the Rhine in 2017, such as those at Leverkusen and Neuenkamp, due to the appearance of cracks. For Henrik Enderlein of the Hertie School of Governance in Berlin, Germany has focused too much on balancing its budget and reducing its deficit and not enough on investment. Statistics show that public investment as a percentage of GDP fell from nearly 5 per cent in 1970 to an all-time low of 1.9 per cent in 2005.[48] Today the government insists public investment is rising but admits that the extra funds made available to local authorities have not triggered much new investment; rather they have been used to 'reduce budgetary deficits and build up surpluses'.[49]

Marcel Fratzscher, head of the in Berlin think tank DIW, says, 'when times are tough and unemployment and social spending go up, regional governments have found that investment is the easiest thing to cut. When the economy does better, Germans prefer to give ourselves a treat rather than invest.' Public attitudes also need to change. 'Politicians are unlikely to get elected by promising to invest in a bridge that might collapse in 30 years if left unattended, says Mr Hover, [a director of a transport lobby group]. For most people, such time horizons are like science fiction.'

This brings us back to one of the root causes of the West's present dysfunctional politics. In the competition for power between professional politicians, there is no reason to suppose that the electorate will vote for socially optimal outcomes, even leaving aside the problems of defining what that is. This is because politicians seeking their own interest will succumb to pressure to offer a more attractive and painless menu of policies to an electorate that does not have the time to research the issues and trade-offs.

Putting it the other way round, maybe there is not such a big conflict of interest between voters and elected representatives after all. If voters have become more selfish, impatient, demanding instant gratification even if it means more pain later, politicians have simply adapted to the new mindset of their electorate and sought to deliver policy accordingly. Our representatives have become as short term in their policy horizons as we are. As the depressing saying goes, people get the governments they deserve, although in Germany this means governments which maintain a structural budget surplus. Stressing bipartisan resistance to increasing public expenditure, then German economics minister Sigmar Gabriel quipped, 'In Germany there is the well-known saying that for the Germans the desire to save on taxes is stronger than the desire to have sex.'[50] However, there are signs that this consensus is collapsing. In 2016

> an opinion poll by the broadcaster ARD showed that a clear majority of the German public wanted the surplus spent on infrastructure rather than used to fund tax cuts or reduce debt … Physical infrastructure in much of the country … is ageing … Germany is also well behind in digital infrastructure, including broadband coverage, hampering the economy's ability to diversify from its traditional manufacturing base into services.[51]

PRESIDENT TRUMP DONATES TO THOSE ALREADY FLUSH WITH CASH

Germany's fiscal hawks only oppose more government spending when the economy is growing, of course. This is in stark contrast to America, where the normally fiscally conservative Republican Party, in a reprise of the Reagan era, was happy to put aside its qualms to pass Trump's massive tax cut programme just when unemployment and slack in the economy was at its lowest for years.

In a hard-hitting article just before the passage of Trump's $1.5 trillion tax cuts for corporations and the wealthy, financier Michael Moritz of Sequoia Capital quoted evidence that suggests that such cuts do not encourage higher investment in America.[52] For example, the top twenty American technology companies spent almost $52 billion on stock buy-backs and $39 billion on dividends to shareholders, compared to $55 billion on investment in the first nine months of 2017. It's not as if there's a cash shortage preventing investment. As Moritz remarked,

> The technology companies would be more likely to increase their long-term investments if consumers had a lot more to spend on pick-up trucks, smartphones, fridges, washing machines and streaming video services – the sorts of items that these days include lots of semiconductor chips and software – than through receiving a tax cut from the Republican administration in Washington … The guaranteed beneficiaries of the corporate tax cuts will be people like me, the shareholders in many of these companies …
>
> This is a tax plan conjured up by people who have spent their lives lining their wallets at the expense of the 'hard working Americans' they so piously claim to protect … Instead of stiffing the banks – as was his past practice – [Trump] is now stiffing the generations who will be left to deal with the consequences of this tax plan.

Given he's a successful financier, it's hard to dismiss Moritz's diatribe against Trump; he's hardly an anti-capitalist, anti-American leftie. Neither is he alone among his mega-wealthy peers. Ray Dalio, founder of the world's largest hedge fund, Bridgewater Associates, wrote in a December 2017 blog that the Trump tax cuts, 'By and large [don't] deal with the impediments that are holding back investment and productivity in the US economy.'

While some large corporations were quick to trumpet pay awards to employees following the passage of the tax cuts, these appeared to be more symbolic than significant. Wells Fargo boosted its minimum wage from $13.50 to $15.00 an hour, while Fifth Third

Bank did the same and added a $1,000 bonus for each of its 13,500 employees. Meanwhile, Boeing announced an extra $300 million of investment.[53] However, this came after it had announced a record programme to buy back $18 billion of its own shares.

It seems likely that many of those who voted Trump into power are benefiting the least from his tax policy. By 2022, the bottom 80 per cent of US earners will receive tax cuts of between 0.9 and 1.7 per cent of income, while the top 1 per cent will enjoy a 2.9 per cent reduction.[54] Moreover, the income tax cuts are due to expire in 2025, but the cuts for corporations (and their shareholders) are permanent.

This is obviously storing up trouble for the future, both economically and socially. Trump's decision to ramp up the budget deficit and so public debt after nine years of economic expansion means there will be nothing left in the tank when the next downturn occurs. Unlike the massive government expenditure and bail-outs of 2009 that helped avert a depression, the public accounts will already be stretched, having not recovered from the previous crisis and the consequences of the tax cuts. That means the only source of emergency funds to prop up the economy during the next recession will be the Fed. The US central bank may have to print even larger amounts of money than last time to finance emergency government expenditure.

Western states are caught in a downward spiral of tax structures that favour corporations over cash-strapped individuals and declining funds for education, security and infrastructure due to a weakening revenue base arising from globalisation. This is degrading their ability to compete and mortgages their future. Populations are waking up to the decline, even if their politicians are mostly still in denial. Like him or loathe him, President Trump is the exception on the trade front. His long-overdue attack on a world trading system that serves the short-term interests of the financial and corporate elite by boosting profits from shifting production to low-cost countries to the detriment of their employees is the first attempt by a Western leader to stop the rot. Whether he is serious enough to succeed remains to be seen. What Trump is not addressing, however (as we have seen, quite the reverse), is the cancer of record inequality in his country.

His popular base elected him in the belief that, as a Washington outsider, Trump would 'drain the swamp', and they would finally recover some of the lost ground of the past decades. The omens do not look promising. Disillusionment is likely to set in as unsustainable policies benefiting the wealthy and the temporary high in the stock market from the tax cuts fail to tackle the root causes of rising popular discontent with the political system. A CNN poll in the week of 21 December 2017 showed that two thirds of Americans thought the tax cuts did more to help the rich than the middle class, evidence that you can't fool all of the people all of the time. In a summer 2018 Gallup poll 51 per cent of Americans between eighteen and twenty-nine said they believed in socialism, while 45 per cent said they supported capitalism. This is unheard of in capitalist America.

BREAKING SYSTEM

Academics Leon Grunberg and Sarah Moore interviewed Boeing employees anonymously over twenty years and in 2010 published their findings, tracking how an engineering-led family business with a strong tradition of employee welfare has morphed into an aggressive, cost-cutting, finance-driven corporation chasing shareholder value and ramping up executive remuneration. Boeing has relocated parts of its production to cheaper countries and treated its workers like disposable commodities. Grunberg and Moore show how the changes at Boeing have contributed to the hollowing-out of the US middle class and a distrust of authority that has prompted a rise in anti-establishment sentiment. The study 'provides a view over two decades of the unwinding of the post-war social contract – where workers felt they could rely on decent pay and benefits in exchange for hard work ... Workers feel more exposed, more vulnerable and anxious, and increasingly abandoned by the establishment.'[55]

The change in corporate behaviour has been partly inspired by the writings of the late economist Milton Friedman. Instead of companies balancing the interests of the various stakeholders in their decision-making, their sole objective should be profit maximisation. 'There is one and only one social responsibility of business – to use its resources and engage in activities designed to increase its profits so long as it stays within the rules of the game, which is to say, engages in open and free competition without deception or fraud.'[56] Shareholder value is the ultimate test for all corporate decisions; employees, the local community, even the environment, should not come into it. This principle is clearly unsustainable today, although so far most top executives have only explicitly acknowledged its limitations with respect to the environment.

Clive Cowdery, a British insurance entrepreneur who donated £50 million to stimulate a debate on how to distribute money and power more fairly, was clear about his motivations: 'It's not a short term thing, it's a 10-, 20-, 30-year erosion in the ability of our economic model to deliver an improved living standard ... And therefore we need a new model.' This is because 'In 1945 you didn't have globalised trade. In 1945 you didn't have machines doing the skilled jobs of skilled workers, and in 1945 you could afford to offer people a pension that paid out at age 65 ... the economic model worked ... because it gave them routine and confidence ... I don't see that confidence today to the same degree among working people.'[57]

Clearly something fundamental has changed in the system we have grown up with, to the point where it appears to be edging towards complete breakdown. As we saw in Chapter 7, this system marries democracy with capitalism. Historians have argued that the rise of capitalism pressured the political system to democratise in order to guarantee property rights to entrepreneurs, the rule of law rather than the whim of the ruler, and incentives to take risks. But if democracy and capitalism evolved in a symbiotic relationship, each needing the other, that is not to say that they were not also subject to contradiction and conflict.

A true democracy – one citizen one vote – is egalitarian by definition. It can also empower political units, such as the nation state or a local authority, using elected representatives to make laws and regulations according to what the majority is thought to have voted for. Capitalism on the other hand, is inherently not egalitarian in outcome or theory, especially in its pure free market form. It aims to maximise the wealth of the owners of capital, who are a minority and who, unrestricted and unregulated, will seek to secure their position by buying out or driving their competitors out of business. Once an unassailable market position is achieved, they will enjoy their protected income as rentiers.

The inherent tension between capitalism and democracy did not prevent this two-headed beast from working well enough to be accepted as legitimate and the best system on offer, as long it could provide security and rising living standard for the majority. It was OK for the rich to get filthy rich, so long as there was enough left over for everyone else to be comfortable too, if somewhat more modestly. Widely shared rising real incomes legitimised both capitalism and democracy. Although there were always winners and losers, the system compensated the latter through transfer payments and by providing good-quality job opportunities.

But the system has now morphed from one organised and

controlled at the national level to one dominated by global companies playing one country off against another. Nation states are losing the power to control their economies, a trend exacerbated by tax policies driven by the fear of losing even more capital and jobs to other jurisdictions. The EU could have resisted this trend, the size of its market enabling some aggregate political sovereignty to survive, but this has only happened in some areas such as competition policy, mobile phone roaming charges and minimum standards. In terms of preserving jobs and the real incomes of the vulnerable, it has manifestly failed, hence the rise of so-called populists across the continent and in the UK.

Logically, a globalised economy needs to be run and regulated by a global government. Multinational businesses can now play one government off against another in a way that was impossible prior to the digital age. As their power has shrunk, national governments have become toothless in defending the interests of the common man or woman, and corporations have ensured that their interests take precedence over those of voters.

10

The rise of China

China is not a superpower nor will she ever seek to be one ...
If one day China should change her colour and turn into a
superpower, if she too should play the tyrant in the world, and
everywhere subject others to her bullying, aggression and
exploitation, the people of the world should identify her as
social-imperialist, expose it and work together with the
Chinese to overthrow it.

Deng Xiaoping

CHINA THE TROJAN HORSE ENTERS THE GLOBAL ECONOMIC CITY

If we go back to the economists' theory that growing trade is a win-win for all concerned, when the West let China join the World Trade Organization (WTO) in 2001, it seemed like everyone would be a winner. Never mind that the theory allegedly holds between similar free-market economies, which China was and is not, or that the theory assumes trading between countries according to their comparative advantage in production, not absolute advantage. These details were perhaps expected to be worked out over time

The opening of China to Western investment and international trade shocked the West's labour market with a vast expansion in the global supply of labour of over one billion new workers between the 1980s and 2010. As we've seen, together with the deregulation of labour markets and technological change, this development significantly undercut Western workers' ability to bargain for higher wages.

China became the new workshop of the world, with Western companies taking advantage of the country's lower absolute costs of production. Some of these savings were passed on to the consumer in the form of cheaper prices, but plenty was also retained from the higher profits for senior management to award themselves bumper pay and retirement packages. In the West the balance of forces and rewards tilted inexorably away from the workers as the share of income going to labour shrank from 64 per cent in the 1970s to below 60 per cent in the 2010s. In a nutshell, most Western workers took a relative pay cut but the return on capital rose.

Chinese workers however prospered. Over 600 million Chinese were lifted out of poverty by moving from farms to factories. China's economy took off, its GDP per head soaring from 1.8 per cent of the level of global GDP in 1979 to 9.3 per cent by 2010.[1] This is illustrated in Figure 10.1, which charts the explosive growth of Chinese real wages between 2005 and 2016 in inflation-adjusted terms, compared with the stagnation experienced by other countries, including Portugal, a member of the EU. Euromonitor International reported in early 2017 that Chinese hourly wages now exceeded those of every country in Latin America, save for Chile, and had reached 70 per cent of wages in poorer European countries.

In fact, Chinese wages in some areas have been overtaking some European countries. Writing in 2017, Kenneth Rapoza reported that median monthly wages in Shanghai ($1,135), Beijing ($983) and Shenzhen ($938) were higher than in the newest European Union member, Croatia, which had joined in 2013. Croatia's median net salary was $887 a month. Shanghai wages were also higher than two of the newest Eurozone members, Lithuania ($956, joined in 2015) and Latvia ($1,005, joined in 2014), with Estonia (joined in 2011)

Figure 10.1: Real wage growth

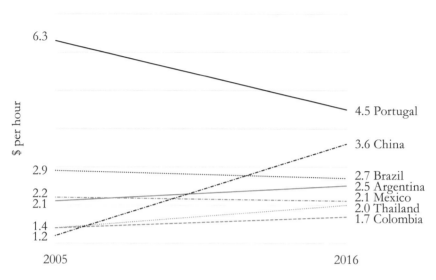

recording a median income of $1,256 per month in 2016, according to government figures. The situation was summarised by Rapoza: 'Over the last 10 years, Europe has sought to incorporate the skilled, lower cost labour pool from Eastern Europe into the fold of the European Union. In 2001, China became more fully integrated into the global labour force when it joined the World Trade Organization. The combination of these two massive labor pools into the workforce set the stage for wage stagnation among lower skilled and assembly line labor worldwide.'[2]

According to the International Labour Organisation (ILO)'s 2016/17 *Global Wage Report*, the average real wage index for the USA, Canada, France and Germany rose by 5–9 per cent, well short of 1 per cent per annum from 2006 to 2015; Italy, Japan and the UK experienced *contractions* of their real wage indexes of around 6, 2 and 7 per cent respectively. Over the same period Chinese real wages increased by around 125 per cent.

Between 1990 and 2014 income per person in China increased thirteen times in real terms. In a delicious irony China's nominally socialist society went from being one of the most equal in the world to one of the most unequal, with a Gini coefficient of 0.49, compared to 0.4 and 0.3 for the capitalist bastions of the US and Germany. China's top 1 per cent could make their Western equivalents pale with envy, controlling around a third of the country's assets, often thanks to hidden or undeclared income. At the same time, President Xi, as far back as 2013, was worried that China was losing its moral compass, bemoaning the numerous food contamination scandals, graft or dereliction of duty by government officials and the country's obsession with money.[3] *The Economist* reported the same lamentation by the official *China Daily* in July 2016, and that trust had become a 'scarce commodity.'[4]

This was not how it was meant to be. Developing countries should grow relatively fast as they catch up, but that should not be at the expense of their trading partners. Otherwise trade becomes a zero-sum game, whereby one party's economic gain becomes the other's pain. Unfortunately, all the evidence points solidly in this direction. Even before its accession to the WTO, China's economy had been growing rapidly since Deng Xiaoping's reforms in the late 1980s. By 2000, China was already stacking up a trade surplus with the US of $84 billion per year.

In a fascinating 2001 paper Nicholas Lardy questioned the rationale for China agreeing to abide by the WTO's stringent rules and conditions in order to become a member, given how well it had fared so far outside. It was already one of the top ten trading countries in the world by 1995, and to join the WTO, China had to be prepared to suffer short-term pain in the form of higher unemployment in industries opened up to unprotected foreign competition. Lardy found this hard to understand, given that politicians are loath to inflict short-term pain for long-term gain.

The protocol governing its accession was clear that China would accept

> significant reductions in tariffs; the introduction of a tariff-rate quota system that brings the tariff rate for key agricultural commodities, such as wheat, almost to zero for a significant volume of imports; the gradual elimination of all quotas and licenses that have restricted the flow of some imports; a substantial reduction in the use of state trading as an instrument to control the volume of imports of agricultural and other key commodities; and the opening of critical service sectors such as telecommunications, distribution, banking, insurance, asset management, and securities to foreign direct investment. In addition, the protocol governing its accession sets forth China's commitment to abide by international standards in the protection of intellectual property and to accept the use by its trading partners of a number of unusual mechanisms that could be used to reduce the flow of Chinese goods into foreign markets.[5]

Lardy speculated that one of the reasons that China was willing to sign up to the WTO and its conditions was that the Chinese regime had staked its legitimacy on being able to deliver rapid growth and rising consumption. These were perhaps tailing off in the 1990s, and China's leaders had calculated that to maintain high growth the country would have to become more integrated into the supply chains being formed through globalisation. Membership would also force China's state-owned banks and enterprises to reform themselves and become more efficient. All this implies that the Chinese understood and accepted the need to develop a market economy even if that meant some short-term pain.

In fact, what we have learned since then, and the Trump

administration has been the first to attempt to rectify, is that the Chinese simply indulged in having their cake and eating it, failing to follow through on any of the conditions they supposedly accepted.

However, Lardy dismissed China's large and growing trade advantage with the US as evidence that it was not playing by the rules, using the frequent non sequitur that America's trade deficit is caused by America's too low savings rate compared to investment rate. Why is this defence weak? Putting aside the government sector for a moment, it is true by definition that, for one country, consumption + investment + exports = consumption + savings + imports = GDP (where investment spending and export revenue boost GDP while savings and imports take money out of the system).

If these are the only broad categories in the economy, they must balance. So, as consumption equals itself on both sides, if imports exceed exports, this implies logically that savings must be less than investment, hence the country needs to borrow from overseas, and overseas countries will oblige since they are earning surpluses from the trade. The mistake or dishonesty of those who defend China is to equate a logical relationship with a necessary one. In fact, any of these variables can change as long as others adjust to preserve the equality of the sides. It is because China is not playing by the rules that imports from China to the US, for example, are about four times exports to China. If trade became balanced, then, necessarily, savings would equal investments. There is no law that says that savings must remain lower than investments.

This disingenuous argument is economic rubbish of the first order. A rise in American exports, or a fall in imports, closing the trade deficit, would increase American income and reduce the savings deficit. And by the same token, China's chronic trade surplus exists because the Chinese save too much, rather than invest or buy more American imports. Nothing prevents the Chinese authorities from encouraging their citizens to spend more and save less, thereby reducing their trade surplus.

This is what is now being negotiated between the Trump administration and China's President Xi Jinping. The Chinese will be happy to oblige and buy more American soybeans and high-tech equipment, but they will not budge on their long-term game plan of overtaking the decadent West politically and economically. It is highly unlikely that China will undertake true structural reforms, opening up its economy, phasing out government funds for 'national champion' companies and ending the acquisition of Western know-how and intellectual property by fair means or foul.

The reasons why America spearheaded the West's welcome of China into the WTO, according to Lardy, were threefold. First, the prospect of easier access by American companies to one of the largest potential markets on the planet was mouth-watering. To be able to sell to the world's most populous nation proved irresistible. Second, American company profits would benefit from the transfer of production to cheaper China. The gains from this switch would be shared out between producers, consumers (lower prices) and Chinese workers (higher wages). In practice, as we have seen, most of the gains were shared between Chinese workers and the global top 1 per cent. Third and perhaps crucial, whether or not US CEOs believed that globalisation would create winners and losers rather than the much touted win-win situation, they were aided and abetted by politicians who either didn't understand the economics of trade or had a naive view of history. This was a colossal strategic blunder, and the West's belated realisation that this was the case is now paving the way for confrontation.

As a result of accepting the notion of the free market in their country, the West assumed the Chinese would adopt a rules-based political system, thereby solidifying the dominant world order devised by the West since the Second World War. Bringing China into the global trading fold was the missionary equivalent of spreading Christianity into Africa in the nineteenth century. Nearly two decades on, America and its allies are recognising that they have been played. Far from living up to its commitments and following the West's playbook of rules-based integration, China has continued to play by its own rules and trade on its own terms. Generations of Western politicians have been forced to look the other way in the hope that their naivety would eventually come good, even as Beijing abused the system. Meanwhile, Beijing has proved masterful at playing for time, with repeated promises of reform and change just around the corner.

The Western strategy of tolerance, patience and hope is no longer tenable. US workers have woken up to their loss of earnings growth at the same time as some big business is switching from appeasement to criticism of its increasingly unfair and predatory treatment by China. The plight of American workers was a significant factor in Trump's rise to power, but their interests conflict with those of his corporate backers who cling to the status quo for their own short-term pecuniary ends. It remains to be seen how forcefully Trump favours the former and the long term, over the defenders-to-the-end of the free market.

Perhaps the most flagrant case of China not playing by the win-win rules of international trade is its controlled currency. If good trade rests on free and open markets, then Beijing's strict control of the yuan, which is not allowed to float or be exchanged against the world's currencies, should have been a deal-breaker by now. The West gave up fixed exchange rates nearly fifty years ago in favour of market-determined rates that move to bring trade into balance. If China is running a large trade surplus with the US, that means, other things being equal, that the US dollar is too high and the yuan too cheap.

In a freely exchangeable currency system, the excess demand for yuan (needed to buy more Chinese goods and services than the Chinese want to buy of American goods and services) would push up its exchange rate. Chinese products would then become more expensive for Americans and vice versa for American products in China, so trade would even out. Fixing the yuan's exchange rate enables China to set the terms of its trade with the US to its own advantage. Those interests in America who have profited from this situation have prevented every administration, until recently, from pronouncing China a currency manipulator, even though it has clearly acted like one.

CHINA'S STEALTH TACTICS TO CATCH UP WITH THE WEST

Rather than complying with the terms of fair trade enshrined by the WTO, China has continued to abuse the international trading system in four ways: by protecting its domestic champions through tariffs, administrative measures and subsidies; by extorting intellectual property (know-how and technology) from foreign companies by forcing them to set up joint ventures in China with local partners, and by stealing it through hacking; by barring foreign competitors in several sectors including technology and banking; and by buying up strategic Western companies while not allowing reciprocal access.

Not content with the dominant share of global manufacturing it has taken, China now wants to move up the food chain and compete in cutting-edge industries where the West still has an edge and something to sell. Now that it has extracted the high-growth benefits from developing its manufacturing base, it needs to move on to new sources of growth to maintain the social contract it has agreed with its citizens: delivering rapidly increasing living standards in exchange for witholding political freedom.

A few examples illustrate the four ways in which China exploits its trade partners.

Protecting domestic champions through tariffs, administrative measures and subsidies

Tariffs vary by type of product and are only one tool that countries use to discourage imports. At a simple level, we can compare the average tariff level between countries. According to IndexMundi, using World Bank staff estimates, China comes in around the middle of the pack globally, with average tariffs on goods of 7.76 per cent, compared to 2.79 per cent for the US and 1.92 per cent for the countries of the EU. Even between WTO members, it is far from a level playing field. However, tariffs are not the main barrier to entry into the vast Chinese market.

In the 2018 edition of the US *National Trade Estimate*, produced by the Office of the United States Trade Representative, the section on China provides stark reading:

> China continued to pursue a wide array of industrial policies in 2017 that seek to limit market access for imported goods, foreign manufacturers and foreign services suppliers.
>
> For example, in technology, China's 2016 cybersecurity law imposed: 'severe restrictions on a wide range of US and other foreign information and communications technology (ICT) products and services with an apparent goal of supporting its technology localisation policies by encouraging the replacement of foreign ICT products and services with domestic ones.
>
> Contrary to its undertakings, the *NTE* notes that, while China agreed to de-link indigenous innovation policies at all levels of the Chinese government from government procurement preferences ... by December 2011 ... this promise had not been fulfilled.

When challenged, China plays for time and makes promises it has apparently no intention of keeping:

China reiterated many of these commitments at the November 2016 JCCT [US–China Joint Commission on Commerce and Trade] meeting, where it affirmed that its 'secure and controllable' policies are not to unnecessarily limit or prevent commercial sales opportunities for foreign ICT suppliers or unnecessarily impose nationality-based conditions and restrictions on commercial ICT purchases, sales or uses. China also agreed that it would notify relevant technical regulations to the WTO Committee on Technical Barriers to Trade (TBT Committee). Again, however, it appears that China does not intend to honor its promises … China's measures do not appear to be consistent with the non-discriminatory, non-trade restrictive approach to which China has committed.[6]

Contrary to its undertakings, China continues to provide substantial subsidies to domestic companies, which have caused injury to US industries. Some of these subsidies also appear to be prohibited under WTO rules.

Studies have shown that China has come to dominate certain industries thanks to state subsidies. These are often provided by local authorities, in cash as well as in the form of cheap loans, cheap land and subsidised utilities. In return, the authorities receive enhanced tax revenues as subsidised companies expand, sometimes to global significance. Laila Khawaja of consultancy Fathom China believes that since local government is controlled by the Communist Party, one path to rapid rise in the party is through being associated with high-growth projects.[7]

China's state direction of key industries, which are set growth targets as well as domestic and international market share targets, aided by state capital (equity, loans and subsidies), distorts market prices and creates excess capacity. The steel industry is one of many where the consequences include excess product being dumped on world markets, threatening to bankrupt foreign competitors.

A 2013 study by Usha and George Haley showed that China, until recently a net importer of steel, glass, paper and auto parts, has turned into the world's largest manufacturer of such products in spite of having no overall comparative advantage in these capital-intensive industries, where labour costs represent a paltry 2–7 per cent of costs. This can only have happened because of state subsidies. And yet no one in industry or government in the West took any notice, blinded by the glittering short-term profits of trading, whatever the long-term cost.[8]

> From 2000 to 2014, China accounted for more than 75 per cent of global steelmaking capacity growth, even though China has no comparative advantage with regard to the energy and raw material inputs that make up the majority of costs for steelmaking. Currently, China's capacity represents about one-half of global capacity and twice the combined steelmaking capacity of the European Union (EU), Japan, the United States and Russia. Meanwhile, China's steel exports grew to be the largest in the world, at 91 million metric tons (MT) in 2014, a 50-per cent increase over 2013 levels, despite sluggish steel demand abroad. In 2015, Chinese exports reached a historic high of 110 million MT, causing increased concerns about the detrimental effects that these exports would have on the already saturated world market for steel.[9]

The story is the same for aluminium and in other industries, causing huge damage to swathes of industry in the West.

China's trade practices do not derive from an adherence to

Ricardo's theory of comparative advantage and a belief in the benefits of free trade. The Chinese system is structurally incentivised to maximise growth, even to the point of overcapacity (which then has to be dumped cheaply abroad). It is all but impossible to imagine how it could reform itself while the one-party state system endures. It appears equally inevitable that such a dynamic must propel China along a collision course with the West, as it cannot back down without disappointing both the ambitions of Communist Party members and the bargain with its citizens of fast growth in exchange for living in a totalitarian surveillance state.

Chinese domestic car companies have also benefited handsomely from subsidies, a fact which did not prompt the European competition authorities stopping the takeover of Volvo cars by Geely in 2010. Geely is a privately held Chinese automotive group although more than 50 per cent of its profits came from subsidies. In contrast, woe betide any European government that provides aid to an ailing domestic company. With friends like the European Commission, mechanically adhering to a mantra which belongs to a time long before China erupted on to the scene, who needs enemies?

The US *National Trade Estimate* notes,

> In its WTO accession agreement, China committed to adopt a single official journal for the publication of all trade-related laws, regulations and other measures, and China adopted a single official journal, to be administered by China's Ministry of Commerce, in 2006. More than 10 years later, it appears that some but not all central-government entities publish trade-related measures in this journal, and these government entities tend to take a narrow view of the types of trade-related measures that need to be published in the official journal.

Lack of transparency makes it difficult to keep track of transgressions of the WTO rules, let alone prove them. The US and other World Trade Organization members have continued to press China to notify all of its subsidies to the WTO in accordance with its obligations. However, 'China has not yet submitted to the WTO a complete notification of subsidies maintained by the central government, and it did not notify a single sub-central government subsidy until July 2016.' Nor is China complying with its commitment to the WTO Government Procurement Agreement (GPA), which would open up its government procurement market to the United States and other GPA parties.

Although the US actually runs a trade surplus in services with China (amounting to $38 billion in 2017), this would probably be much larger if the services market were open rather than being constrained by 'case-by-case approvals, discriminatory regulatory processes, informal bans on entry and expansion, overly burdensome licensing and operating requirements, and other means to frustrate the efforts of US suppliers of services to achieve their full market potential in China'.[10]

In banking, foreign banks' share of the Chinese market has actually declined – not surprising given that China imposes asset and capital requirements on foreign banks that it does not apply to domestic banks and is notoriously slow to act upon the applications of foreign banks to set up new branches. It also restricts the activities that can be conducted by foreign banks, while discriminatory and non-transparent regulations also limit the potential of foreign banks to take full advantage of China's capital markets.

In 1994 China introduced a rule forcing foreign automobile companies to set up joint ventures with Chinese companies in order to manufacture and sell their products in China. This served the twin purposes of providing a captive source of revenue and profits for the Chinese partners and ensuring rapid technological transfer. Furthermore, Beijing imposed a rule whereby joint ventures with state companies were required to set up internal Communist Party cells to be involved in decision-making. In April 2018, under pressure from President Trump, China promised to phase out the joint venture requirement by 2022. Whether Western companies actually take advantage of this change remains to be seen. Their statements so far suggest few planned changes in their structures. As has been pointed out, this relaxation is probably too late given that the Chinese car market grew from about 4 million to 20 million sales between 2003 and 2018, so the costs and logistical complications required for foreign companies to buy back their Chinese partners' stakes and go it alone may be prohibitive.

When it comes to technology that China judges to be of prime importance for the future, Beijing aggressively pursues its own interests. For example, requests by Seat, part of the VW group, to use its name on electric vehicles produced under a joint venture with Chinese car maker JAC were rejected by the National Development and Reform Commission, even though Seat sells conventional cars under that name. China intends to lead the world in advanced manufacturing (see below), including electric vehicles, so does not want foreign brands to gain recognition in this area.

Extortion and theft of intellectual property (IP)

The US Trade Representative's (USTR) office has investigated the various direct or indirect practices that put foreign firms at a disadvantage in China, including the theft or extortion of intellectual property. It has identified four categories of reported Chinese government conduct for investigation including but not limited to:

- the use of a variety of tools to require or pressure the

transfer of technologies and intellectual property to Chinese companies

- depriving US companies of the ability to set market-based terms in licensing negotiations with Chinese companies
- intervention in markets by directing or unfairly facilitating the acquisition of US companies and assets by Chinese companies to obtain cutting-edge technologies and intellectual property
- conducting or supporting unauthorised intrusions into US commercial computer networks or cyber-enabled theft for commercial gains

In March 2018 the USTR issued a report stating that the four categories of acts, policies and practices covered in the investigation are 'unreasonable or discriminatory and burden and/or restrict US commerce'.

Famously, China forces foreigners to transfer intellectual property in exchange for access to its market.

> China seeks to protect many domestic industries through a restrictive investment regime, which adversely affects foreign investors in key services sectors, agriculture, extractive industries and certain manufacturing sectors … evidenced by the continued application of foreign equity caps and joint venture requirements … In addition, foreign enterprises report that Chinese government officials may condition investment approval on a requirement that a foreign enterprise transfer technology, conduct research and development in China.

If China cannot obtain technology and know-how to accelerate its ability to compete with the West further up the value chain, it may resort to theft or take-overs: 'the protection of trade secrets and IP more broadly represents yet another area where China has failed to comply with its promises for a more market-oriented system, particularly to the extent that the state itself sponsors the theft of trade secrets or actively frustrates the effective protection of trade secrets'.[11]

China's cybersecurity law gives the government control over encryption and the flow of data. Hanna Müller, head of the German business lobby BDI has said, 'You have to disclose a lot of data, and there is the risk that commercial secrets are just no longer protected.'

Foreign companies reported to the USTR various forms of pressure to share technology; if they resisted, permits to operate were withheld. Often, the pressure came through private channels with no paper trail, a violation of WTO rules. Companies that comply with demands are likely to have their competitive advantage rapidly eroded as local players master the technology. Foreign cloud service companies, for example, have had to share their know-how with Chinese partners.

Hacking is also a problem. US Steel was on the receiving end when Ugly Gorilla, allegedly a Chinese hacker, broke into 1,700 of the firm's computers and mobile devices in 2010. One year later, the computer of a researcher at the company was hacked and details of how to produce ultra-high-strength steel were stolen. China's Baosteel was rolling out such products two years later using techniques US Steel took a decade to develop.

Most legal systems and international institutions such as the WTO were not crafted to cope with the digital era. Cyber theft is difficult to prove, making it difficult to bring a case through conventional channels. This is one reason President Trump is circumventing such avenues of redress (which are also slow) in favour of executive orders, using the justification of threats to national security.

There has long been a problem with knock-offs made in China, including pirated videos and movies. Allegedly, factories in southern China produce components for iPhone or iPad imitations alongside the manufacture of the real thing, and the quality of knock-offs is now in some cases as good as or better than that of the real products. Local versions of GoPro cameras, for example, are as good as the originals and cheaper. Chinese drones are said to be the best available. Innovators such as GoPro are teetering on the brink of extinction due to their failure to realise the dangers of availing themselves of a cheap Chinese manufacturing base. Ironically, even Chinese manufacturers of high-quality products are complaining that they are being undercut by cheap imitations. Lei Jun, founder of Xiaomi, has griped that 30–40 per cent of supposedly Xiaomi phones on the market are in fact fake.

Barring foreign competitors

In the all-important technology sector the Chinese government has mandated that local information technology firms purchase Chinese products and use Chinese service suppliers, has imposed local content and research and development requirements, designated the location of R & D as a cybersecurity risk factor and required the transfer or disclosure of source codes and other intellectual property. China has nurtured its domestic Internet companies through cheap loans and land, access to the state-run banking and payments infrastructure and crucially by effectively barring Google, Facebook, Twitter, Instagram and YouTube using the so-called Great Firewall of China.[12] Amazon operates in China, but can't compete effectively with its Chinese rivals for locally sourced products and so enjoys only a modest 6 per cent market share. eBay and Walmart sold their unsuccessful operations.

China's censorship rules and the Great Firewall have allowed its domestic tech companies like Baidu (search engine), Alibaba and

JD.com (e-commerce) and Tencent (Facebook equivalent) to grow and thrive in the world's most populous market, safe from foreign competitors. Tencent has 1 billion users in China, and Alibaba's online platforms reported 654 million active users in the first quarter of 2019, probably more than Amazon and eBay put together.[13] Chinese online companies work with the state's artificial-intelligence-enabled censorship apparatus, scrubbing their services for undesirable content.

Their protected profits enable them to reinvest in new start-ups, such as ride-hailing Didi Chuxing. At the end of 2017, according to Chinese brokerage outfit CICC, China boasted half the world's billion-dollar start-ups. The Chinese tech industry is graduating from copycat to innovator and will undoubtedly use its protected domestic customer base as the foundation for an eventual push abroad. Richard Liu, founder of JD.com, openly boasts that his company and its Chinese peers will one day challenge Google, Facebook and Amazon.

But protection is also a double-edged sword. Chinese companies have struggled to gain traction even next door in Hong Kong, let alone the US, where Tencent app WeChat operates. Perhaps this has something to do with the fact that people outside China do not trust the privacy settings on Chinese apps and services. Whatever the eventual outcome, China's ambitions are plain to see, but it may have overplayed its hand.

Buying up Western companies
According to Bloomberg, China has bought at least $318 billion-worth of companies in Europe alone over the last ten years, and over $900 billion globally.[14] This is probably an underestimate since it excludes companies taken over by foreign subsidiaries of Chinese companies. The US was the single largest target country, representing $175 billion of acquisitions.

These are often businesses that own key infrastructure. In Europe alone this category includes at least four airports, six sea ports (including Piraeus in Greece) and wind farms in nine countries. Iconic industrial brands such as Pirelli have been taken over, and the Zhejiang Geely Holding Group has struck at the very heart of German industry and pride by taking a $9 billion stake in Daimler AG, parent of Mercedes-Benz, which has a large development budget for electric vehicles. Li Shufu, founder of Geely, is said to want to cooperate in the area of e-mobility – vehicles powered by electricity. As we have seen, Geely also owns Volvo and has used Volvo technology in its own cars. Bill Russo, CEO of advisory firm Automobility Ltd, says Chinese carmakers are 'hungry for partners to help build capabilities to improve the[ir] competitiveness'. Speaking on Chinese State TV channel CCTV, Li Shufu explained this was to 'support the growth of the Chinese auto industry ... [and] serve our national strategies'.

Li Shufu built up his 9 per cent stake in Daimler AG by stealth, exploiting loopholes in German financial rules that require investors to inform the authorities once their stake exceeds 3 per cent of the voting rights of a company. He used a combination of bank financing, share options and complicated derivative contracts. Such tactics are hardly those of a partner with pure and transparent motives. Unsurprisingly, the banks were as usual happy to aid and abet transactions that evaded the spirit and the letter of the rules.

The suspicion is that this is a piece in the jigsaw of the *Made in China 2025* plan (see below) for world domination in the key industries of the future. As Thorsten Benner, director of the global Public Policy Institute in Berlin put it, 'If *Made in China 2025* succeeds, German industry might as well pack up and go home.'[15] The Daimler acquisitions, the Chinese purchase of Kuka, Germany's largest maker of industrial robots, for €4.5 billion in 2016, and other deals that have been stopped just in time, plus the centralisation and increasing assertiveness of power in China and the refusal to open its own markets, have combined to flip the mood among the Western elite. China is seen less as a partner and more as an adversary, moving in on high-end manufacturing. If the plan succeeds, what will the West have left to sell to China?

In the UK, Chinese interests have bought about a dozen office towers in the City and Canary Wharf. Pin Ang Insurance group has taken a $10 billion stake in HSBC. In Switzerland, the China National Chemical Corporation paid $44 billion for agribusiness Syngenta and all the knowledge it possesses on plants, seeds, herbicides, pesticides, fungicides and fertilisers. In Portugal, China's State Administration of Foreign Exchange (SAFE) bought a 5 per cent stake in EDP, the national electricity company. China Three Gorges (CTG) acquired a 23 per cent stake in 2011, and another Chinese entity, CNIC, majority owned by SAFE, also owns 5 per cent. Tim Buckley, a director at the Institute for Energy Economics and Financial Analysis, commented, 'I see this as China going global. They are building a global network not by military adventurism, but by economic imperialism.'[16]

Chinese direct investment in Europe has jumped from €2.1 billion in 2010 to €37.2 billion in 2016, but declined to €17.3 billion in 2018. Around 60 per cent of takeovers have come from state-controlled groups who enjoy subsidies from the Chinese government.[17]

Western politicians such as David Cameron, who as UK prime minister welcomed Chinese investments with open arms, have done so from a position of weakness. With huge public debts racked up since the GFC, low growth and increasingly angry electorates, Western governments have seen Chinese capital as an easy short-term source of funds for infrastructure projects. And in the private sector, corporate management and shareholders are happy to take the short-term gain from selling shareholdings at a premium. In contrast, China is playing a long game to which the West has been blind.

Made in China 2025

China has set self-sufficiency targets in technology-related industries. For example, in telecommunications and aerospace the government has mandated that at least 70 per cent of key components be sourced from domestic companies by 2025, and seeks dominance in world markets by 2049, the hundredth anniversary of the foundation of the People's Republic of China. That does not bode well for the West.

Made in China 2025 is a ten-year plan spearheaded by the Chinese Ministry of Industry and Information Technology (MIIT) which targets ten strategic industries including, among other things, advanced IT, automated machine tools and robotics, aviation and space-flight equipment and new energy vehicles. According to the 2018 US *Naional Trade Estimate*, *Made in China 2025* is 'emblematic of China's evolving and increasingly sophisticated approach to indigenous innovation, which is evident in numerous supporting and related industrial plans. Their common, overriding aim is to replace foreign technology, products and services with Chinese technology, products and services in the China market through any means possible so as to ready Chinese companies for dominating international markets.'

The initial goal of *Made in China 2025* is to ensure that Chinese companies develop, extract or acquire their own technology, intellectual property and know-how and their own brands. The next goal is to substitute domestic technologies, products and services for foreign technologies, products and services in the China market. The final goal is to capture much larger worldwide market shares in the ten targeted industries.

Many of the policy tools being used by the Chinese government to achieve the goals of *Made in China 2025* raise serious concerns. These tools include a wide array of state interventions and support mechanisms designed to promote the development of Chinese industry in large part by restricting, taking advantage of, discriminating against or otherwise creating disadvantages for foreign enterprises and their technologies, products and services.

The digital economy already represents about one third of China's GDP.[18] No longer content with being a supplier of components or hardware, China is moving up to compete at the highest level. Payments using smartphones and Alibaba's Alipay or Tencent's WeChat are making cash obsolete. Yahoo and the Japanese Softbank were the largest initial shareholders in Alibaba, until founder Jack Ma told them that the Chinese government would not allow foreign investors to control a part of the country's payments system. When Ma carved out Alipay, Yahoo was told the susidiary was no longer included in its investment.

China is currently aiming to raise over $30 billion through its state-backed China Integrated Circuit Industry Investment Fund to invest in domestic computer chip companies, an area where it is still overwhelmingly dependent on foreign producers. China represents a large proportion of global demand for semi-conductors, yet produces only a small fraction of the supply.[19] Only 16 per cent of chips used in China are produced domestically and only half of those by Chinese-owned firms.[20] China's aim is to reduce its reliance on chip imports for national security reasons but also to become a global leader in the design and manufacture of sophisticated products to maintain its high economic growth rate. Increasingly squeezed by lower-cost Asian countries at the bottom end of the manufacturing food chain, and having achieved rapid growth during the period of migration of the labour force from fields to factories, China cannot stand still if it wants to avert the fate of Japan, mired in stagnation since 1990.

Chinese labour costs have risen so fast, the country is in danger of becoming uncompetitive in basic manufacturing. In order to preserve market share, some companies are replacing workers by robots, but as China's manufacturing moves up the sophistication spectrum, it ceases to complement the West's, and the notion of division of labour and specialisation by country creating the basis for mutually beneficial trade completely falls by the wayside.

China published a separate development strategy governing artificial intelligence in 2017, in which it set out its plans to dominate the 'fourth industrial revolution'. It expects to be at the level of the most advanced countries by 2020, and according to a government statement issued in July 2018 will be the world's primary AI innovation centre by 2030. In 2018 the AI market in China expanded 52.8 per cent to 33.9 billion yuan and is projected to pass 70 billion by 2020.[21] Industry output is targeted to explode towards 1 trillion yuan by 2030. As well as nurturing home-grown talent, China is importing foreign talent, such as Lu Qi, hired from Microsoft in 2016 to head up its AI effort. The Berlin-based Mercator Institute for China Studies described the plan as 'the building blocks of an overarching political program ... In the long run, China wants to obtain control over the most profitable segments of global supply chains and production networks.'

Russian president Vladimir Putin is said to have remarked that the country that takes the lead in AI will rule the world, and China has declared AI superiority a strategic goal.

ESCALATING TRADE WAR AND THE BATTLE FOR WORLD DOMINATION

President Trump has ordered a probe into what he considers China's unfair trade practices. As well as the first set of tariffs effective on up to $250 billion of Chinese goods, with further tariffs to follow if the Chinese do not change their ways, the US administration is also looking at enforcing reciprocity of access for foreign investment. The idea is that America will only permit Chinese takeovers in sectors where the Chinese allow similar US companies access.

America is strengthening the mandate of its Committee on Foreign Investment in the United States (CFIUS) to investigate and block deals. Similarly, Germany, Italy and France are tightening up their laws on overseas takeovers, introducing tougher screening and enhancing powers to block transactions; these initiatives are not, it should be noted, at the EU level. Meanwhile China has been caught flat-footed in its response to the pushback against its practices. This is perhaps not surprising given the decades of appeasement by the West. China's meteoric rise to challenge the US for the title of the world's top economy has encouraged a hubristic reinflation of national pride and the reinforcement of the notion of the superiority of its centralised, controlled, closed and undemocratic system as the most effective state model for the twenty-first century. Why should it compromise, faced by a weak, craven, divided and decadent West unable to follow a consistent course through the swings and roundabouts of the electoral pendulum?

But rather than heeding the wise advice of Deng Xiaoping, China's success has gone to its head. It has let the proverbial cat out of the bag with its *Made in China 2025* plan, presuming that it was already too late for anyone to block its path to global domination of cutting-edge industries and hence the world.

Ironically, as the prospect of realising its revanchist agenda finally comes into view, the very rigidity and closed characteristics of China's system appear to have tripped it up. At home, with power concentrated at the top in the hands of a leader with no term limit, there are no checks to its exercise, as long as power continues to deliver rapid increases in living standards. That means there is only risk and no reward for anyone in the entourage of Xi Jinping who expresses a divergent opinion, in other words, who speaks truth to power. In particular, would any of his entourage have dared warn him of the provocative effect of the *Made in China 2025* declaration or the AI manifesto? Did Mr Xi not consider the possibility that Western companies would tire of the inhospitable conditions for doing business in China? Last, but not least, did his contempt for the West's democratic system blind him to the ability of the system to self-correct *at the base.*

For all the talk of win-win and the universal benefits of globalisation, ordinary people in the West are beginning to realise that they have been tricked by the actual winners' self-serving propaganda and have lost badly. As some wag noted a few years back, the United States lost millions of jobs, indebted itself to China by $1.4 trillion and received in return a host of consumer goods, many of which now reside in landfills across the country.

Sigmar Gabriel, a German politician, has said that China is the only country with a truly global, geostrategic idea, and the West has no strategy of its own to offer in response. In 2017 the German security services revealed that Chinese intelligence agencies were setting up fake profiles on social networks such as LinkedIn to establish contact and potentially recruit German politicians and officials. These are not the actions of a friendly partner without ulterior motives. Meanwhile China apologists and Western beneficiaries of a system that reached its sell-by date at the time of the GFC and now smells rotten try to hold back the rising tide of change by disparaging it as 'populism', implying that its leaders are ignorant of economics and exploiting the masses' base nationalistic instincts for their own cynical political ends.

There are also fatalists who realise what is happening but have given up trying to prevent it. According to this point of view, China's rise is inevitable and we might as well accept it gracefully rather than shoot ourselves in the foot with a futile attempt to halt the Chinese bulldozer via a trade war. It is exemplified by declarations such as: 'There is a legitimate argument that Daimler will ultimately survive by becoming a little less German and a little more Chinese,' the opinion of one German official.[22]

China's self-proclaimed return to the glories of the Middle Kingdom, around which the rest of the world rotates, coincides with the establishment of President Xi as its modern emperor for life. As James Stavridis eloquently noted, if Western democracy lives by following the short-term policies of the revolving door, what happens to a system where there is no mechanism for changing the leader, if the going gets tough?[23] And it will get tough in a country that is ageing, has a huge gender skew in favour of males and will not be able to keep its high-growth show on the road to justify the absence of freedom.

Machiavelli provided an answer centuries ago: distract the masses' attention from their domestic problems by channelling their frustrated aspirations into nationalism, if necessary to the point of conflict. It is no accident that China has siezed control of huge swathes of the South China Sea by enlarging small atolls into military bases equipped with runways, ignoring the ruling of an international tribunal against its claims. Defence spending is rising sharply, and China has built the first of several planned aircraft carriers which will enable it to project its military power well beyond its shores for the first time in modern history, thereby increasing the risk of a clash with the US in the Pacific. Reneging on its international commitments, in 2017 China's foreign ministry casually declared the Sino-British joint declaration guaranteeing political autonomy for Hong Kong a 'historical document' that no longer has any significance.

Trade negotiations between China and the US to de-escalate the developing trade war are at an advanced stage at the time of writing and are likely to conclude with some sort of deal. Even if an agreement is sealed in time to suit Trump's re-election calendar, it is likely to be cosmetic and will probably not alter China's behaviour. This is because of the powerful deep structural forces at play within China that have been outlined above. Its business model – high growth, state and local government sponsorship of business, monopoly of power by the Communist Party – does not permit any slowdown in growth that would result from adherence to an open economy and abandoning its pursuit of foreign intellectual property. China is more likely to put up with tariffs than slam the brakes on its drive for domination of the key industries of the future.

Alibaba boss Jack Ma has remarked that war starts when trade stops. Ominously, he warned: 'The first technology revolution caused the First World War, the second technology revolution caused the Second World War – and now we have the third.'[24]

If he's right, the world needs wise leaders. Instead we have rulers with an inadequate understanding of history and a dangerous excess of personal vanity and national pride. In short, everything but the wisdom of Deng Xiaoping.

PART FOUR

The Failure of the Free Market and Democracy – and what to do about it

11

Solutions

We would rather be ruined than changed.

W. H. Auden

Keeping the zombie system from expiring and covering up the corruption with propaganda is what's actually destroying the world as we know it.

Heinz Blasnik

MARXIAN DETERMINISM OR THE FREEDOM TO SAVE DEMOCRACY?

The diagnosis of the West's ailments is now complete. Economic numbers may say that our average real income has never been higher, but the lived experience of most remains one of stagnant living standards and an uncertain future. The shocking prospect of our children being poorer than us over their lifetime, many of them unable to buy a home or start a family as they search for security in a market of precarious employment prospects undermined by globalisation and automation, has set off a ticking political time bomb.

America, the arch promoter of free-market economics, likes to think of itself as the land of opportunity. The reality today is that social mobility is lower in America than in Europe. The probability of escaping from the bottom quintile of earnings is lower than in

Britain, France, Italy and Sweden.[1] The American dream has become a mirage. US unemployment may be at historic lows, but the proportion of decently paid and secure jobs, not only in manufacturing, is down, with digitisation eating into white-collar jobs, not just repetitive manual tasks. Deregulation and the transfer of jobs to China, India, Mexico and other cheap-labour locations has contributed to weak income growth.

At an absolute level, global equality remains obscenely skewed. As we saw in Chapter 4, an Oxfam report suggests that the world's twenty-six wealthiest people own as much ($426 billion) as the entire bottom half of the world population – 3.8 billion people.[2] More Americans and Europeans are having trouble making ends meet, while governments' austerity policies impose cuts on programmes that help the less affluent. In contrast, those who have accumulated some capital or control companies that have become near-monopolies have seen their fortunes soar since the Great Financial Crisis. No wonder people are angry and beginning to express their rage not only through the ballot box, but also in the street, with rising levels of violence.

At the same time, the GFC caused national debt loads and deficits to soar as governments rescued the banks from collapse. This has meant years of spending cuts in public services and neglect of core infrastructure. For decades the mania for deregulation and privatisation championed by the free marketeers from the time of Thatcher in the UK and Reagan in the US has worked its corrosive effect on the very fabric of society. This decay has become so advanced it is now clearly visible; hence the collective disillusionment with our political and economic systems, shaking the very foundations of democracy.

Indiscriminate deregulation of business, globalisation based on fraudulent economic premises and the march of technology and automation have not resulted in better lives for Western workers;

the beneficiaries have been the captains of industry, monopoly technology entrepreneurs and workers in some emerging markets, principally China. So greater global equality has been achieved at the expense of Western workers. But with democratic institutions organised at the nation-state level, electorates vote for what they consider to be in their best interests, not for the global good, whatever that is. Such decisions would require a global government voted in by a global electorate. An unlikely scenario.

There is a clear disconnect between political units built for a bygone age and the twenty-first-century globalised digital world. National political institutions were efficient at offering political choices to citizens when nations had some control. In a globalised world dominated by monopolistic technology rentiers and international corporate titans, the quaint historic ritual of national elections seems pathetically anachronistic.

The US constitution, devised two centuries ago, was admirably suited to managing and balancing the competing and collective interests of a population totalling that of a present-day medium-sized town with limited means of communication. The UK, lacking a written constitution, has demonstrated during its tortured processing of the Brexit vote that its quaint rituals and conventions, originating centuries ago, are as decrepit as the physical fabric of the Palace of Westminster, and no longer fit for purpose.

When a large slice of a company's profits is earned abroad, and production or even its headquarters can be moved across borders with ease, it is clear how little power national governments have when it comes to controlling business and protecting the common good. Perhaps that's why politicians prefer to devote more and more of their time to policy areas where they can still exercise power, like health-and-safety regulations or tinkering with highway speed limits. It gives them something to do.

In France the *gilets jaunes* (yellow vests) movement has emerged as an anti-political party protest movement with no leaders. It is a rejection of the conventional channelling of political discourse through a hierarchy of professional politicians and institutions. Its prominence is all the more remarkable given its appearance just eighteen months after the election of a president affiliated to no pre-existing political party. The election of Emmanuel Macron, a political outsider and novice, was the last hope of those in France who wanted to reform the system to preserve it, but it did not take long for those left behind to realise that his reforms were simply those of a free-market ideologue.

Similar trends are evident in other large Western countries. The dwindling support for Germany's main parties of the centre left and centre right, and the rise of the Alternative für Deutschland (AfD) signal a breakdown of the post-war consensus. Italy's coalition government comprising the Five Star Movement and the League was a partnership of anti-establishment parties. Ukraine's election to the presidency of an actor who played a fictional president in a TV series demonstrates how far people will go in their quest for genuine change. Last but not least, the election of Donald Trump in the US in 2016 is testimony to the level of desperation in America and the disillusionment of many with conventional politics.

The realisation of many in the West that they have been sold a chimera by their leaders, disenfranchised and betrayed by their institutions, has triggered a backlash. This backlash threatens the survival of a political model that had prevailed against its only alternative, communism, since the collapse of the Soviet Union. We have reached the crossroads between Marxian determinism – a certain sense of the inevitable decline and fall of all empires and civilisations – and a more hopeful belief that the very act of understanding our predicament empowers us to formulate and implement an escape.

The central purpose of this book has been to set out an

explanation of why and how we arrived at our current predicament. It does not constitute proof, as history, economics and politics are not susceptible to proof; its logic will always be open to attack and counter-argument, especially by those in favour of the status quo either out of ideological conviction or financial interest. But my interpretation should resonate with those of good faith who love the freedom, creativity and respect for the individual that comes with democracy, and know how good society can be when democracy functions as it should. There is no guarantee that my diagnosis can be successfully applied to implement a cure. It may already be too late. However, that does not relieve us of the duty to try to change the way the game is played and bring democracy back from the brink.

This is not the first time that democratic societies and capitalism have faced an existential crisis. The revolts of the mid-eighteenth century; the Great Depression of the 1930s; the two world wars; the Cuban Missile Crisis; the inflation of the 1970s: these all came close to ending Western society as we know it. Yet, even if only just, we succeeded each time in saving capitalism and democracy. It can be done.

This time, however, is different; the challenges are more serious than in the past. This is not only because our political institutions were designed for an altogether smaller and more cohesive body politic in a simpler economy, but also because technological change has brought us to a tipping point. Previously, technological advances were symbiotic with human labour – jobs destroyed were replaced by more productive and enriching jobs as labour worked *with* machines. That is no longer true except for a dwindling band of highly educated workers at the top end of the skills pyramid. As we have seen, we cannot transform laid-off factory workers or checkout counter assistants into lawyers or surgeons or software writers or successful entrepreneurs.

In the past, crises brought about their own solutions: Keynesian injections of demand into faltering economies, such as the New Deal in the USA, deregulation and a more rigorous control of central bank money in the early 1980s. But the solutions we've used in the past seem to have outstayed their welcome. As they became entrenched in the political establishment and acquired the power of quasi-religious orthodoxies, inertia set in. No one seems able to call time or adapt the system even when the signs are that it's going off the rails.

Unfortunately, the lesson of history is that political systems only rise to the challenge after a crisis has occurred. Today, it is clear that our institutions only doused the flames of the GFC by borrowing vast sums of money from the public and flooring interest rates to nothing to bail out private commercial interests. But this was a short-term fix and no solution to the underlying problems of the crisis. In fact, if anything, the fix exacerbated the core problems of inequality, debt, sky-high house prices, prolonged weak income growth, intergenerational regression, crumbling infrastructure and declining public services.

The political class has simply papered over the cracks with our own money. But these cracks are reappearing in the more serious form of political disaffection and disillusionment. People are switching off and no longer listening to the old mantras. Those reactionary forces who have been the winners are either in denial or too greedy to accept the need for change and force our politicians towards ditching the pre-crisis orthodoxy of market fundamentalism.

So what are the solutions? Logically, these should be mirror images of the multiple factors that have hurt our societies. In some cases the clock cannot and should not be wound back – for example, the advance of technology cannot be reversed. But we can propose measures to mitigate the negative effects of the growing redundancy of human labour. We can re-apply the rules of fair competition, dissolve monopolies and protect the political machine from the corrupting influence of money.

In the economic sphere, we have yet to find the right balance between distrust of markets and belief in state intervention (1930s–70s) and the subsequent reverence for unencumbered markets as the wisest allocator of resources and rewards. It is clear, though, that the current worship of the free market is excessive, and that there must be some readjustment towards a more interventionist state. This will be hard for those who cannot remember a time before free market ideology held sway and accept it as the norm, although perhaps easier for the generation that have come of age since the GFC. They are not impressed by the ideology of their parents; they have the energy and, with poor prospects, much less to lose.

Although economic and political solutions must be applied together, and economic changes will need to be implemented by politicians, we can look at these areas separately. Some of the nine measures outlined below are emergency first steps. Deep changes to the political system, such as more direct democracy, will take time to gain acceptance, and time is in short supply. Measures to transfer income and employment from the strong to the weak must be implemented soon, and cannot wait for the outcome of debates on institutions.

THE SOLUTIONS

1. Invest in public services and infrastructure

In post-industrial, post-service economies we should face the facts and update for the modern world our notions of work and reward. Keynes's insight that there is no God-given law guaranteeing jobs for all at rates determined by the market now needs to be interpreted for the long term, not just cyclically.

In the past, jobs disappeared when the economy received a shock and demand fell. The economy would then turn over at a slower pace and could stay stuck there for a considerable length of time if there was nothing to break the vicious circle of no job and income growth, so no investment and demand growth, hence no job growth and so on. Governments could act as economic defibrillators, restarting the virtuous circle of rising demand, rising jobs and incomes and rising investment. The problem was that governments couldn't resist juicing the system for political gain even after the slump had passed.

Surrendering to the temptation to cut taxes or boost spending to fulfil election promises or pay for wars risks running the economic engine too hot. It also weakens public finances through rising debt from accumulated deficits. The pressure is then on the central bank to print enough money to accommodate the government's profligacy. This raises inflation to a level which becomes socially divisive and economically damaging, as happened in the 1970s. If left to spiral out of control, hyper-inflation ensues, as in 1920s Germany, or more recently, Argentina, Venezuela and Zimbabwe. So, while we need governments to play a bigger role in economic policy, we also need to avoid uncontrolled government spending. We need a more stable system.

However, the quest for a solution to cyclical swings in the economic consensus has been complicated by a new structural and permanent damper on the demand for human labour – technology and automation. For the first time in human history, human workers risk becoming redundant en masse. Keynes also foresaw this but envisaged it not as a problem but rather as sunny uplands where humans would be liberated from the chore of full-time work to concentrate on leisure and pursuing creative activities.

Of course, many people would be happy to be relieved of the tedious obligation to work. If machines can build and drive cars, provide furniture, electrical appliances, legal advice, banking services, medical diagnostics, security services, laundry, warehouse management and deliveries while we sit at home or visit theme parks to be entertained or exercise our creative talents, what's not to like?

Two things. First, humans crave respect, including a sense of self-worth and purpose. People need to be part of society, not burdens that subsist on charity from those whom society still values highly enough to pay. Second, how will society finance decent incomes for the growing mass of redundant people? In fact, solutions combining both needs are not that complicated – with a little imagination.

The market is not good at pricing and delivering infrastructure and public goods such as safety, health and education in a society that has been trained to value *personal* consumption and profits highly. This is because it is difficult to market and commercialise certain things even though they have value. At the most basic, most of us would derive some satisfaction from seeing bridges, walls or shop shutters cleaned of graffiti, but can we and would we pay much to have it removed? Enough for this to be commercially viable? The answer in both cases is probably not. The same goes for weeds overrunning old sports facilities in public areas or parks, or even along highways. Therefore …

- Public goods, such as a safe, clean, adequate and modern infrastructure, could do with a metaphorical coat of paint, as well as expansion. Our public spaces in many cases have become run-down, dirty and outdated. Our roads are crumbling and potholed and our bridges are often safety hazards. In short, we could usefully employ an army of people to reverse the decline, clean up, upgrade and expand our vast network of transport facilities, public roads and buildings, leisure facilities, parks, schools and hospitals.

- Crime and violence are symptoms of stress and decline and a measure of how much the social fabric is tearing. Expanding policing resources to help staunch a rising crime wave that could tip out of control, while necessary, is not sufficient. We need to provide facilities to train young disenfranchised citizens to (re-)integrate them into society and provide them with a sense of hope, self-respect and belonging. This needs another small army of people. At the same time, cultural and sporting facilities should be built in problem areas to provide pleasurable and creative outlets for restless young energy.

- The effective delivery of public health services has declined over the decades because spending and investment has not kept up with rising needs. In some countries, the dramatic rise in demand from large net immigration and an ageing population has led to scenes of people being parked for hours on trolleys in the corridors of hospital A & E departments. This was unthinkable in rich countries twenty years ago. Waiting times in the UK's National Health Service for diagnostics and serious interventions routinely run into months, placing patient health at risk. Meanwhile, doctors' surgeries are so overwhelmed that it can take well over a week to obtain an appointment.

- No doubt the UK's unique system of free access to medical treatment does act as a magnet for health tourists from all over the world, since none can be refused. Introducing a modest charge that can be recouped by citizens below a certain income would put an end to rationing by queuing. If the system is being overwhelmed by numbers and the state is unable to expand capacity, then there is no other solution than to restrict demand by tightening the rules governing access by citizens of other countries.

- The soaring healthcare and care-home demands of ageing baby boomers also present challenges. Few governments have invested enough to meet this, and, rather like global warming, waiting for the crisis to strike is not a tenable policy. A response is needed now. In short, billions of pounds, dollars, yen and euros need to be spent on new hospitals, care homes and all the hardware. A small army of professionals needs to be trained. This is at least a ten-year programme, perhaps beyond the political horizon of our current crop of careerist politicians. Not all of the jobs created, especially carers', can be automated, and there will be many vacancies in socially valuable occupations that can absorb those whose commercial skills have been automated.

- Even reactionaries agree on the need to improve education in order to equip workers with the skills necessary to compete globally and be sufficiently productive to earn a good and secure wage. The trouble is that few governments – with notable exceptions – are willing to put up the necessary money. Standard class sizes of thirty or more cannot provide adequate, let alone targeted and tailored, teaching catering to the needs of a wide range of pupils. Those who struggle, often from underprivileged backgrounds, are at risk of getting left behind, becoming demotivated and dropping out.

- What is wrong with building more schools, training and hiring more teachers and paying them a wage that recognises their huge social value? This is the purest investment in the future of a country, as the Chinese well know. A teacher's contribution to society is undoubtedly considerable, which is probably not the case for the average financier paid multiples of a teacher's salary. Society allows the market to richly reward the latter because the related profit is quickly quantifiable, whereas there is no easily quantifiable measure of a teacher's contribution to society. We must adjust our methodology for justifying rewards. To paraphrase the immortal remark of Paul Volcker, it is hard to point to any really useful innovation by the financial industry over recent decades other than the cash machine.

- If the market continues to reward activities of dubious social value but pays those making visible and often life-changing contributions a fraction of the former, then the market is misallocating resources at a societal level. The state, as the representative of society, must either regulate or tax the first so as to redistribute rewards adequately to the second.

- Infrastructure and public service needs should provide plenty of work in roles that cannot easily be automated because they require the human touch at its most personal. This should absorb a substantial proportion of those workers who have become commercially obsolete. The only difficulty with all this, and it is not a negligible problem, is that such a regime implies higher taxation of commerce, bringing with it the familiar risk of the more heavily taxed skipping to lower-taxed jurisdictions. The question is: would a country be worse off in the long term with more teachers, doctors and nurses, but fewer, say, bankers?

If private enterprise will not supply good infrastructure and associated services at affordable prices, then the state must step up to the plate. But how to finance this? Again, the logical answer is as simple as the politics may be difficult.

2. Introduce a living wage

Those still not working in our brave new world, perhaps due to disability or by choice, should still earn a state-sponsored income that covers life's necessities. Unemployment benefit should be scrapped and replaced by a living wage paid to all below a certain level of income. This should be calibrated to enable everyone to live with dignity. Anyone with a job that pays less would have their income topped up to the living wage level by the state because some work is better than none, both for individuals and society, even if its commercial value is below the subsistence level. This recognises the imperfections of the labour market.

Citizens not employed in the commercial private sector would have a choice between the public/social sector, undergoing further education and training, or engaging in other activities. As people could risk leaving paid employment, it is likely we would discover certain talents that would otherwise not have revealed themselves. This in itself is valuable to society.

There is growing interest in this idea, to the point where such a scheme has entered political debate. In Italy the government has instituted a monthly €780 so-called Citizen's Income for those who qualify, at an estimated cost of about €7 billion in the first year. But because it ceases after eighteen months and has various strings attached, this is in fact closer to unemployment benefit.

The key hurdle to overcome is the antiquated belief that people *have to earn* a living. Work would become voluntary for people with those skills that have been automated. Financing such a system would be taken care of by the next two measures.

3. Tax the robots

It is indisputable that technology, in the form of robots, machines and software, is replacing an increasing range of human occupations. One 2018 estimate concluded that 14 per cent of jobs are highly automatable, and another 32 per cent are highly likely to change in character due to automation. Clearly these percentages are only going to rise.[3]

This is another example of the generalisation principle. Automation works to the extent that the owners of businesses calculate that replacing humans increases their profits. Their reckoning may be correct at the individual business level – same revenue, lower cost of production. But, as we have seen, companies taking decisions in their self-interest at the micro level end up hurting themselves and society at the aggregate macro level if they deprive their future customers of jobs. How can that be a sustainable business model? Yet private markets do not appear able to deal with this dilemma constructively, so the state must intervene. Therefore …

- As has been suggested by many, the logical solution is to either slow the replacement of humans by machines or to compensate them and thereby create a level playing field by taxing the robots. Why should only human work be taxed, thereby penalising it? The exact methodology need not be complicated. For example, the tax on the introduction of a machine or software application that results in the redundancy of X number of workers could be equal to the tax that would have been paid by the company and the workers when they were employed, thus providing the state with revenue to employ those same workers in socially productive but 'unprofitable' jobs such as those identified above. That robots are not taxed is in effect a tax loophole and an anomaly in the system, as well as being socially pernicious.

- The same goes for those who live off income derived from their privileged and protected position in the market – originally land but now also capital in the form of intellectual property. Today, this definition is applicable to major shareholders in monopoly or near-monopoly businesses. In the West, huge technology-driven companies such as Google, Facebook, Amazon and Microsoft have all but cornered their markets in blatant contradiction to the pure theory of the unrivalled beneficial effects of relying on free-market competition. Furthermore, they have proved expert at circumventing an antiquated tax system designed for physical goods and services. This needs to be rectified. Tired of waiting for a European consensus, France has unilaterally announced a 'tech tax' based on revenue rather than profit, but it remains to be seen how this would work in practice.
- Alternatively, the state could break up monopolies, and reintroduce competition via antitrust measures. It is ironic that the only authority that has battled to preserve free-market competition against the uncompetitive practices of giant companies has been the European Commission, that much-derided bastion of European bureaucracy.

It is immaterial which solution is employed to bring down excess profits to levels consistent with competitive industries, as the end result will be similar. Cap abnormal profits and you will take away the incentive to create monopolies in the first place. Whatever works.

4. Tax finance

Society needs to reduce the importance of finance within the economy. Finance should revert to being a utility, keeping deposited money safe in banks and lending it out for investment for very low fees.

There is very little evidence that bankers and most investment advisers or managers generate activity that is useful socially. Mergers and acquisitions often end in disaster with bankers earning fees to break up conglomerates that their predecessors put together. Most investment managers underperform the market over time. If these companies insist on paying their employees Hollywood star salaries, governments should tax them to bring their net incomes in line with other occupations that society considers at least as valuable – teachers perhaps. Irrespective of considerations of social value, eliminating outsized incentives to pump up credit would by itself cut out a major source of economic instability and inequality.

Congresswoman Ocasio-Cortez's 70 per cent tax proposal for annual incomes over $10 million is hardly radically new and would simply reset the top US tax rate to around where it was in 1981.

5. Outlaw lobbying and nationalise campaign finance

The political machine has become paralysed in its ability to implement laws and regulations in the best interests of the majority by the corrupting influence of private money. This is at its most extreme in the US, but Europe is also plagued. Emmanuel Macron, a rank outsider with no political party backing, managed to amass the biggest campaign fund of all candidates in the 2017 French presidential election in part thanks to substantial sums channelled his way by the rich and powerful. In the US, Trump's election campaign enjoyed the luxury of being largely self-funded. Therefore …

- If political parties need to raise funds from third parties to maintain their structures between elections, these should be limited by law. Election campaigns should be state funded, since democratic elections are a public good and candidates should be free from influence by unrepresentative special interests. For presidential elections, all candidates that have won through their party primaries to be present on the final ballot should receive the same amount of public money. For Congressional and parliamentary elections, all parties should receive from the public purse a fixed sum per candidate, plus a variable bonus commensurate with their share of the vote at the last election, to be spent equally by each candidate.

- Trying to influence the legislative agenda towards the interests of businesses or foreign governments through private contacts with elected representatives has no jus-tification and should be outlawed. Lobbying is distorting the democratic machine throughout the Western world and is the cause of countless harmful decisions. This is shameful and scandalous. If companies want to draw the attention of legislators to unintended potential conse-quences for business and employment of proposed laws and regulations, this should take place in an open public forum or by written submissions to civil servants.

6. Enforce shareholder control over top executive compensation and contract terms and outlaw stock options

We need to roll back the capture of companies by senior managers for their own enrichment, often at the expense of shareholders, the company's long-term interests, customers and society. Managers are not unique talents and are easily replaceable, while successful founding entrepreneurs do not need to game the company pay scheme to get rich.

- Senior managers' compensation should revert to consisting mainly of a fixed salary, with a bonus related to annual performance worth no more than 100 per cent of salary. Long-term incentive plans that grant share participation to managers should be in the form of loans for the purchase of the company's shares after a sufficiently long delay, for example, five years. This would end short-term gaming of the system and the granting of share options as riskless lottery tickets, which is the ultimate example of (legal) insider trading since the beneficiaries can manipulate the value of shares to their own advantage. Executive compensation committees should include a substantial number of delegates from the workforce and unions. Consultants should be banned.
- Compensation packages for top executives should be subject to legally binding approval or rejection by shareholders. It is not enough for companies to pay lip service to reconciling shareholder and executive interests by holding advisory votes on top pay, which can be disregarded or lead to only marginal tweaked outcomes.
- All public companies should be legally required to publish annually the ratio of the CEO's compensation to that of the average full-time employee in the company.

7. In the absence of world government, impose minimum local production-content rules and reinforce anti-dumping rules

This is probably the trickiest reform of the global economic system to try to enact. The logic is simple. Ricardo's theory of the benefits from free trade could work in practice if participant countries stuck to the rules rather than trying to gain market share at each other's expense. Countries would be limited to selling goods according to their *comparative advantage*, not *absolute advantage*. This could be monitored and policed by a global body such as a redesigned World Trade Organization with teeth.

In practice, however, this is almost bound to fail. Such a body would not have the necessary clout to compel any country to desist from cheating, as has been demonstrated over decades, and anyway sanctions take too long to implement. But most damningly, unless the members of such a body are directly elected by the people, they will have no direct incentive to work in the interests of the people. If appointed or nominated by national governments, they will depend on the goodwill of politicians whose interests may not coincide with those of the people they represent.

- Nation states possess institutions, laws, courts and police to resolve and enforce disputes and conflicts within their jurisdictions. In a globalised world, an equivalent global super-state should carry out the equivalent responsibilities but could only have legitimacy and sufficient power to act if duly elected by the world's citizens. Just as the United States and Germany are composed of states with their own political powers at the local level, so a world government would maintain national governments to run education, health, infrastructure and internal security. A directly elected world government would only have powers over matters which need to be resolved at the global level: trade, pollution, territorial disputes. This is a long-term goal.

- Any plan to export production to another country should be reviewed by the authorities of the country that stands to lose, with a view to demanding an exit tax equal to the loss of tax revenue from redundant workers and lost output for up to, say, ten years. In cases where a nation's comparative advantage in an industry is involved, the movement of its production against this law should be banned. A nationally elected government exists to protect the interests of its citizens, not of corporations or other countries.

- To guard against imports made artificially cheap by state subsidies, all imports should be subject to full transparency on the entire financial chain implicated in their production.

- To level the playing field, no foreign goods or services should be allowed into a country unless there is complete reciprocity of export to the source country of the same goods and services.

8. Impose an effective tax on carbon emissions and ban the use of chemicals and pesticides that have not passed rigorous food-safety tests

It is clear that the current geopolitical and economic system is unable to cope with a variety of environmental problems. Quite apart from the harmful long-term consequences of carbon emissions and the use of plastics, the employment of pesticides in farming and the use of chemical additives in the production of foods to enhance taste or colour and for preservation is increasingly recognised as a public health danger. Inadequate regulatory standards and oversight are tolerated as a result of pressure from the food and farm industries on governments. Nor are governments innocent, happy to reap the electoral rewards of short-term attempts to protect the purchasing power of consumers by turning a blind eye to the hazards of cheap industrial food.

This would be less explosive politically were real wages rising at a healthy pace. Tackling this problem implies a profound change in our model of economic production and growth. We cannot continue to account for wealth only by adding up the goods and services produced, without subtracting the pollution, disease and other negative side-effects of current means of production. The rising incidence of some serious diseases, such as diabetes and cancer, may be linked to the presence of chemical additives in processed food. Clearly it is unfair that only the wealthy are able to avoid the risk of being slowly poisoned because they can afford to buy better-quality 'organic' food. At the very least, we require …

- An effective tax on carbon emissions at a rate that finances investments to neutralise the effects of carbon emissions over and above a sustainable rate (defined as a rate expected not to increase planet temperatures by more than 2° Celsius in the long run). Pending a binding treaty at the global level that can be effectively policed, individual states, countries and the EU should proceed unilaterally. In order to deter companies from moving operations to lower-taxed regions, appropriate exit taxes should be imposed, as well as naming and shaming to encourage consumers to avoid brands that pursue environmentally damaging policies and procedures.
- Laws banning the use of plastic for retail purposes and the dumping of plastic waste in the sea.
- Laws requiring pesticides and other artificial compounds used in agriculture to pass rigorous tests proving they have no adverse effects on the environment and those directly exposed to them, as well as causing no long-

term damage through their ingestion into the food chain and leakage into the water supply. The onus of proof for safety should be inverted: chemicals in the food chain should be considered guilty unless proved innocent.

- The phasing out of hormones and routine use of antibiotics on animals, and a return to organic farming. The consequent rise in the cost of food would be met by a corresponding rise in the minimum wage, guaranteed incomes and allowances to enable the poorest sections of society to afford healthy natural food.

9. Upgrade national constitutions

The underlying political problems threatening to destroy our democracies stem from three sources.

a) Political institutions have been perverted by the power and influence of money. Instead of one citizen, one vote, we have been sliding towards one dollar/pound/ euro, one effective vote.

b) Communications technology and the speed of information transfer have transformed social and economic relations. Our political institutions and constitutional arrangements need updating to catch up with the modern world.

c) The fundamental paradox of political economy remains. There is no political system or collective decision-making logic that consistently and demonstrably provides the best social outcomes (Kenneth Arrow's voter paradox proves how voting can be inconclusive; see Chapter 7). Even if we could measure each person's happiness in different outcomes (which we cannot), this would not guarantee fairness since it could be used to justify the tyranny of the majority.

So what to do?

By definition, there is no foolproof solution because of c. This does not mean we cannot improve the system in ways that would be generally recognised along the following lines …

- Curtail the influence of private money over the political system (see 5 above). This at least reduces the risk of oligarchy.

Trust in the people; after all, it is their interests that matter. Modern communications have, in theory, liberated us from the need for assemblies like Congress, the Houses of Parliament, l'Assemblée nationale or the Bundestag, to which we send our elected professional politicians to represent us and debate and decide the law. Technology can empower us and eliminate the conflicts of interest inherent in delegating the political side of government to intermediaries pursuing their own agendas. We could simply all vote on key issues using our TV remotes or smartphones; we certainly don't need to go through the antiquated process of visiting a polling station to cast a paper ballot. All that would be required is for civil servants at each level – local, regional, national, federal – to order and present questions to be put to the vote. Citizens wishing to put a question to a national vote would need to gather a threshold number of signatures. Professional politicians could be replaced by expert moderators for the issue in question, who would guide the presentation of key information and trade-offs to the people, arrange public debates face to face and over the Internet and media, and phrase the question for the popular vote.

In order to lessen the problem of decisions being taken by uninformed, busy citizens, time would be carved out of the working week for the study of information relating to upcoming votes. Furthermore, the state would train and employ teams of educators to meet members of the public on a regular basis to listen to their grievances and suggestions and debate the issues of the day. This is analogous to the time some states require from their citizens in the form of military service. This would be political service, taken out of the working week with no financial penalty for those in paid work. While the measured output of goods and services might reduce in the short term, the greater chances of socially harmonious decision-making in the long term would enhance and prolong the stability of the system.

All this necessitates a radical updating of Western constitutions. The greatest objection is not that it is technically impossible or too costly; it is that we are asking the current system to euthanise itself. The probability of elected politicians advocating constitutional reforms that abolish their own functions is akin to the chance of turkeys voting for Christmas. History shows us that institutions resist change until pushed to breaking point, so it will only come from a growing swell of popular opinion as a consensus forms that we need to move from the political equivalent of gold and silver coins to digital money. It will be a grass-roots movement, perhaps, to start with, grafting itself onto existing political formations. Today, we can identify potentially friendly groups within the Democratic Party in the US, certain centre and left-leaning elements within the UK, and strands such as the yellow vests in France, as well as elements of the governmental alliance in Italy, and Podemos in Spain. By cutting out the middle-man, technology can act as midwife for the re-birth of direct democracy.

This leaves us with the last and most intractable problem: the quest for the best political system has no hope of any *theoretical* solution. The dismal truth is that the finest political, philosophical and economic minds have pored over this enigma across the millennia without success. Anyone who claims to have solved this riddle is a charlatan. The right approach must therefore be to abandon theory and trust in the people in *practice*, under certain conditions. Their assent, their collective judgement, will be the ultimate test.

Given a situation where everyone lives in material security and basic comfort, where inequalities are not outrageously divisive and patently unfair, and where citizens are well educated, engaged and informed about the political issues and involved with their fellow citizens, feeling a sense of community and collective responsibility and respect, then direct democracy has a good shot at working. It will likely generate decisions on questions of principle that we generally see as socially good and fair, correctly balancing various interests for the common good in the long term. It should restore one person, one vote, untainted by the power of money.

Of all the solutions proposed in this chapter, this will probably take the most time to implement. Not only must the consensus build to a point where it becomes compelling, but the details of its implementation need to be agreed and put in place. Judging by our current febrile state of political discourse, this will be a long and challenging process.

At the same time, given our current predicament, no partial implementation will do. Simply restoring income tax rates to a more progressive pattern will not raise enough money to deal with the effects on labour of technology and globalisation. Nor will outlawing private cash in politics remove all conflicts of interest between voters and elected. Such individual measures will help, but if we are serious about giving our twin economic and democratic engines an overdue full service that will keep us safe for the long term and confound Marxian fatalists, then *all* of these measures are probably needed. What is heartening is that these issues are now being talked about more widely and are sure to figure prominently in upcoming national elections across Western countries.

It will require huge efforts to break with deeply ingrained bad habits. We must relinquish instant gratification and extreme individualism and relearn the discipline of making short-term term sacrifices for long-term gains. It is achievable, should we so decide. Our fate is in our own hands.

Notes

1 Globalisation and its perversions

1. 'Globalization: a brief overview', International Monetary Fund (IMF), May 2008, accessed at: www.imf.org/external/np/exr/ib/2008/053008. htm, 4 October 2019.

2. David Ricardo, *On the Principles of Political Economy and Taxation*, first published 1817.

3. Adam Smith, *An Inquiry into the Nature and Causes of the Wealth of Nations*, Vol. 1, first published 1776.

4. Joan Robinson, *Aspects of Development and Underdevelopment*, Cambridge University Press, 1979, p.103.

5. 'Exports of goods and services (% of GDP)', World Bank databank, accessed at: www.data.worldbank.org/indicator/NE.EXP.GNFS.ZS, 22 October 2019.

6. Janet L. Yellen, 'Recent developments and the outlook for the economy', Speech by Ms Janet L. Yellen, Chair of the Board of Governors of the Federal Reserve System, at the City Club of Cleveland, Cleveland, Ohio, 10 July 2015.

7. Susan Houseman, Christopher Kurz, Paul Lengermann and Benjamin Mandel, 'Offshoring Bias in U.S. Manufacturing', *Journal of Economic Perspectives*, Vol. 25, No. 2, 2011.

8. Gwynn Guilford, 'The epic mistake about manufacturing that's cost Americans millions of jobs', *Quartz*, 3 May 2018, accessed at: www.qz. com, 22 October 2019.

9. Jill Petzinger, 'Germany has way more industrial robots than the US, but they haven't caused job losses,' *Quartz*, 10 October 2017, accessed at: www.qz.com, 25 October 2019.

10. Scott Andes and Mark Muro, 'Don't blame the robots for lost

manufacturing jobs', Brookings Institution blog, accessed at: www.brookings.edu/blog/the-avenue/2015/04/29/, 25 October 2019.

11. Davis H. Autor, David Dorn and Gordon H. Hanson, 'The China Syndrome: Local Labor Market Effects of Import Competition in the United States', *American Economic Review*, Vol. 103, No. 6, 2013.

12. David Acemoglu, David Autor, David Dorn, Gordon H. Hanson and Brendan Price, 'Import Competition and the Great US Employment Sag of the 2000s', *Journal of Labor Economics*, Vol. 34, No. 1. Part 2, 2016.

13. Justin K. Pierce and Peter K. Schott, 'The Surprisingly Swift Decline of US Manufacturing Employment', National Bureau of Economic Research (NBER), Working Paper No. 18655, December 2012.

14. Robert E. Scott, 'Growth in U.S.–China trade deficit between 2001 and 2015 cost 3.4 million jobs', Economic Policy Institute, 31 January 2017, accessed at: www.epi.org/publication/growth-in-u-s-china-trade-deficit-between-2001-and-2015, 25 October 2019.

15. Ibid.

16. Joseph E. Stiglitz, 'On the Wrong Side of Globalization', *The New York Times*, 15 March 2014.

17. David E. Bonior, 'Obama's Free-Trade Conundrum', *The New York Times*, 29 January 2014.

18. Ibid.

19. 'Age – People (Both Sexes Combined – All Races) by Median and Mean Income: 1974–2018', United States Census Bureau, Historical Income Tables, Table P-10, accessed at: www.census.gov/data/tables/time-series/demo/income-poverty/historical-income-people, 26 October 2019.

20. 'Germany real wage growth YoY', Trading Economics, accessed at: www.tradingeconomics.com/germany/wage-growth, 26 October 2019.

21. Federal Reserve Bank of St Louis, Economic data, accessed at: www.fred.stlouisfed.org/series/NYGDPPCAPKDDEU, 26 October 2019.

22. 'Globalization and the Crisis (2005–Present)', IMF, accessed at: www.imf.org/external/about/histglob.htm, 26 October 2019.

23. International Labour Organization (ILO), Global Wage Report 2018/19, accessed at: www.hbs.edu/competitiveness/Documents/competitiveness-at-a-crossroads.pdf.

24. ILO World Employment Social Outlook Trends 2019, accessed at: www.ilo.org/global/research/global-reports/weso/2019/lang--en/index. htm

25. Homi Kharas, 'The unprecedented expansion of the global middle class', Brookings Institution, Global Economy and Development Working Paper 100, February 2017, accessed at www.brookings.edu/ wp-content/uploads/2017/02/global_20170228_global-middle-class. pdf.

26. Hyman P. Minsky, *Stabilizing an Unstable Economy*, McGraw Hill Education, 2008.

27. F. Fukuyama, 'The End of History?', *The National Interest*, No. 16, Summer 1989.

28. F. Fukuyama, 'At the "End of History" Still Stands Democracy', *Wall Street Journal*, 6 June 2014.

29. J. Huang and S. Rozelle, 'Agricultural development, nutrition, and the policies behind China's success', *Asian Journal of Agriculture & Development*, 2010, Vol. 7, No. 1, pp.93–126.

30. IMF data library.

31. World Bank data library.

32. Thomas Piketty, *Capital in the Twenty-First Century*, Harvard University Press, 2014.

33. Martin Wolf, 'The British economy after the coalition', *Financial Times*, 28 April 2015.

34. Michael Porter, Jan Rivkin and Rosabeth Kanter, 'Competitiveness at a Crossroads: Findings of Harvard Business School's 2012 Survey on U.S. Competitiveness', Harvard Business School, February 2013, accessed at www.hbs.edu/competitiveness/Documents/ competitiveness-at-a-crossroads.pdf.

35. Robert Skidelsky, 'Meeting our makers: Britain's long Industrial decline', *New Statesman*, 23 January 2013.

2 What to do with obsolete humans

1. Peter Brabeck, 'Davos: Smart machines set to transform society', *Financial Times*, 21 January 2016, citation, accessed at: www.ft.com/ content/c5cf07c4-bf8e-11e5-846f-79b0e3d20eaf.

2. Martin Wolf, 'Enslave the robots and free the poor', *Financial Times*,

21 January 2014, accessed at: www.ft.com/content/dfe218d6-9038-11e3-a776-00144feab7de.

3. Aaron Smith and Janna Andersen, 'AI, Robotics and the Future of Jobs', Pew Research Center, 6 August 2014, accessed: at www.pewresearch.org/internet/2014/08/06/future-of-jobs/.

4. Georg Graetz and Guy Michaels, 'Robots at Work', Centre for Economic Policy Research, March 2015.

5. Martin Ford, *The Rise of the Robots*, Basic Books, 2015, p.35.

6. Glen White, 'Volkswagen to replace human workforce with robots to meet demand', *The Manufacturer*, 7 October 2014, citation, accessed at: www.manufacturingglobal.com/people-and-skills/volkswagen-replace-human-workforce-robots-germany-meet-demand.

7. Wassily Leontief, 'National Perspective: The Definition of Problems and Opportunities', National Academy Press, 30 June 1983, Part of National Academy of Engineering Symposium on the Long-Term Impact of Technology on Employment and Unemployment.

8. Craig Holmes and Ken Mayhew, CIPD Policy Report, 'Over-qualification and skills mismatch in the graduate labour market', August 2015, accessed at: www.cipd.co.uk/knowledge/work/skills/graduate-labour-market-report.

9. Larry Page, Khosla Ventures CEO Summit, 3 July 2014, accessed at: www.khoslaventures.com/fireside-chat-with-google-co-founders-larry-page-and-sergey-brin, 29 October 2019.

10. Eric Schmidt, widely reported speech at Davos World Economic Forum, January 2014.

11. Martin Ford, *The Lights in the Tunnel*, Acculant Publishing, 2009.

12. Marc Andreessen, 'Why software is eating the world', *Wall Street Journal*, 10 August 2011.

13. Ford, *The Rise of the Robots*, p.11.

14. Minsky, *Stabilizing an Unstable Economy*.

15. Robert Gordon, *The Rise and Fall of American Growth*, Princeton University Press, 2015.

16. Shawn Sprague, 'Below trend: The US productivity slowdown since the great recession', Bureau of Labor Statistics, Vol. 6, No. 2, January 2017.

17. 'Real Median Personal Income in the United States,' Federal Reserve

Bank of St Louis, Economic research, accessed at: www.fred.stlouisfed.org/series/MEPAINUSA672N.

18. 'Technology does not possess a divine right', *Financial Times* leader, 26 January 2015.

19. Brian Groom, 'Weak productivity cited as main reason for falling wages', *Financial Times*, 31 January 2014.

20. 'Automation and the threat to jobs', *Financial Times* leader, 27 January 2014.

21. Carl Benedikt Frey and Michael A. Osborne, 'The future of employment: How susceptible are jobs to computerization', Oxford Martin Programme on Technology and Employment, 17 September 2013, accessed at: www.fhi.ox.ac.uk/wp-content/uploads/The-Future-of-Em%22ployment-How-Susceptible-Are-Jobs-to-Computerization.pdf.

22. Ford, *The Rise of the Robots*, p.55.

23. Ibid.

24. Erik Brynjolfsson and Andrew MacAfee, *Race Against the Machine: How the digital revolution is accelerating innovation, driving productivity, and irreversibly transforming employment and the economy*, Digital Frontier Press, 2011.

25. Robert Reich, 'Why we'll need a universal basic income', 29 September 2016, accessed at: www.Robertreich.org, 30 October 2019.

26. Guy Standing, 'Basic Income as Common Dividends: Piloting a Transformative Policy', Report for the Shadow Chancellor of the Exchequer, 7 May 2019.

3 The falling share of labour in the economy

1. Bureau of Labor Statistics, US Department of Labor and S&P 500 index.

2. 'Playing to win: The new global competition for global profits', McKinsey Global Institute, September 2015.

3. 'UK corporate profits as a percentage of GDP, 1988–2015', Thomson Reuters Datastream and Office for National Statistics (ONS).

4. Piketty, *Capital in the Twenty-First Century*.

5. Henry Ford, 6 June 1913, accessed at: www.quoteswise.com/henry-ford-quotes.

6. S&P 500 Historical Return Calculator to July 2019, accessed at: www. dqydj.com/sp-500-historical-return-calculator/.

7. Stephen Machin, 'Real Wages and Living Standards', Chart from the Centre for Economic Performance, London School of Economics, 26 March 2015, accessed at: www.cep.lse.ac.uk/pubs/download/EA024. pdf.

8. 'Analysis of real earnings and contributions to nominal earnings growth, Great Britain, September 2018', Office for National Statistics (ONS), accessed at: www.ons.gov.uk/employmentandlabourmarket/ peopleinwork/earningsandworkinghours/articles/ supplementaryanalysisofaverageweeklyearnings/september2018, 5 November 2019.

9. Machin, 'Real Wages and Living Standards', 26 March 2015.

10. Stephen Machin, Conference, Bank of England, 23 and 24 September 2015.

11. Lenny Aizenman and Richard Lane, 'US companies' cash holdings down 15.2% as capex, dividends, buy-backs and acquisitions hit new record highs', Moody's Investor Services, 10 June 2019, accessed at: www.moodys.com/research/, 5 November 2019.

4 Rising inequality in developed countries

1. Gustavo Gonzales, OECD Secretary General on Twitter, 29 January 2018.

2. Emmanuel Saez and Gabriel Zucman, 'Wealth Inequality in the United States Since 1913: Evidence from Capitalized Income Tax Data', NBER, Working Paper No. 20625, October 2014.

3. 'Savings as % of adjusted disposable income, by equivalised disposable income quintile, 2008, 2012 and 2013', Office for National Statistics (ONS), accessed at: www.ons.gov.uk/economy/nationalaccounts/ uksectoraccounts/articles/thedistributionofhouseholdincome consumptionandsavingsanoecdstudy/2015-11-30

4. Era Dabal-Norris, Kalpana Kochbar et al., 'Causes and Consequences of Income Inequality: A Global Perspective', IMF Staff discussion note, June 2015.

5. 'In It Together: Why Less Inequality Benefits All', OECD, May 2015,

accessed at: www.oecd.org/social/in-it-together-why-less-inequality-benefits-all-9789264235120-en.htm .

6. *The Bank Credit Analyst*, Issue of March 2015

7. Caroline Binham, 'UK reviews impact of student debt on financial stability', *Financial Times*, 16 January 2019.

8. Angela Moneghan and Sally Weale, 'UK student debt soars to more than £100 billion', *The Guardian*, 15 June 2017.

9. Sutirtha Bagchi and Jan Svejnar, 'Does wealth inequality matter for growth?: The effect of billionaire wealth, income distribution and poverty', Institute of Labor Economics (IZA) Discussion Paper No. 7733, November 2013.

10. 'Focus on Inequality and Growth', OECD, December 2014, accessed at: www.oecd.org/social/Focus-Inequality-and-Growth-2014.pdf.

11. Gabriel Wildau and Tom Mitchell, 'China income inequality among the world's worst', *Financial Times*, 15 January 2016.

12. Sean Gorman, 'Bernie Sanders says Walmart heirs are wealthier than bottom 40 percent of Americans', Politifact Virginia, 14 March 2016, accessed at: www.politifact.com/virginia/statements/2016/mar/14/bernie-s/bernie-sanders-says-walmart-heirs-are-wealthier-bo/, 6 November 2019.

13. Emmanuel Saenz and Gabriel Zucman, 'Wealth inequality in the United States since 1913; Evidence from capitalized income data', *The Quarterly Journal of Economics*, May 2016.

14. 'The American middle class is losing ground', Pew Research Center, 9 December 2015, accessed at: www.pewsocialtrends.org/2015/12/09/the-american-middle-class-is-losing-ground/.

15. Sydney Leng, 'China's dirty little secret: Its growing wealth gap', *South China Morning Post*, 7 July 2017.

16. 'Proportion of aggregate wealth owned by the top 5% and top 1% 2006–2016', ONS, 10 May 2018.

17. Bobby Duffy, 'Comprehending the growing divide', Director of The Policy Institute, King's College London, 8 November 2018, accessed on www.bbc.com, 6 November 2019.

18. 'An economy for the 1%', Oxfam, 18 January 2016.

19. Noam Chomsky, Quora, 1 March 2016.

20. A. B. Atkinson and S. Morelli, 'The Chartbook of Economic

Inequality', 2014, accessed at: www.ecineq.org/milano/WP/ECINEQ2014-324.pdf, 6 November 2019.

21. Thomas Piketty and Emmanuel Saez, 'The Evolution of Top Incomes: A Historical and International Perspective', NBER, Working Paper No. 11955, January *2006*.

22. 'Income share held by the highest 10% – United States, United Kingdom', World Bank Development Research Group, accessed at: data.worldbank.org/indicator/SI.DST.10TH.10?locations=US-GB, 6 November 2019.

23. Megan Murphy, 'US ponders inequality amid economic rebound', *Financial Times*, 12 January 2015.

24. 'Income Inequality, Italy, 1980–2016', World Inequality Database, accessed at: www.wid.world/country/italy/, 6 November 2019.

25. Bertrand Garbinti, Jonathan Goupille-Lebret and Thomas Piketty, 'Income inequality in France: Economic growth and the gender gap', Vox CEPR Policy Portal, 5 September 2018, accessed at: www.voxeu.org/article/income-inequality-france, 6 November 2019.

26. John Kay, 'Rise in US and UK inequality principally due to financialisation and executive pay', 6 January 2015, accessed at: www.johnkay.com/2015/01/06/rise-in-us-and-uk-inequality-principally-due-to-financialisation-and-executive-pay/, 6 November 2019.

27. Employee earnings in the UK, ONS, 25 October 2018.

28. 'Finance Salaries: Average Base Pay', Glassdoor, accessed at: www.glassdoor.co.uk/Salaries/finance-salary-SRCH_KO0,7.htm.

29. Lawrence Mishal and Jessica Schieder, 'CEO compensation surged in 2017', Economic Policy Institute (EPI), 16 April 2018, accessed at: www.epi.org/publication/ceo-compensation-surged-in-2017/, 6 November 2019.

30. Olga Khazan, 'US corporate executives aren't the only ones making tons of money', *The Atlantic*, 19 March 2013, accessed at: www.theatlantic.com/international/archive/2013/03/us-corporate-executives-arent-the-only-ones-making-tons-of-money/274136/, 6 November 2019.

31. 'Executive pay: Review of FTSE 100 executive pay packages', CIPD, accessed at: www.cipd.co.uk/Images/7571-ceo-pay-in-the-ftse100-report-web_tcm18-26441.pdf

32. Robert Colville, 'Yes, CEOs are ludicrously overpaid. And yes it's getting worse', *Daily Telegraph*, 13 October 2014.
33. Jonas Cho Walsgard, 'Steering clear of the top paid CEOs pays off for a Nordea fund', re Robert Naes, investment manager at Nordea Bank, Bloomberg, 6 March 2019, accessed at www.bloomberg.com/news/articles/2019-03-06/steering-clear-of-the-top-paid-ceos-is-paying-off-for-this-fund.
34. Henry Mance, 'Quidell under fire over new appointments', *Financial Times*, 13 January 2015, accessed at: www.ft.com/content/a6eca70a-9a30-11e4-8426-00144feabdc0.
35. David Oakley and Alison Smith, 'Temperature rising again on corporate pay', *Financial Times*, 5 May 2014, accessed at: www.ft.com/content/c3890eaa-d44a-11e3-a122-00144feabdc0.

5 The debt explosion in the West

1. Bruce Western and Jake Rosenfeld, 'Unions, Norms, and the Rise in U.S. Wage Inequality', *American Sociological Review*, 4 August 2011.
2. Union Members Summary, Bureau of Labor Statistics, 18 January 2019.
3. Carl Roper, 'Trade union membership is growing but there's still work to do', TUC blog, 31 May 2018, accessed at: www.tuc.org.uk/blogs/trade-union-membership-growing-there's-still-work-do, 31 May 2018.
4. 'How the decline of unions will change America', *The Economist*, 19 June 2018, accessed at: www.economist.com/united-states, 7 November 2019.
5. Jaumotte and Osorio Buitron, 'Union Power and Inequality', CEPR's Policy Portal, 22 October 2015. The advanced economies in this study are Australia, Austria, Belgium, Canada, Denmark, Finland, France, Germany, Ireland, Italy, Japan, the Netherlands, New Zealand, Norway, Portugal, Spain, Sweden, Switzerland, the UK and the US.
6. Felix Richter, '50 years of US wages, in one chart', World Economic Forum (WEF), 12 April 2019, accessed at: www.weforum.org/agenda/2019/04/50-years-of-us-wages-in-one-chart, 7 November 2019.
7. 'The state of American jobs', Pew Research Center, 6 October 2016, accessed at: www.pewsocialtrends.org/2016/10/06/the-state-of-american-jobs/.

8. Adair Turner, *Between Debt and the Devil*, Princeton University Press, 2016, p.178.

9. 'The hollowing of the American middle class', Pew Research Center, 9 December 2015, accessed at: www.pewsocialtrends.org/2015/12/09/1-the-hollowing-of-the-american-middle-class/.

10. 'Global productivity growth remains weak', Total Economy Database™ – Key Findings, The Conference Board, April 2019, accessed at: www.conference-board.org/data/economydatabase/.

11. Luigi Buttiglione, Philip Lane, Lucretia Reichlin and Vincent Reinhart, 'Deleveraging? What de-leveraging?', International Center for Monetary and Banking Studies, September 2014, accessed at: www.ycsg.yale.edu/sites/default/files/files/deleveraging_geneva.pdf.

12. Atif Mian and Amir Sufi, *House of Debt*, University of Chicago Press, 2014.

13. Ben McLannahan on Jack Guttentag, 'The nonagenarian taking on home lenders', *Financial Times*, 17 April 2016.

14. Buttiglione et al., 'Deleveraging? What de-leveraging?'

15. Turner, *Between Debt and the Devil*, p.7.

16. 'The diminishing impact of debt on U.S. economic growth', Disruptive Investor, 14 January 2009, accessed at: www.seekingalpha.com/article/143089-the-diminishing-impact-of-debt-on-u-s-economic-growth, 7 November 2019.

17. Charles Finch, *Financial Times*, Letters, 15 May 2015.

18. Turner, *Between Debt and the Devil*, Preface.

19. Alan Greenspan, 'Risk Transfer and Financial Stability', Remarks to the Federal Reserve Bank of Chicago's 41st annual conference, 5 May 2005.

20. Alan Greenspan in a speech to the Commercial Finance Association on 26 October 2006, as reported by the Associated Press ('Finally, Greenspan can speak his mind').

21. Alan Greenspan, *The Age of Turbulence*, Penguin, 2007.

22. 'Greenspan admits mistake that helped crisis', NBC News, 23 October 2008, accessed at: www.nbcnews.com/id/27335454/ns/business-stocks_and_economy/t/greenspan-admits-mistake-helped-crisis/#.XUneGi2QiN0, 7 November 2019.

23. 'Average annual wages', OECD.Stat, accessed at: stats.oecd.org/Index. aspx?DataSetCode=AV_AN_WAGE, 7 November 2019.
24. Buttiglione et al., 'Deleveraging? What de-leveraging?'
25. Ibid.

6 The free market, politics and the road to the Great Financial Crisis
1. Minsky, *Stabilizing an Unstable Economy.*
2. Ibid., p.191.
3. 'Greenspan says he would pre-empt asset bubbles financed by debt', Newsmax, 4 December 2013, accessed at: www.newsmax.com/finance/greenspan-bubble-federal-reserve-economy/2014/12/04/id/611129/, 7 November 2019.
4. Remarks by Mr Alan Greenspan, Chairman of the Board of Governors of the US Federal Reserve System, before the Economic Club of New York, New York City, 19 December 2002.
5. Ayn Rand, The Ayn Rand Institute, accessed at: aynrand.org.
6. Greenspan, *The Age of Turbulence.*
7. 'Greenspan Says Tariffs on China Would Hurt U.S. Economy, Jobs', Bloomberg News, accessed on 7 January 2013.
8. Jesse Colombo, 'Black Monday, the stock market crash of 1987', The Bubble, 3 August 2012, accessed at: www.thebubblebubble.com/1987-crash/, 10 November 2019.
9. Kimberley Amadeo, 'Savings and loan crisis explained', The Balance, 25 June 2019, accessed at: www.thebalance.com/savings-and-loans-crisis-causes-cost-3306035, 8 November 2019.
10. Federal Deposit Insurance Corporation (FDIC) and James R. Barth, 'History of the eighties, lessons for the future', *The Great Savings and Loan Debacle*, American Enterprise Institute Press, 1991, Chapter 4, accessed at: www.fdic.gov/bank/historical/history/167_188.pdf, 8 November 2019.
11. Timothy Curry and Lynn Shibut, 'The Cost of the Savings and Loans Crisis: Truth and Consequences', *FDIC Banking Review*, 1 January 2000, accessed at: www.fdic.gov/bank/analytical/banking/br2000v13n2.pdf, 8 November 2019.
12. William Seidman, 'Lessons of the eighties, what does the evidence

show?', accessed at: www.fdic.gov/bank/historical/history/vol2/panel3. pdf, 8 November 2019.

13. FDIC and Barth, 'History of the eighties, lessons for the future', Chapter 4.

14. 'US Housing Starts Fall from 12-Year High', Trading Economics, accessed at: www.tradingeconomics.com/united-states/housing-starts, 8 November 2019.

15. Joseph Whit, 'The Mexican Peso Crisis', Federal Reserve Bank of Atlanta, *Economic Review*, accessed at: www.frbatlanta.org/-/media/ documents/research/publications/economic-review/1996/vol81no1_ whitt.pdf, 8 November 2019.

16. Ibid.

17. Giancarlo Corsetti, Paolo Pesenti and Nouriel Roubini, 'What caused the Asian currency and financial crisis', NBER, December 1998, accessed at: www.nber.org/papers/w6833.pdf, 8 November 2019.

18. IMF Staff, 'Recovery from the Asian crisis and the role of the IMF', accessed at: www.imf.org/external/np/exr/ib/2000/062300.htm#VI, 8 November 2019.

19. Sergei Ulatov and Brian Pinto, 'Financial Globalization and the Russian Crisis of 1998', The World Bank Managing Director's Office, May 2010.

20. Abigail Chiodo and Michael Owyang, 'A Case Study of a Financial Crisis: The Russian Default of 1998', Federal Reserve Bank of St Louis, November / December 2002, accessed at: www.files.stlouisfed.org/ files/htdocs/publications/review/02/11/ChiodoOwyang.pdf.

21. Alan Greenspan, 'The economic outlook', Testimony to the Joint Economic Committee, US Congress, 13 November 2002, accessed at: www.bis.org/review/r021114a.pdf, 8 November 2019.

22. Alan Greenspan, 'Understanding household debt obligations', Federal Reserve Board, 23 February 2004, accessed at: www.federalreserve.gov/ boarddocs/speeches/2004/20040223/, 8 November 2019.

23. Alex Pollock, 'Mugged by Uncertainty. What can Alan Greenspan still teach us?', Law & Liberty, 29 December 2013, accessed at: www. lawliberty.org/book-review/mugged-by-uncertainty-what-can-alan- greenspan-still-teach-us/, 8 November 2019.

24. Andy Blatchford, 'Explosion of global debt biggest risk to world

financial system, Bank of Canada warns', *Financial Post*, 15 March 2019, accessed at: www.business.financialpost.com/news/economy/rising-global-debt-holding-back-growth-opening-up-vulnerabilities-central-bank, 8 November 2019.

25. Minsky, *Stabilizing an Unstable Economy*.

26. Federal Reserve Bank of St Louis, Economic data, accessed at: www. fred.stlouisfed.org/series/USHOWN, 8 November 2019.

27. Mark Zandi, '*Financial Shock: Global panic and government bail-outs – how we got here and what must be done to fix it*, Pearson Education, 2010.

28. 'US National Debt and Deficit History', US Government Spending, accessed at: www.usgovernmentspending.com/debt_deficit_history, 8 November 2019.

29. Gautam Mukunda. 'The social and political cost of the financial crisis, ten years later', *Harvard Business Review*, 25 September 2018, accessed at: www.hbr.org/2018/09/the-social-and-political-costs-of-the-financial-crisis-10-years-later, 8 November 2019. The combination of increased expenditures and decreased revenues resulting from the crisis from 2008–10 is likely to cost the United States government well over $2 trillion, more than twice the cost of the 17-year-long war in Afghanistan. Broader measures are even more damning. Measured by decrease in per capita United States GDP compared to the pre-crisis trend, by 2016 the crisis had cost the country 15% of GDP, or $4.6 trillion.

30. Tom Clark and Andrew Dilnot, 'Measuring the UK fiscal stance since the Second World War', Institute for Fiscal Studies, Briefing Note No. 6, 2002.

31. 'Annual consolidate balance sheet of the eurosystem', European Central Bank, accessed at: www.ecb.europa.eu/pub/annual/balance/html/index.en.html, and Federal Reserve Board, accessed at: www. federalreserve.gov/monetarypolicy/bst_recenttrends.htm

7 The challenge to democracy

1. Paul Krugman, 'Reagan was a Keynseian', Economist's View, 8 June 2012, accessed at: economistsview.typepad.com/

economistsview/2012/06/paul-krugman-reagan-was-a-keynesian.html, 8 November 2019.

2. 'Revenue Effects of Major Tax Bills', Office of Tax Analysis, Dept of the Treasury, February 2013, accessed at: www.treasury.gov/resource-center/tax-policy/tax-analysis/Documents/WP81-Table2013.pdf, 9November 2019.

3. William Greider, The Atlantic Monthly Company, 22 November 1981.

4. Stuart Auerbach, 'America the diminished giant', *Washington Post*, 15 April 1987, accessed at: www.washingtonpost.com.

5. Ed Harris and Frank Sammartino, 'Trends in the distribution of household income, 1979–2009', Congressional Budget Office, *6 August 2012, accessed at: www.cbo.gov/publication/43524.*

6. Noam Chomsky, *Requiem for the American Dream*, Seven Stories Press, 2017.

7. House of Commons Library Briefing Paper No. 01942, 12 November 2018.

8. John Stuart Mill, *Utilitarianism*, first published 1861.

9. Kenneth Arrow, *Social Choice and Individual Values*, Yale University Press, 1951.

10. Anthony Downs, *An Economic Theory of Democracy*, Harper, 1957.

11. Mark Cartwright, 'Athenian Democracy', Ancient History Encyclopaedia, 3 April 2018.

12. Colin Brennan, 'Millennials are falling behind their boomer parents', *USA Today*, accessed at: www.usatoday.com/story/money/2017/01/13/millennials-falling-behind-boomer-parents/96530338/; updated 13 January 2017, Telegraph Forum.

13. Raj Chetty, David Grusky et al., 'The fading American dream: trends in absolute income mobility since 1940', NBER, Working Paper No. 22910, December 2016.

14. 'Youth better or worse than parents', IPSOS survey, 11 October 2016, accessed at: www.ipsosglobaltrends.com/youth-better-or-worse-than-parents/, 9 November 2019.

15. Fahmina Rahman and Daniel Tomlinson, 'Intergenerational Commission Report', Resolution Foundation, February 2018, accessed at: www.resolutionfoundation.org/app/uploads/2018/02/IC-international.pdf.

16. Hansard Society, *2019 Audit of Political Engagement*, accessed at: www.hansardsociety.org.uk/blog/finding-of-support-for-a-'strong-leader'-helps-provoke-responses-to-2019.

17. John Plender, 'Capitalism in crisis: The code that forms a bar to harmony', *Financial Times*, 9 January 2012, accessed at: www.ft.com/content/fb95b4fe-3863-11e1-9d07-00144feabdc0.

18. John Maynard Keynes, *Essays in Persuasion*, Macmillan, first published 1931.

19. Lawrence Summers, 'Voters deserve responsible nationalism, not reflex globalism', *Financial Times*, 10 July 2016.

20. Alistair Gray, 'Top financier warns on anti-business sentiment', *Financial Times*, 29 September 2015.

21. Deepanshu Bagchee, 'The American dream is now a myth: Joseph Stiglitz', CNBC, 26 June 2012, accessed at: www.cnbc.com/id/47957186, 8 November 2019.

22. Economist Intelligence Unit, Democracy Index 2018.

23. Anne Case and Angus Deaton, 'Mortality and morbidity in the 21st century', Brookings Institution Paper, April 2017.

24. Drake Baer and Thrive Global, 'Why are American men getting less marriageable', Business Insider, 20 January 2018.

25. 'Share of births outside of marriage', *OECD Family Database 2018*, accessed at: www.oecd.org/els/family/SF_2_4_Share_births_outside_marriage.pdf, 8 November 2019.

26. Gillian Tett, 'Bridgewater billionaire Ray Dalio: "I have an affinity for mistakes"', *Financial Times* interview, 12 January 2018.

27. 'Italy GDP per capita', Trading Economics, accessed at: www.tradingeconomics.com/italy/gdp-per-capita, 8 November 2019.

28. Mark Mazower, 'Ideas that fed the beast of fascism flourish today', *Financial Times*, 6 November 2016.

29. Ibid.

8 The capture of the political system by private interest groups

1. 'Public Good or Private Wealth?', Oxfam Brief, January 2019, accessed at: www.oxfamilibrary.openrepository.com/bitstream/handle/10546/620599/bp-public-good-or-private-wealth-210119-summ-en.pdf?utm_source=indepth.

2. United Nations Sustainable Development Goals, accessed at: www.un.org/sustainabledevelopment/poverty/, 9 November 2019.

3. Bernie Sanders, 'Let's wrench power back from the billionaires', *The Guardian*, 14 January 2018, accessed at: www.theguardian.com/commentisfree/2018/jan/14/power-billionaires-bernie-sanders-poverty-life-expectancy-climate-change.

4. Jill Abramson, 'Return of the secret donors', *The New York Times*, 16 October 2010, accessed at: www.nytimes.com/2010/10/17/weekinreview/17abramson.html.

5. Federal Election Commission, 'McCutchon v. FEC: Supreme court finds biennial limits unconstitutional', 15 April 2014, accessed at: www.fec.gov/updates/mccutcheon-v-fec-supreme-court-finds-aggregate-biennial-limits-unconstitutional/.

6. Bill Allisson and Elizabeth Dexheimer, 'Wall Street and Kochs fuel most expensive U.S. senate race ever', Bloomberg, 'U.S. Campaign Finance', 3 November 2016, accessed at: www.bloomberg.com/news/articles/2016-11-03/wall-street-and-kochs-fuel-most-expensive-u-s-senate-race-ever.

7. Bill Allisson, Mira Rojanasakul, Brittany Harris and Cedric Sam, 'Tracking the 2016 presidential race', Bloomberg, 9 December 2016.

8. Joshua L. Kalla and David E. Brookman, *American Journal of Political Science*, July 2016.

9. Christopher Witko, 'Campaign contributions, access, and government contracting', *Journal of Public Administration and Theory*, 18 March 2011, accessed at: www.academic.oup.com/jpart/article-abstract/21/4/761/955742.

10. Eleanor Neff Powell and Justin Grimmer, 'Money in exile: campaign contributions and committee access', *The Journal of Politics*, August 2016.

11. Anthony Fowler, Haritz Garro and Jörg L. Spenkuch, 'Quid pro quo? Corporate returns to campaign contributions,' June 2017, accessed at: www.pdfs.semanticscholar.org/e981/58bbc9f3bac640a370b88870c166caf7a855.pdf.

12. Thomas Bassetti and Filippo Pavesi, 'Electoral Contributions and the Cost of Unpopularity', *Economic Inquiry*, 2017, Vol. 55, No. 4, pp.1771–91; doi: 10.1111/ecin.12461.

13. Michael Traugott, Reuters, 9 November 2016.
14. Chris Morris, 'The 10 politicians who have benefited the most from NRA funding', fortune.com, 15 February 2018, accessed at: www.fortune.com/2018/02/15/nra-contributions-politicians-senators/.
15. Aaron Kessler, 'Why the NRA is so powerful, by the numbers', CNN, 23 February 2018, accessed at: www.edition.cnn.com/2018/02/23/politics/nra-political-money-clout/index.html.
16. Charlotte Hill, 'The real reason the NRA's money matters in elections', Vox, updated 24 March 2018, accessed at: www.vox.com/the-big-idea/2018/2/27/17051560/money-nra-guns-contributions-donations-parkland-march.
17. The Library of Congress, Campaign finance in Germany, accessed at: www.loc.gov/law/help/campaign-finance/germany.php#t53.
18. Martin Gilens and Benjamin Page, 'Testing theories of American politics: elites, interest groups, and average citizens', American Political Science Association, 2014, accessed at: www.scholar.princeton.edu/sites/default/files/mgilens/files/gilens_and_page_2014_-testing_theories_of_american_politics.doc.pdf.
19. Karl Evers-Hillstrom, 'Lobbying reaches $3.4 billion in 2018, highest in 8 years', Open Secrets News, 25 January 2019, accessed at: www.opensecrets.org/news/2019/01/lobbying-spending-reaches-3-4-billion-in-18/.
20. 'Wall Street lobby and campaign cash tops $2 billion for 2016 elections', Americans for Financial Reform, March 2017, accessed at: www.ourfinancialsecurity.org/2017/03/afr-report-wall-street-lobby-campaign-cash-tops-2-billion-2016-elections/.
21. 'Industries', Centre for Responsive Politics, Open Secrets, accessed at: www.opensecrets.org/federal-lobbying/industries?cycle=2018.
22. Zachary Mider and Ben Elkin, 'How Hedge Funds (Secretly) Get Their Way in Washington', *Bloomberg Businessweek*, 25 January 2018.
23. Alan Rappeport and Emily Flitter, 'Congress approves first big Dodd-Frank rollback', *The New York Times*, 22 May 2019, accessed at: www.nytimes.com/2018/05/22/business/congress-passes-dodd-frank-rollback-for-smaller-banks.html.
24. Alan Rappeport and Emily Flitter, 'Regulators move to ease post-crisis relation of Wall Street', *The New York Times*, 6 March 2019,

accessed at: www.nytimes.com/2019/03/06/business/bank-regulation.
html.

25. Charles Calomiris and Stephen Haber, *Fragile by Design: The Political Origins of Banking Crises and Scarce Credit*, Princeton University Press, 2014.

26. Susanne Craig and Deborah Solomon, 'Bank Bonus Tab: $33 Billion', *Wall Street Journal*, 31 July 2009, re. Andrew Cuomo, The Bank Bonus Report, July 2009, accessed at: www.wsj.com/articles/SB124896891815094085, 9 November 2019.

27. David Luttrell, Tyler Atkinson and Harvey Rosenblum, 'Assessing the cost and consequences of the 2007–09 financial crisis and its aftermath', Federal Reserve Bank of Dallas, 7 September 2013, accessed at: www.dallasfed.org/research/eclett/2013/el1307.cfm.

28. 'Taxpayer support for UK banks: FAQs', National Audit Office, updated November 2019, accessed at: www.nao.org.uk/highlights/taxpayer-support-for-uk-banks-faqs/.

29. Robert Strauss, 'It was the Greeks who paid to bail out those bankers', *Financial Times*, Letters, 21 December 2017.

30. 'Annual consolidate balance sheet of the eurosystem', European Central Bank, accessed at: www.ecb.europa.eu/pub/annual/balance/html/index.en.html.

31. Michael MacKenzie, 'Charts that matter: The importance of central banks for equity prices', *Financial Times*, 14 July 2017.

32. Paul Marshall, 'Central banks have made the rich richer,' *Financial Times*, 22 September 2015.

33. Writing in Marc Faber's *Gloom, Boom & Doom Report*, 23 September 2013.

34. 'Lobbying expenses spiked as Congress shaped tax overhaul', The Independent Ledger, 10 February 2018, accessed at: www.maysville-online.com/news/40673/lobbying-expenses-spiked-as-congress-shaped-tax-overhaul.

35. Lee Fang, 'Lawmakers who championed repeal of web browsing privacy protections raked in telecom campaign cash', *The Intercept*, 14 April 2017, accessed at: theintercept.com/2017/04/13/telecom-cash-isp/, 9 November 2019.

36. Ben Brody, 'Google topped peers in lobbying as Washington beat up big tech', Bloomberg, 24 January 2018.

37. Geoff West, 'Lobbying by Telecom industry spikes to end 2017', Open Secrets, 23 January 2018, accessed at: www.opensecrets.org/news/2018/01/lobbying-by-telecoms-industry-2017/, 9 November 2019.

38. 'Lawrence Lessig on Money, Corruption and Politics', On Point, 2 January 2012, accessed at: www.wbur.org/onpoint/2012/01/02/lawrence-lessig-on-money-corruption-and-politics, 10 November 2019.

39. Jack Abramof, 'Lobbying Reforms haven't fixed flawed system', CNN, 9 November 2011, accessed at: www.edition.cnn.com/2011/11/06/politics/abramoff-ethics/index.html, 9 November 2019.

40. Gary Rivlin and Susan Antilla, 'No protection for protectors', *The Intercept*, 18 November 2017, accessed at: www.theintercept.com/2017/11/18/wall-street-wants-to-kill-the-agency-protecting-americans-from-financial-scams/, 10 November 2019.

41. Pete Schroeder, 'U.S. regulators hand Wall Street a major win with stripped-down "Volcker rule"', Reuters, 20 August 2019, accessed at: www.reuters.com/article/us-usa-banks-volcker/u-s-regulators-hand-wall-street-a-major-win-with-stripped-down-volcker-rule-idUSKCN1VA1B8, 9 November 2019.

42. Greg Robb, 'Aggressive Volcker rule changes to come quickly, top Fed official in charge of regulation says', Marketwatch, 5 March 2018, accessed at: www.marketwatch.com/story/aggressive-volcker-rule-changes-to-come-quickly-top-fed-official-in-charge-of-regulation-says-2018-03-05, 9 November 2019.

43. 'Payday, vehicle title and certain high-cost instalment loans', Consumer Financial Protection Bureau, 6 February 2019, accessed at: www.consumerfinance.gov/policy-compliance/rulemaking/rules-under-development/payday-vehicle-title-and-certain-high-cost-installment-loans/, 9 November 2019.

44. Barney Jopson, 'Obama holdout stands in the way of US bank deregulatory wave', *Financial Times*, 3 May 2018, accessed at: www.app.ft.com/content/cd8d0576-4e00-11e8-8a8e-22951a2d8493.

45. Donald Light, Joel Lexchin and Jonathan Darrow, 'Institutional Corruption of Pharmaceuticals and the Myth of Safe and Effective

Drugs', *The Journal of Law, Medicine & Ethics*, September 2013, Vol. 41, pp.590–600; doi.org/ 10.1111/jlme.12068.

46. Ibid.

47. 'Opinion of the Scientific Committee on Veterinary Measures Relating to Public Health', European Commission, 30 April 1999, accessed at: www.ec.europa.eu/food/sites/food/files/safety/docs/sci-com_scv_out21_en.pdf., 9 November 2019.

48. 'Driving into Disaster', Corporate Europe Observatory, 23 February 2017, accessed at: www.corporateeurope.org/en/pressreleases/2017/02/european-commission-complicit-dieselgate-scandal-say-ngos, 9 November 2019.

49. 'Evaluation of five organophosphate insecticides and herbicides', International Agency for Research on Cancer, World Health Organization, *IARC Monographs*, Vol. 112, 20 March 2015, accessed at: www.iarc.fr/wp-content/uploads/2018/07/MonographVolume112-1.pdf., 9 November 2019.

50. Tina Bellon, 'California jury hits Bayer with $2 billion award in California Roundup cancer trial', Reuters, 14 May 2019, accessed at: www.reuters.com/article/us-bayer-glyphosate-lawsuit/california-jury-hits-bayer-with-2-billion-award-in-roundup-cancer-trial-idUSKCN1SJ29F, 9 November 2019.

51. Arthur Neslen, 'EU report on weedkiller safety copied report from Monsanto study', *The Guardian*, 15 September 2017, accessed at: www.theguardian.com/environment/2017/sep/15/eu-report-on-weedkiller-safety-copied-text-from-monsanto-study, 9 November 2019.

52. Arthur Neslen, 'EU on brink of historic decision on pervasive glyphosate weedkiller', *The Guardian*, 24 October 2017, accessed at: www.theguardian.com/environment/2017/oct/24/eu-brink-historic-decision-pervasive-glyphosate-weedkiller, 9 November 2019.

53. Diane Coyle, 'Protect faith in privatised monopolies with tougher regulation', *Financial Times*, 6 October 2017.

9 Declining taxes and the pauperisation of the nation state

1. Erica York, 'Income taxes on the top 0.1 per cent weren't much higher in the 1950s', Tax Foundation, 31 January 2019, accessed at: www.taxfoundation.org/income-taxes-on-the-rich-1950s-not-high/.

2. Kimberly Amadeo, 'Fiscal year 2019: Trump's Budget Request', The Balance, updated 8 August 2019, accessed at: www.thebalance.com/ fy-2019-federal-budget-summary-of-revenue-and-spending-4589082.

3. Helen Miller, 'What's been happening to corporation tax?', Institute for Fiscal Studies, 10 May 2017, accessed at: www.ifs.org.uk/ publications/9207.

4. 'Tax revenue trends in the OECD', OECD Revenue Statistics 2018, accessed at: www.oecd.org/tax/tax-policy/revenue-statistics-highlights-brochure.pdf.

5. National Insurance, accessed at: www.gov.uk/national-insurance, 9 November 2019.

6. 'The effects of taxes and benefits on income inequality: 1977 to financial year ending 2015', ONS, 8 April 2016, accessed at: www.ons. gov.uk/peoplepopulationandcommunity/ personalandhouseholdfinances/incomeandwealth/bulletins/ theeffectsoftaxesandbenefitsonincomeinequality/ 1977tofinancialyearending2015.

7. Robert Bellafiore, 'Summary of the latest federal income tax update, 2018 update', Tax Foundation, 13 November 2018, accessed at: www. taxfoundation.org/summary-latest-federal-income-tax-data-2018-update/.

8. Frank Samartino, 'Taxes and Income Inequality', Tax Policy Center, 15 June 2017, accessed at: www.taxpolicycenter.org/publications/taxes-and-income-inequality/full.

9. 'Focus on top incomes and taxation in OECD: Was the crisis a game changer?', OECD, May 2014, accessed at: www.oecd.org/social/ OECD2014-FocusOnTopIncomes.pdf, 9 November 2019.

10. 'Part II – Trends in global inequality', World Inequality Lab, accessed at: www.wir2018.wid.world/part-2.html, 9 November 2019.

11. Duncan Robinson, 'Report links McDonalds to EU tax avoidance scandal', *Financial Times*, 25 February 2015, accessed at: www.ft.com/ content/aeeaf598-bcfd-11e4-9902-00144feab7de.Duncan, 9 November 2019.

12. Robert-Jan Bartunek, 'EU orders Amazon to repay $295 million in back taxes', Reuters, 4 October 2017, accessed at: www.reuters.com/

article/us-eu-amazon-taxavoidance/eu-orders-amazon-to-repay-295-million-in-luxembourg-back-taxes-idUSKCN1C913S.

13. Kamal Ahmed, 'Google's tax bill rises to £50 million', BBC News, 28 March 2018, accessed at: www.bbc.com/news/business-4356675, 9 November 2019.

14. Colm Keena, 'Apple records $119 billion of global sales', *Irish Times*, 7 November 2017, accessed at: www.irishtimes.com/business/technology/apple-records-global-sales-of-119bn-in-ireland-1.3283066e, 9 November 2019.

15. Ibid.

16. 'State aid: Ireland gave illegal tax benefits to Apple worth up to Euros 13 billion', European Commission Press Release Database, 30 August 2016, accessed at: europa.eu/rapid/press-release_IP-16-2923_en.htm.

17. Mehreen Kahn, 'Vestager's sweethearts', *Financial Times*, 25 September 2019.

18. 'Tax revenue trends in the OECD', OECD Revenue Statistics 2018, accessed at: www.oecd.org/tax/tax-policy/revenue-statistics-highlights-brochure.pdf.

19. OECD Revenue Statistics 2018, The United Kingdom.

20. John Plender, 'Corporate aristocracy holding out against tax revolution', *Financial Times*, 2 March 2015.

21. 'Breaking the dilemma on global corporation tax', *Financial Times* editorial, 12 March 2018.

22. Edward Luce, 'US share buybacks loot the future', *Financial Times*, 26 April 2015.

23. Lucinda Chen, 'General Electric's value plummeted under Jeffrey Immelt', *Fortune*, 12 June 2017.

24. Thomas Gryta, 'GE probed who knew about spare jet for Immelt', *Wall Street Journal*, updated 12 December 2017, accessed at: www.wsj.com/articles/ge-probed-who-knew-about-spare-jet-for-immelt-1513078200, 9 November 2019.

25. 'No routine riches: Reforms to performance-related pay', High Pay Centre (HPC), May 2015, accessed at: www.highpaycentre.org/pubs/no-routine-riches-reforms-to-performance-related-pay, 9 November 2019.

26. 'HPC responds to select committee inquiry on executive pay', HPC,

16 May 2018, accessed at: www.highpaycentre.org/pubs/hpc-responds-to-select-committee-inquiry-on-executive-pay, 9 November 2019.

27. Suzanne Fitzpatrick et al., 'The homelessness monitor: England 2018', Crisis, April 2018, accessed at: www.crisis.org.uk/media/238700/homelessness_monitor_england_2018.pdf, November 2019.

28. 'Briefing: health and care of older people in England 2017', Age UK, February 2017, accessed at: www.ageuk.org.uk/Documents/EN-GB/For-professionals/Research/The_Health_and_Care_of_Older_People_in_England_2016.pdf?dtrk=true.

29. 'Education Expenditures by Country', *The Condition of Education 2019*, Chapter 4, accessed at: nces.ed.gov/programs/coe/pdf/coe_cmd.pdf, 9 November 2019.

30. Hannah Richardson, 'All state schools in England "to face funding gap by 2020"', BBC News, 17 March 2017, accessed at: www.bbc.com/news/education-39292344, 9 November 2019.

31. Chris Belfield, Christine Farquharson and Luke Sibieta, '2018 Annual report on education spending in England', IFS/Nuffield Foundation, September 2018, accessed at: www.ifs.org.uk/uploads/publications/comms/R150.pdf, 9 November 2019.

32. 'The implications of the National Funding Formula for schools', Education funding report, Education Policy Institute, 17 March 2017, accessed at: epi.org.uk/publications-and-research/implications-national-funding-formula-schools/, 9 November 2019.

33. 'Education at a Glance 2017: How much are teachers paid?', OECD iLibrary, accessed at: www.oecd-ilibrary.org/docserver/eag-2017-31-en.pdf?expires=1566134251&id=id&accname=guest&checksum=6B9917A0BD0ABE83D42749AAB17606B6, 9 November 2019.

34. 'Not practical to investigate all crimes', BBC News, 16 October 2017, accessed at: www.bbc.com/news/uk-england-london-41633205, 9 November 2019.

35. 'Shoplifters taking under £200 worth of goods "not pursued"', BBC News, 27 December 2017, accessed at: www.bbc.com/news/uk-42492488, 9 November 2019.

36. 'Met chief says budget cuts have contributed to the rise in violent crime', *The Guardian*, 18 May 2018, accessed at: www.theguardian.

com/uk-news/2018/may/18/metropolitan-police-cressida-dick-budget-cuts-violent-crime-rise-london, 9 November 2019.

37. 'London killings: Why are they happening?', BBC News, 6 April 2018, accessed at: www.bbc.com/news/uk-england-43654831.6, 9 November 2019.

38. 'Insécurité et délinquance en 2017: Un premier bilan', Report of 24 January 2018, Ministère de l'Intérieur, France, accessed at: www.interieur.gouv.fr/Interstats/Actualites/Insecurite-et-delinquance-en-2017-premier-bilan-statistique.

39. 'Revealed: Shocking 25 percent of evening and week-end GP appointments empty', *The Pulse*, 1 October 2018, accessed at: www.pulsetoday.co.uk/news/hot-topics/seven-day-gp-access/revealed-shocking-25-of-evening-and-weekend-gp-appointments-empty/20037533.article.

40. Siva Anandaciva, 'NHS Myth-busters', The King's Fund, 20 November 2017, accessed at: www.kingsfund.org.uk/publications/nhs-myth-busters, 9 November 2019.

41. Emma Rosser, 'Revealed: GP vacancy rates rocket with one in six roles unfilled', *The Pulse*, 6 July 2018, accessed at: www.pulsetoday.co.uk/partners-/practice-business/revealed-gp-vacancy-rates-rocket-with-one-in-six-roles-unfilled/20036995.article, 9 November 2019.

42. Emily Andrews, Graham Atkins et al., 'Performance tracker 2018: A data-driven analysis of the performance of public services', Institute for Government / CIPFA, accessed at: www.instituteforgovernment.org.uk/sites/default/files/publications/Performance%20Tracker%20 2018%20web.pdf, 9 November 2019.

43. Harris Meyer, 'Why does the US spend so much more on healthcare? It's the prices', *Modern Healthcare*, 7 April 2019, accessed at: www.modernhealthcare.com/article/20180407/NEWS/180409939/why-does-the-u-s-spend-so-much-more-on-healthcare-it-s-the-prices, 9 November 2019.

44. OECD Health Statistics 2019, accessed at: www.oecd.org/els/health-systems/health-data.htm, 9 November 2019.

45. 'Health expenditure per capita, 2016 (or nearest year)', in *Health expenditure*, OECD Publishing, Paris, www.doi.org/10.1787/health_glance-2017-graph110-en.

OECD (2017). See also 'Annual average growth rate in per capita health expenditure, real terms, 2003 to 2016 (or nearest year)', in *Health expenditure*, OECD Publishing, Paris, www.doi.org/10.1787/health_glance-2017-graph111-en.

46. François Beguin, 'Apres huit années de baisse, les tarifs hospitaliers vont augmenter de 0.5%', *Le Monde*, 26 February 2018.

47. 'Chart of the day: Infrastructure spending over 60 years', *The Fiscal Times*, 19 October 2018, accessed at www.thefiscaltimes.com/2018/10/19/Chart-Day-Infrastructure-Spending-Over-60-Years, 9 Novemeber 2019.

48. 'Is German public investment heading for a sustained upswing?', Federal Ministry of Finance, 19 June 2017, accessed at: www.bundesfinanzministerium.de/Content/EN/Standardartikel/Topics/Public-Finances/Articles/2017-06-19-german-public-investment.html, 9 November 2019

49. Guy Chazan, 'Cracks appear in Germany's cash-starved infrastructure', *Financial Times*, 4 August 2017, accessed at: www.ft.com/content/a98f7b30-776a-11e7-90c0-90a9d1bc9691.

50. Paul Taylor and Ingrid Melander, 'French, German economists offer plan to counter stagnation', Reuters, 27 November 2014, accessed at: www.reuters.com/article/us-eurozone-economy-france-germany/french-german-economists-offer-plan-to-counter-eu-stagnation-idUSKCN0JB1I220141127, 9 November 2019.

51. Op-ed, 'The fiscal surplus that Germany should spend', *Financial Times*, 21 December 2017, accessed at: www.ft.com/content/2848ce2e-e640-11e7-97e2-916d4fbac0da, 9 November 2019.

52. Michael Moritz, 'US tax reform will benefit shareholders more than workers', *Financial Times*, 5 December 2017, accessed at: www.ft.com/content/ba834dca-d9af-11e7-9504-59efdb70e12f.

53. Edward Greenberg, *Turbulence: Boeing and the state of American workers and managers*, Yale University Press, 2010.

54. Huaqun Li and Kyle Pommerleau, 'The distribution impact of the tax cuts and jobs act over the next decade', Tax Foundation, 28 June 2018, accessed at: www.taxfoundation.org/the-distributional-impact-of-the-tax-cuts-and-jobs-act-over-the-next-decade/, 9 November 2019.

55. Gill Plimmer, 'Boeing and the decline of the US middle class',

Financial Times, 20 January 2016, accessed at: www.ft.com/
content/5487ad7c-b5fd-11e5-b147-e5e5bba42e51, 9 November 2019.

56. Milton Friedman, 'The social responsibility of business is to increase
its profits', *New York Times Magazine*, 13 September 1970, cited by
Andrew Edgcliffe-Johnsson in 'Beyond the bottom line: Should
business put purpose before profit?', *Financial Times*, 4 January 2019,
accessed at: www.ft.com/content/5487ad7c-b5fd-11e5-b147-
e5e5bba42e51, 9 November 2019.

57. Sarah Neville, 'Clive Cowdery donates £50 million to research living
standards', *Financial Times*, 20 April 2015, accessed at: www.ft.com/
content/3abfe1fc-eaab-11e4-96ec-00144feab7de, 9 November 2019.

10 The rise of China

1. Justin Yifu Lin, 'China and the Global Economy', 2011, Asia
Economic Policy Conference, Lunchtime address, accessed at: www.
frbsf.org/economic-research/files/Lin.pdf, 9 November 2019.

2. Kenneth Rapoza, 'China Wage Levels Equal to or Surpass Parts of
Europe', *Forbes,* 16 August 2017, accessed at: www.forbes.com, 9
November 2019.

3. Reuters in Beijing, 'Be more tolerant of traditional faiths, Xi Jinping
urges Communist Party', *South China Morning Post*, 30 September
2013, accessed at: www.scmp.com, 9 November 2019.

4. 'Special Report: Chinese Society', *The Economist*, 9 July 2016, accessed
at: www.economist.com/sites/default/files/sr_china_mailout_09.07.16.
pdf, 9 November 2019.

5. Nicholas R. Lardy, 'Issues in China's WTO Accession', The Brookings
Institution, 9 May 2001, accessed at: www.brookings.edu, 9 November
2019.

6. Robert Lighthizer, 'National Trade Estimate Report on Foreign Trade
Barriers 2018' (NTE), Office of the US Trade Representative, accessed
at: www.sice.oas.org/ctyindex/USA/USTR_Reports/2018/2018_
NTE_e.pdf, 10 November 2019.

7. James Anderlini, 'Chinese industry: Ambitions in excess', *The
Financial Times*, 16 June 2013, accessed at: www.ft.com/
content/4d5528ec-d412-11e2-8639-00144feab7de, 9 November 2019.

8. Usha C. V. Haley and George T. Hayley, *Subsidies to Chinese Industry*, Oxford University Press, 2013.

9. Lighthizer, 'National Trade Estimate Report on Foreign Trade Barriers 2018'.

10. Ibid.

11. Ibid.

12. Paige Leskin, 'Here are all the major US tech companies locked behind China's Great Firewall', *Business Insider*, 10 October 2019, accessed at: www.businessinsider.com/major-us-tech-companies-blocked-from-operating-in-china-2019-5?r=US&IR=T, 9 November 2019.

13. Agne Blazyte, 'Alibaba: cumulative active online buyers Q2 2014–Q2 2019', Statista, 27 September 2019, accessed at: www.statista.com/statistics/226927/alibaba-cumulative-active-online-buyers-taobao-tmall/, 9 November 2019.

14. Andre Tartar, Mira Rojanasakul and Jeremy Scott Diamond, 'How China is Buying Its Way Into Europe', Bloomberg, accessed at: www.bloomberg.com/graphics/2018-china-business-in-europe/, 9 November 2019.

15. Guy Chazan, 'Backlash grows over Chinese deals for Germany's corporate jewels', *Financial Times*, 12 March 2018, accessed at: www.ft.com/content/391637d2-215a-11e8-a895-1ba1f72c2c11, 9 November 2019.

16. Tim Buckley, 'China Regulator Safe revealed as controller of 5% stake in EDP', *Financial Times*, 19 June 2019, accessed at: www.ft.com/content/72bcb14a-73db-11e8-aa31-31da4279a601, 9 November 2019.

17. Agence France-Presse, 'Chinese investment in Europe: A story of cash and concerns', 28 March 2019, *European Data News Hub*, accessed at: www.ednh.news, 9 November 2019. And 'Is "Made in China 2025" a Threat to Global Trade?', Council on Foreign Relations, May 2019, accessed at: www.cfr.org/backgrounder/made-china-2025-threat-global-trade, 9 November 2019.

18. Ann Tang, 'China's tech race throws up thorny issues', *Financial Times*, 25 April 2018, accessed at: www.ft.com/content/78177942-488c-11e8-8ee8-cae73aab7ccb, 9 November 2019.

19. Christopher Thomas, 'A new world under construction: China and

semiconductors', McKinsey, November 2015, accessed at: www.mckinsey.com/featured-insights/asia-pacific/a-new-world-under-construction-china-and-semiconductors, 11 November 2019.

20. James Lewis, 'China's Pursuit of Semiconductor Independence', 27 February 2019, Center for Strategic and International Studies, accessed at: www.csis.org/analysis/chinas-pursuit-semiconductor-independence, 9 November 2019.

21. D. M. Chan, 'China's AI market to hit 71 billion yuan', *Asia Times*, 11 July 2019, accessed at: www.asiatimes.com/2019/07/article/chinas-ai-market-to-hit-71-bn-yuan/, 11 November 2019.

22. Guy Chazan, 'Backlash grows over Chinese deals for Germany's corporate jewels', *Financial Times*, 13 March 2018, accessed at: www.ft.com/content/391637d2-215a-11e8-a895-1ba1f72c2c11, 9 November 2019.

23. James Stavridis, 'Why China's emperor Xi should worry the US', Bloomberg, 27 February 2018, as also reported in *The Japan Times*, accessed 11 November 2019.

24. Ryan Brown, 'Alibaba's Jack Ma suggests technology could result in a new world war', Jack Ma at the WEF, Davos, 23 January 2019, as reported by CNBC, accessed at: www.cnbc.com/2019/01/23/alibaba-jack-ma-suggests-technology-could-result-in-a-new-world-war.html, 11 November 2019.

11 Solutions

1. 'Movin' on up', *The Economist*, 14 February 2018.

2. Max Lawson et al., 'Public Good or Private Wealth?', Oxfam report, January 2019, accessed at: oxfamilibrary.openrepository.com/bitstream/handle/10546/620599/bp-public-good-or-private-wealth-210119-summ-en.pdf?utm_source=indepth.

3. Ljubica Nedelkoska and Glenda Quintini, 'Automation, skills use and training', OECD Social, Employment and Migration Working Paper No. 202, 14 March 2018, accessed at: www.read.oecd-ilibrary.org/employment/automation-skills-use-and-training_2e2f4eea-en#page1.

Illustration sources

The publisher and author wish to thank the following sources for the use of their website information and other copyright material:

p.22, Figure 1.1, 'International comparisons of annual labor force statistics', The Conference Board, 2014, accessed at: www.conference-board.org/.

p.23, Table 1.1, Nicholas Lardy, 'Manufacturing employment in China', Peterson Institute for International Economics, 21 December 2015, accessed at: www.piie.com/blogs/china-economic-watch/manufacturing-employment-china.

p.37, Figure 1.2, Stephen Machin, 'Real wage trends' from 'Understanding the Great Recession' conference, Bank of England, 23 and 24 September 2015, accessed at: www.ifs.org.uk/uploads/Presentations/Understanding%20the%20recession_230915/SMachin.pdf.

p.60, Figure 3.1, 'The labour share in G20 economies', Organisation for Economic Co-operation and Development (OECD), accessed at: www.oecd.org/g20/topics/employment-and-social-policy/The-Labour-Share-in-G20-Economies.pdf.

p.61, Figure 3.2, Bank of America Merrill Lynch.

p.63, Figure 3.3, 'Share of labour compensation in GDP at current national prices for United States', University of Groningen and University of California, Davis, retrieved from FRED, Federal Reserve Bank of St. Louis, accessed at: www.fred.stlouisfed.org/series/LABSHPUSA156NRUG.

p.63, Figure 3.4, 'The labour share in G20 economies', Organisation for Economic Co-operation and Development (OECD), accessed at: www.oecd.org/g20/topics/employment-and-social-policy/The-Labour-Share-in-G20-Economies.pdf.

p.70, Figure 3.5, 'Why wages have stagnated while GDP has grown', chart by aneconomicsense.com, data from Bureau of Economic Analysis (BEA) and Bureau of Labor Statistics (BLS).

p.71, Table 3.1, data from World Inequality Database by Thomas Piketty, Emmanuel Saez et al., accessed at: www.wid.world.

p.72–3, Figures 3.6–8, Stephen Machin, 'Real wage trends' from 'Understanding the Great Recession: from micro to macro' conference, Bank of England, 23 and 24 September 2015, accessed at: www.ifs.org.uk/uploads/Presentations/Understanding%20the%20 recession_230915/SMachin.pdf.

p.89, Figure 4.2, Office for National Statistics.

p.90, Figure 4.3, Evan Soltas, originally accessed at: esoltas.blogspot.co.uk; now accessed at: www.industrious.info/45/07767-finance-graphs-and-charts.html.

p.107, Figure 5.1, Caroline Fairchild, 'Middle-class decline mirrors the fall of unions', *Huffington Post*, accessed at: www.huffpost.com/entry/ union-membership-middle-class-income_n_3948543.

p.109, Figure 5.2, 'Effective federal funds rate', Board of Governors of the Federal Reserve System (US), accessed at FRED, Federal Reserve Bank of St. Louis: www.fred.stlouisfed.org/series/FEDFUNDS.

p.110, Figure 5.3, 'United Kingdom interest rate', Tradingeconomics.com / Bank of England.

p.113 Figure 5.4, 'United States wages and salaries growth', Tradingeconomics.com / US Bureau of Economic Analysis.

p.115 Figure 5.5, Sarah O'Connor, 'Millenials poorer than previous generations, data shows', Luxembourg Income Study Database © *Financial Times*.

p.126 Figure 5.6, Bank of America Merrill Lynch Global Investment Strategy, Federal Reserve, DataStream, US Global Investors, accessed at: goldsilverworlds.com.

p.127 Figure 5.7, 'United States household debt to GDP', Trading Economics / Bank for International Settlements, accessed at: tradingeconomics.com.

p.128 Figure 5.8, based on data from Standard and Poor's Case–Shiller National Composite Home Price Index and made available by the Federal Reserve Bank of St. Louis. The index is a standardised representation of prices, with the average home price in Q1 2000 representing '100'. Trend Line is based on 1987 Q1–1999 Q1.

p.128 Figure 5.9, 'United Kingdom household debt to GDP', Trading Economics / Bank of International Settlements, accessed at: tradingeconomics.com.

p.132 Figure 5.10, 'France household debt to GDP', Trading Economics / Bank for International Settlements, accessed at: tradingeconomics.com.

p.132 Figure 5.11, 'Germany household debt to GDP', Trading Eonomics / Bank for International Settlements, accessed at: tradingeconomics.com.

p.150 Figure 6.1, 'Effective federal funds rate', Board of Governors of the Federal Reserve System (US), accessed at FRED, Federal Reserve Bank of St. Louis: www.fred.stlouisfed.org/series/FEDFUNDS.

p.152, Figure 6.2, Trading Economics / US Bureau of Economic Analysis, accessed at: www.tradingeconomics.com.

p.183 Figure 7.1, 'Federal deficit in the 20th century', accessed at: usgovernmentspending.com.

p.212 Table 8.1, 'Cost of election', Center for Responsive Politics, accessed at: www.opensecrets.org/overview/cost.php?display=T&infl=N.

p.212 Table 8.2, 'Donor Demographics', Center for Responsive Politics, accessed at: www.opensecrets.org/overview/donordemographics.php.

p.213 Figure 8.1, 'How money affects elections', Center for Responsive Politics, accessed at: www.fivethirtyeight.com/features/money-and-elections-a-complicated-love-story/.

p.241 Figure 9.1, chart combines data from 'Corporate top tax rate and bracket' accessed at: www.taxpolicycenter.org/statistics/corporate-top-tax-rate-and-bracket and US Bureau of Economic Analysis, Federal Government: 'Tax receipts on corporate income [FCTAX]', accessed at: FRED, Federal Reserve Bank of St. Louis: www.fred.stlouisfed.org/series/FCTAX, November 29, 2019.

p.242 Figure 9.2, data from research.stlouisfed.org.

p.279 Figure 10.1, Euromonitor International.

Index

Abramoff, Jack, 229
absolute advantage, 12–13, 24, 115, 325
Abu Dhabi, United Arab Emirates, 266
Adelson, Sheldon, 211
adjustable-rate mortgages (ARMs), 162
Affordable Care Act (2010), 267, 268
AIG, 171, 174, 226
Alibaba, 294, 299
Alipay, 299
Alphabet, 227
Alternative für Deutschland (AfD), 310
Amazon, 52, 53, 249, 250, 294, 295
American Bankers' Association, 231
American Journal of Political Science,
  214
Anandaciva, Siva, 266
Andreessen, Marc, 48
anti-dumping rules, 324–6
Apple, 45, 52, 53, 227, 249, 251–3
ARD, 270
Argentina, 220, 314
Aristophanes, 194
Aristotle, 189
Arrow, Kenneth, 328
artificial intelligence, 47, 50, 195, 295, 300
Asian Development Bank, 156
Asian financial crisis (1997), 154–6
asset price inflation, 69, 123, 139, 141–2,
  154, 164, 224
asset-backed securities, 125
AstraZeneca, 97
AT&T, 226
Athens, 194, 195
Atkinson, Anthony, 86
Auden, Wystan Hugh, 307

austerity, 124, 131, 134, 201, 226, 254,
  261–70, 308
Australia, 20
Austria, 229, 249
automated transport systems, 54
automation, 19–20, 36, 39, 40, 42–56, 62,
  314, 320–21
Automobility Ltd, 296
Aviva, 97

Baby boom generation (1946–65), 45, 114,
  115, 201–2, 239, 317
Bagchi, Sutirtha, 81
Baidu, 294
bail-outs, 4, 121, 131, 133, 150–51, 155, 159,
  163, 167, 175, 222–6, 261
Ballard, Brian, 219
Bank Credit Analyst (BCA), 79, 84
Bank of England, 92, 175
Bank of Japan, 223
Baosteel, 293
Barclays, 93
basic income, 55
Bayer, 237
BDI, 293
Bear Stearns, 169, 171
Beijing, China, 278
Belgium, 84
Benner, Thorsten, 296
Berlin Wall, 2, 119
Better Regulation Agenda, 235
Between Debt and the Devil (Turner), 117
Black Monday (1987), 147–8, 166
Blackburn, Marsha, 227
Blackrock, 256

365

election campaigns in, 210, 217, 323
gilets jaunes movement, 309–10, 330
Gini coefficient, 83, 84
healthcare in, 268
household debt in, 131, 132
income inequality in, 88, 248
life expectancy in, 267
lobbying in, 229
manufacturing in, 19
McDonald's in, 250
offshoring of labour in, 62
Revolution (1789–99), 186, 194, 253
taxation in, 250, 253
unions in, 108
wages in, 30, 37, 279, 308
Franco, Francisco, 248
Franz Ferdinand, Archduke of Austria-
Este, 167
Fratzscher, Marcel, 270
Frey, Carl, 51
Friedman, Milton, 104, 274
Friends of the Earth, 235
FTSE (Financial Times Stock Exchange),
93
Fukuyama, Francis, 33–4

G7 club, 87
G20 club, 30, 60
Gabriel, Sigmar, 270, 302
Gallup, 273
Garn-St. Germain Depository Institutions
Act (1982), 149
Garro, Haritz, 215
Geely, 289, 296
General Electric, 257–8
General Motors, 52–3, 174, 226
generalisation principle, 49, 65–6, 74,
139–40, 141, 191–2
generations
Baby boom generation (1946–65), 45, 114,
115, 201–202, 239, 317
Generation X (1966–80), 115, 202
Millenial generation (1981–2000), 1, 28,
64, 114, 115, 201–202
Silent generation (1928–45), 115, 202

German Institute for Economic Research,
88
Germany
Alternative für Deutschland (AfD), 310
automation in, 45, 62
Bundestag, 195
Chinese acquisitions in, 296, 301, 303
Dieselgate (2015), 236
election campaigns in, 217
Eurozone, leadership of, 207
executive pay in, 94
Greek debt crisis (2009–), 223
gross domestic product (GDP), 28
household debt in, 131, 132, 134
hyper-inflation (1921–3), 314
income inequality in, 87–8, 94
infrastructure, 269–70
interest rates in, 109
life expectancy in, 267
manufacturing in, 19, 39, 45
Nazi period (1933–45), 192
offshoring of labour in, 62
populism in, 249, 310
taxation in, 253
unions in, 108
wages in, 28, 88, 279
Gilens, Martin, 209, 219
gilets jaunes movement, 309–10, 330
Gini coefficient, 82–5, 107, 245
Glass-Steagall Act (1933), 90, 92, 220–21
Glassman, James, 220
Global Wage Report, 279
globalisation, 2–4, 11–40, 87, 115, 172–3,
206, 265, 274, 276, 281, 283, 302, 331
education and, 200, 263
China and, 20–24, 28, 35–6
nation state and, 249
offshoring of jobs, 20–28, 39, 45, 62,
89–90, 120, 184, 273, 307, 308
taxation and, 239, 240, 248–9, 252, 272,
276
technology and, 42, 52, 309
wages and, 20, 21, 25–30, 32–3, 36–8,
40, 239
world government and, 276, 325